Happy Birthday, Tom
Love, , Carl,
Kathleen, Frances, and

THE DINGLE TRAIN

by

David Rowlands, Walter McGrath and Tom Francis

DEDICATION

This book is dedicated to the memory of Ivo Peters.

We also wish to associate with it the memories of Patrick B Whitehouse and A. John Powell who, together, wrote the history of the Tralee and Dingle Railway; and of Cyril Fry, Robin N. Clements and W. Arthur Camwell ('Cam') who all made magnificent contributions to recording the history of "the Dingle Train."

Plateway Press, PO Box 973, Brighton, BN2 2TG

ISBN 1871980 27 5

British Library Cataloguing in Publication Data

Rowlands, David
Dingle Train
I. Title
385. 52094196

ISBN 1-871980-27-5

Printed in Great Britain by Amadeus Press Ltd., Huddersfield.

Typesetting by Highlight Type Bureau Ltd., Bradford.

Book Design and Cover artwork by David H. Smith, Hebden Bridge

THE DINGLE TRAIN

Pinch of pepper, pinch of pepper,
Westwards went the Dingle train;
Pinch of pepper, pinch of pepper
Was the theme of its refrain.
Pinch of pepper, pinch of pepper,
Sure it seems but yesterday
Since I made the journey westward
O'er the hills and far away.

'The Dingle train is whistling now,
'Tis time to make the tay.'
That's what they said in Tralee town
When evening came the way;
For then the train went slowly west
The trail, uphill and down,
By many a little country home
To far-off Dingle town.

The scholars all sat in the front
Returning home from school;
The quiet ones read Bello Gallico,
The wild ones played the fool.
And they kept time with a tune they had
To the chatter of the train,
Pinch of pepper, pinch of pepper,
Up the hills and down again.

The good folk out at Blennerville
Looked up with kindly eye
And nodded as if it had been
An old friend passing by.
The children waved their little hands
By Derrymore with glee
As the engine butted up the line
Between the hill and sea.

And at Camp Junction they unyoked
The horses from the plough;
'The ploughing's done,' the farmers said,
'Time now to milk the cow.'
And further west at Annascaul
As the train puffed on its way
The young folk downed their tools and said,
'So ends another day.'

And as it went uphill and down
By vale and mountain pass
The driver and the fireman waved
To many a lad and lass.
And Dan the Blacksmith at Lispole
Thought he would work no more,
For the Dingle train was steaming by
Outside the smithy door.

Said the housewife back near Dingle town,
'The day is growing late,'
When the train at Ballintaggart height
Proclaimed 'twas turned eight.
And a little short of journey's end
Its whistle loud did fill
The evening from the harbour's mouth
To the Pass of Connor Hill.

But the train that went o'er hill and dale
Goes by no more that way,
Nor will its whistle at Tralee
Announce the evening tay.
No more the western people hear
Full thirty miles away
The once familiar homely peal
Proclaim the close of day.

Now often in my dreams I see
Tralee, the sea, the sky,
And a small train struggle bravely on
Across the mountains high.
A memory of the days that were,
A ghost from out the years
Climbing the heights of Gleannagalt
Like an old man full of tears.

—Tim O'Donnell.

Front cover illustration: **With the broad sweep of Tralee Bay providing a breathtaking background, Nos 8T and 1T build up a head of steam for the assault on Glenagalt bank, in the dying days of the Dingle Train, June 1952.**

From an original watercolour by Mike Turner G.R.A., based on a photograph by Henry Orbach

Back cover illustration: **STEAMING BACK TO BLENNERVILLE – a portrait of No. 5 in action on the restored section of the Tralee and Dingle.**

(courtesy Kerry UDC)

Frontispiece: **HIGH SUMMER: June 29th 1951 and cattle specials meet at Annascaul. In distance No. 8T is on a Relief working that left Tralee at 8.20am with empty wagons and "Cam's" party, returning same day, fully loaded. Nos. 1T and 2T (foreground) have left Tralee at noon with the main working of cattle empties. They will return next day (fully loaded). 8T will probably work back again to Dingle with her rake of empties and also return on the Saturday (Fair Day). 8T is taking water into her left hand tanks; she will soon move toward us and fill the right hand tanks at the standpipe at the Tralee end of the island platform. Mike Davies just in front of 1T, centre picture.** *(Ivo Peters, copyright Julian Peters)*

CONTENTS

ACKNOWLEDGEMENTS

Our thanks go to all those mentioned in the text, but particularly in chapters 4, 7 and 8 who gave so willingly of their time and recollections of The Dingle; not forgetting the photographers whose skills in capturing the T&DR complement the text so fully.

Particular thanks are due to:

Coras Iompair Eirann for making the Minute Books of the T&DLR Company available to Tom Francis in Dublin; Allan C Baker, for his invaluable input into the "Locomotives" and "Carriages and Wagons" chapters (though final responsibility for their content rests with the Authors and Publisher); and David Pinniger for his excellent drawings – the outcome of many hours of research, studying photographs with a magnifying lens!

We have throughout our researches approached the T&DLR by tracking down the railfans and other visitors who recorded its uniqueness in notebook, on photographic plates and film and on ciné film. Without the efforts of these chroniclers there would be no story and the Train would, one day, be forgotten.

D.G.R. W.McG. T.F.

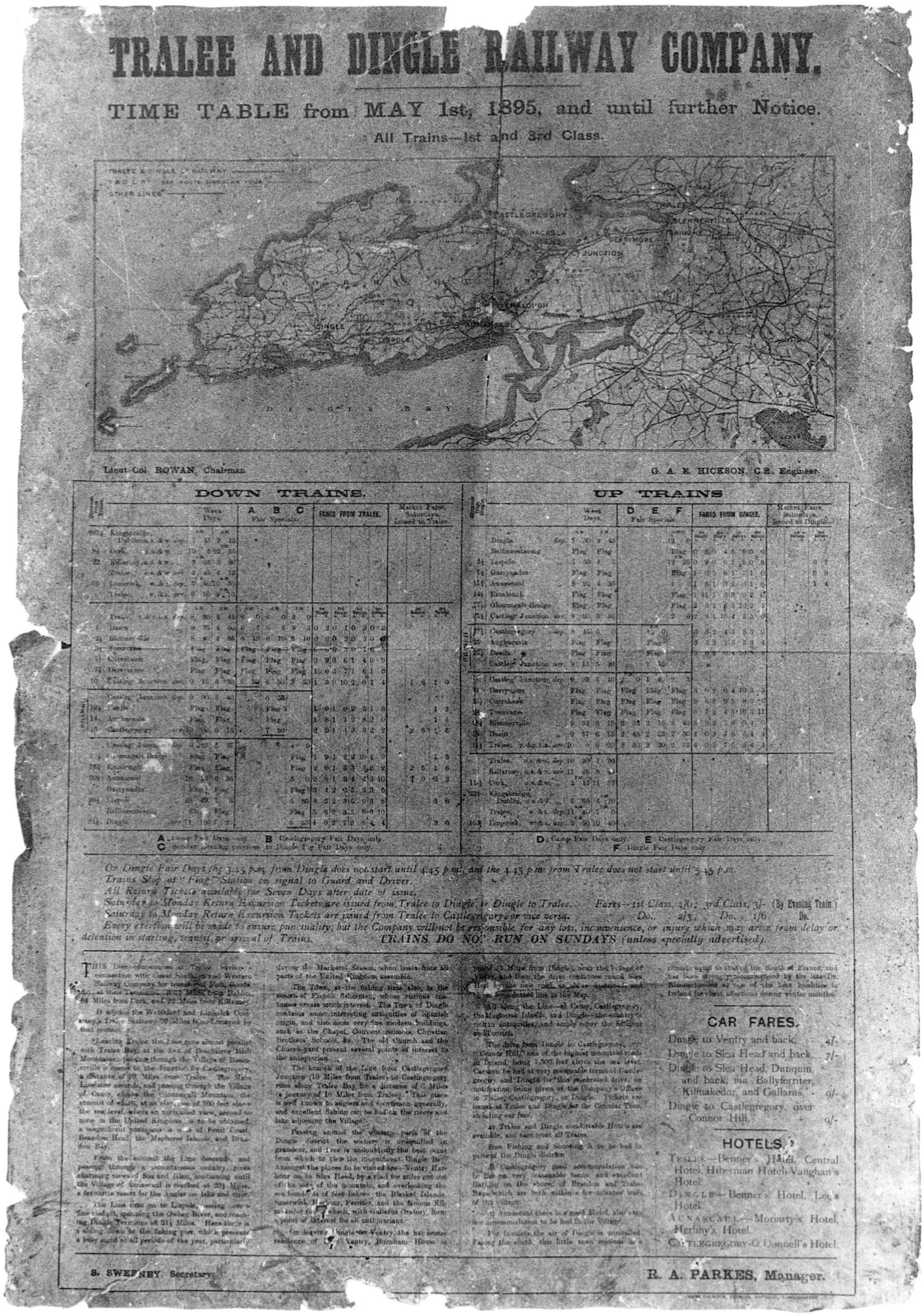

TRALEE AND DINGLE RAILWAY COMPANY.

TIME TABLE from MAY 1st, 1895, and until further Notice.

All Trains—1st and 3rd Class.

Lieut.-Col. ROWAN, Chairman.

G. A. E. HICKSON, C.E., Engineer.

DOWN TRAINS.

UP TRAINS

A Camp Fair Days only. B Castlegregory Fair Days only. C Sunday Evening Excursion to Dingle Fair Days only.

D Camp Fair Days only. E Castlegregory Fair Days only. F Dingle Fair Days only.

On Dingle Fair Days the 3.45 p.m. from Dingle does not start until 4.45 p.m., and the 4.45 p.m. from Tralee does not start until 5.45 p.m.
Trains Stop at "Flag" Station on signal to Guard and Driver.
All Return Tickets available for Seven Days after date of issue.
Saturday to Monday Return Excursion Tickets are issued from Tralee to Dingle, or Dingle to Tralee. Fares—1st Class, 4/6; 3rd Class, 3/- (By Evening Train.)
Saturday to Monday Return Excursion Tickets are issued from Tralee to Castlegregory, or vice versa. Do. 2/3. Do. 1/6. Do.
Every exertion will be made to ensure punctuality; but the Company will not be responsible for any loss, inconvenience, or injury which may arise from delay or detention in starting, transit, or arrival of Trains. TRAINS DO NOT RUN ON SUNDAYS (unless specially advertised).

CAR FARES.

Dingle to Ventry and back, 4/-
Dingle to Slea Head and back, 7/-
Dingle to Slea Head, Dunquin, and back, via Ballyferriter, Kilmakedor, and Gallarus, 9/-
Dingle to Castlegregory, over Connor Hill, 9/-

HOTELS.

TRALEE—Benner's Hotel, Central Hotel, Hibernian Hotel, Vaughan's Hotel.
DINGLE—Benner's Hotel, Lee's Hotel.
AUNASCAUL—Moriarty's Hotel, Herlihy's Hotel.
CASTLEGREGORY—O'Donnell's Hotel.

S. SWEENEY, Secretary.

R. A. PARKES, Manager.

Timetable for Summer 1895 as given to Guest Houses. Note the halts marked as "flag" stops and the fares printed alongside the times in similar-looking units: how to confuse the Public! *(Author's Collection)*

PREFACE

It was an unique line! How often have you heard that said of an independent rural railway? Yet the Tralee & Dingle could most reasonably justify this claim. Not only has its spirit of adventure and at times comic persistence appealed mightily to the railway enthusiast in search of something different and original, but it has featured far more than any other minor railway in literature, and has secured a permanent place in the annals of Kerry.

The aim of this book is to show what manner of line the Tralee & Dingle was. For those who wish to read more about it and to savour the contribution it made to Kerry history, we have included many references. These are indicated in the text but are placed in an appendix to each chapter, so that the flow of the narrative is not broken by hundreds of footnotes. These can thus be ignored by the casual reader, yet are readily available to those who would know far more of this wonderful railway than any one book can hope to convey.

The Dingle Train was many things to many people, as you will see; but most importantly it played a major role in the development of the area, as explained more fully in Chapter 7.

INTRODUCTION

'To the little station of the Dingle line the country people come at the tail of a market day with their motley purchases; you forget London and Dublin, all the cities of the earth, and with Gaelic faces and Gaelic voices about you, stand in the gateway of an older and simpler world.[1]

With these words, Robin Flower introduced the Dingle Railway, a narrow-gauge[2] line which was unique in its appeal to connoisseurs of railway practice throughout the world, and which served the people of Corkaguiny and Tralee for more than 60 years (1891-1953).

It is more than fifty years since the last regular passengers left Tralee for Dingle by train,[3] and over forty years since any sort of train made its undulating way westward. For, with the coming of the motor bus and the re-surfacing of the roads in the 1930s, it was no longer the 'easiest and quickest way to get to Dingle', as advised C. P. Crane in 1907.[4] Far from it [5] – the numerous speed restrictions applied on a railway of sharp curves and steep gradients and numerous crossings,[6] made the journey time excessive by comparison with road transport. So the passenger service ceased. Such a comparison was inevitably made – as it had been fifty years earlier between mail coach and train – because 'this little up-and-down narrow gauge line follows as closely as possible the old mail coach route'.[7] In fact of the total 31 miles and 52 chains of main line to Dingle, some 27 miles and 61 chains were alongside the public road, the exceptions being where gradients or curves on the road were so severe as to make rail traction impossible. Then the railway would diverge on to its own right of way.

An excellent history of the railway by P. B. Whitehouse and A. J. Powell,[8] albeit directed to the interests of the railway enthusiast, was published in 1958, but is long out of print and unobtainable, so that a brief synopsis of the railway's history would seem to be appropriate here. Further to this there has been a pictorial album portraying the journey from Tralee to Dingle and the locomotives and rolling stock in some detail [9]. Two more recent books of considerable interest are Tom Ferris's "The Irish Narrow Gauge: a Pictorial History", volume one of which contains a section on the Tralee & Dingle[10] and Patrick Taylor's "The West Clare Railway" which covers the history of those Tralee & Dingle locomotives and stock that were transferred to that Section[11].

1. R. Flower, *The Western Island* (London) Preface.
2. In railway parlance anything less than 'standard' gauge (5ft 3ins in Ireland, 4ft 8½ins in England) is 'narrow' gauge. The T&DLR was 3ft gauge.
3. Passenger services and all branch services (to Castlegregory) were withdrawn by GSR in April 1939. Complete closure of Tralee & Dingle section by CIE was from July 1953.
4. C. P. Crane, *Kerry* (London 1907) 197-201.
5. At time of closure in 1939, buses took 105 minutes Tralee-Dingle; the train took 155 minutes for an almost identical route. Intermediate shunting and goods unloading accounted for much of the difference. A railcar as used on the Donegal and West Clare lines could have reduced rail passenger journey times considerably.
6. There were 70 or more between Tralee and Dingle: nearly all ungated.
7. C. P. Crane *op cit;* see also J. O'Connor, *Hostage to Fortune,* (Dublin 1951) 5-8. And an interesting inter-relation of the railway with the social and historical records of the barony can be found in T. F. O'Sullivan *Romantic Hidden Kerry,* (Tralee 1931).
8. P. B. Whitehouse and A. J. Powell, *The Tralee & Dingle Railway* (London 1958). 1-60.
9. D. G. Rowlands, *The Tralee and Dingle Railway* (Truro 1977). 1-96.
10. T. Ferris, *The Irish Narrow Gauge: A Pictorial History, Vol. 1, From Cork to Cavan.* Midland Publishing, 1993.
11. P. Taylor, *The West Clare Railway,* Plateway Press, 1994.

1. This is the earliest known picture of a train in service on the T&D, and is included despite the poor quality for its historical interest. TRALEE 1891: An excursion train for the Cambrian Archaeological Society on a field trip to Corcaguiny. Locomotive No. 1 in near original condition (before the Curraduff disaster) still with some evidence of side skirts. Standing fourth from the left is Driver Harry Quinn, with his fireman (Murphy) third from left. Note the lining out on the elegant oil lamp. *(The Kerryman)*

2. PAUSE for a blow-up at Glenmore, Fair Day, September 1952. Loco No. 2T on one of her last workings, returning from Dingle with a relief special, following in the wake of Nos. 1T and 8T with the main portion. Between her toolboxes she is carrying No. 5T's metal toolbox as an extra sandbox. *(R. N. Clements)*

Chapter 1
A SHORT HISTORY OF THE RAILWAY

The passing of the Tramways (Ireland) Act of 1883 awoke, or revived, much interest in railway communication for places off the beaten track. With general merchandise and fish traffic in mind, a line to Dingle was sanctioned by the Privy Council in 1884, but lapsed for want of a contractor. Two main obstacles had to be surmounted, the Slieve Marsh range which, in the event, was crossed via the pass at Gleann na nGealt, and the more westerly hills south of Brandon, which were crossed near Baunogue. The sanction was renewed on appeal on the 17th September 1888 when the proposers (chairman Sir M. Fitzgerald, Knight of Kerry) were supported by an experienced contractor, Robert Worthington J.P., who had built many other railways in Ireland. Total capital authorised was £150,000 of which £120,000 was guaranteed locally at 4 per cent: Corkaguiny bearing half the burden, Trughanacmy £39,000, Clanmaurice £15,000 and Tralee Sanitary District making up the balance. Of this £120,000, some £20,000 went in promotion and legal expenses. Under this arrangement, the guarantors were held liable for any working deficit and, under the Act of Incorporation, if this pertained for four years, the railway was to be surrendered to the Grand Jury which would appoint a committee to manage it. This is precisely what happened in 1896, although it proved to be only a paper transaction – a mere change of title – and the heavy operating losses continued, reported now by a Committee of Management, rather than a Board of Directors.

Construction began late in 1888 and took three years. Right from the start, Worthington pressed for adoption of the Irish standard gauge, but no satisfactory arrangement could be made with the Great Southern & Western Company, which had an important station in Tralee; and consequently the cheaper sub-standard gauge of 3ft was adopted.[1]

Within a few years of operation one guide book was to echo Worthington's disquietude: 'The cautious traveller will go by rail to Castlegregory and thence by road over Connor Hill to Dingle. He will thus avoid a none-too-safe bit of railway. It is much to be regretted that the Dingle line was not made of full gauge and on safe inclines'.[2]

The wisdom of this advice was to be demonstrated many times in the ensuing years. No doubt the shrewd writer had in mind the hideous disaster at Curraduff Bridge, Camp, (Chapter 2); at any rate he pinpointed two major defects of the line's cheap construction, which added greatly to the dangers of operation, to say nothing of the day-to-day difficulty – and yet which contributed to making working practice on 'The Dingle' unique.

It is easy now, in retrospect, to diagnose the troubles which were to cause daily problems to the management until the big amalgamation in to the Great Southern Railways took place in 1925. With hindsight, it can be said that the railway was built too cheaply [3] and never had enough working capital to maintain equipment properly or securely (especially engines and rolling stock) nor to hold supervisory staff of the requisite calibre. No forward planning was possible; working on a day-to-day basis was the only way to keep the line going. These economic facts decided the character of the railway.

For construction, Worthington set up his base at Blennerville and worked westward. The *Kerry Evening Post,* February 5th 1890, reports a meeting of the T&DLR Directors at which a progress report was given by Messrs Ryan & Hickson, Engineers to the Company, as follows:

'The formation of the main line is complete from Blennerville to Ballinasare Lower, a distance of 19$^1/_2$ miles and from Dingle to Baunogue, a distance of seven miles, leaving only 2 miles to complete the formation through and 3 miles from Blennerville to Tralee. All the Castlegregory branch has been completed with the exception of a short deviation at Bunnow Mills. Most of the line laid has been ballasted but the quality of the ballast between Blennerville and Camp is, generally speaking, indifferent. This will however be rectified. All the farmed portions of the line have been fenced, and the necessary farm gates to crossings and other accommodation works provided. Lispole viaduct has

3. Dingle taken from the pier/Mole in 1899. Just discernible, centre of picture, is a rake of T&DLR wagons standing on the Pier extension, as the harbour branch was called. *(John Wills)*

4. AFTERNOON MIXED: 3T with the 5.30pm mixed for Dingle, including coach for Castlegregory that will be detached at Camp Junction. *(R. W. Kidner)*

been completed during the past month and the rails laid down across it. Masonry bridges have been built over two of the rivers at Annascaul, and the abutments for the girder bridge over the third river are finished. The only bridges now remaining to be built are the Finglas river at Bunnow and over the Clahane and Lee Rivers on the deviation between Blennerville and Tralee. Three of the Gatekeepers' houses at public road level crossings are complete and a fourth is in the course of construction. All the rails, fastenings, switches etc. required for the time being, have been first tested at the mills by your Inspector. The working of the engines supplied continues to give satisfaction, they being able to work the steepest gradient without any difficulty. Nineteen more waggons and two carriage trucks have been supplied since the last report, the total number of waggons supplied being thirty-nine. The entire work is being carried out in a suitable and substantial manner, and with the exception of a few slight alterations of curves and other matters incidental to finishing up, work done by the contractor has given us every satisfaction.'

The section into Tralee was left until last, as he had finally persuaded the then directors[4] to reconsider their original plan to bring the track through the streets of Tralee.[5] This, Worthington rightly thought, would cause serious traffic congestion problems, even in the 1890s. He favoured an alternative route back from Blennerville on a separate right of way: to the Basin and round by the Christian Brothers' Monastery and convent grounds, to link up in Tralee with the North Kerry line of the Waterford and Limerick Railway with which they had a working agreement and whose station adjoined the new terminus. A connection to the GSWR terminus was for freight movement only. Passengers for Dingle arriving at the GSWR terminus thus had the annoyance of walking along the street, bag and baggage, to 'the Dingle' terminus. This nuisance, which was to remain throughout the passenger life of the T&D, was remembered by Ernest Blythe in recounting his 1913 journey to Dingle:

> At the big railway station in Tralee two strong youths accosted me, offering to carry my suitcase. I told them to bring it to the small railway station. It was a very short journey and I gave them sixpence each – a sum approximately half-a-crown in today's money. They were dissatisfied and demanded more. They became abusive and shouted to the crowd on the platform how

mean the 'Yank' had been to them. My accent must have given them the impression that I was American, and that as a Yank I would be much more generous. Two or three people joined in and said I should pay the boys more. But I was working on a very tight budget, with only five pounds for my trip and I was determined not to be browbeaten by a couple of Tralee 'alfraits'.[6]

J. M. Synge had a better experience:

> I found a boy who carried my bag some way along the road to an open yard, where the light railway starts for the West. There was a confused mass of peasants struggling on the platform with all sorts of baggage, which the people lifted into the train for themselves as well as they were able. The seats ran up either side of the cars, and the space between them was soon filled with sacks of flour, cases of porter, chairs rolled in straw and other household goods.[7]

Westward from Tralee the stations were Basin, Blennerville, Curraheen, Derrymore, Castlegregory Junction (with a branch of 6 miles to Deelis, Aughacasla and Castlegregory), Camp, Gleann na nGealt Bridge, Glenmore, Emalough, Annascaul, Ballinasare, Garrynadur, Lispole, Ballinasteenig and Dingle, with a half-mile extension to Dingle Pier.

There were stone buildings at Tralee, Basin, Blennerville, Castlegregory (branch) and Dingle; corrugated iron at Castlegregory Junction, Lispole and Annascaul. The other stations were merely low-platformed halts, each originally with a small shelter. There were keepers' cottages at Tralee (Pembroke, Strand and Basin crossings), Skirlough (Driscoll's), Ballinclare and Ballinacourty; also at the end of Dingle yard for the pier extension. Passenger trains often made courtesy stops at such places as Tonevane, Ballinclare, Ballinacourty, Skirlough, Lougher school etc.

Only an understanding of the gradient profile, with its 'Alpine' shape, can convey the way in which the line of railway climbed from just above sea level at Lower Camp, where Castlegregory Junction was situated, to the summit at Gleann na nGealt (usually anglicised to Glenagalt) Bridge at 680ft. in a little under four miles; only to descend steeply over 6 miles to the level at Annascaul before climbing back to the second summit (450ft.) at Baunogue, and finally drop back to sea level at Dingle Pier. The steepest descents were 1 in 29 approaching Camp from the west, and in the opposite direction the section from Emalough to Annascaul and from Baunogue to Lispole. These were the steepest gradients on any Irish railway.

The danger was considerable, even to efficiently vacuum-braked trains, and this fact, together with the cheap construction, was blamed on the Irish Board of Works. This was most unfair since the Board was limited to advising on the (engineering) practicality of the scheme and had no powers to inspect during construction to see if its recommendations were being heeded.

The first fatality on the Dingle Railway occurred when one Jeremiah O'Malley was fatally struck by a flying hatchet, propelled when timber baulks collapsed during their unloading from a wagon at Blennerville on 27th January 1890.

The trackway laid consisted of 30ft. lengths of steel rail (45lbs/yard weight) joined by fishplates and secured to sleepers by fang bolts and dogspikes. Ballast was of broken stone. Few sections were ever re-ballasted after 1905.

It must be wondered what the impact was on the local people of the arrival of construction gangs and the first steam locomotives in the Dingle Peninsula. There seems to be no record extant, but Joseph O'Connor described a typical construction train which gave his family a welcome ride into Dingle. Sitting on the bumpy Bianconi coach hauled by four sturdy horses, holding on to his brothers who were asleep, he drowsed too . . .

> Only the Mot and Johnny (Connor) remember the change of horses at Annascaul and the winding road to the top of Garry Na Dur, where the whistle of a train woke us to a scene of noisy activity. We had reached the open gap in the railway line. The gangs we saw were closing it at high pressure, shouldering new rails to their appointed places, laying them and binding them with fishplates and bolts. Johnny got down and told Harry Quinn, the engine driver, who we were. Harry could do no less than jump off his footplate and come across, wiping his hands on cotton waste, to welcome us into the fold. His shining red face and beaming smile were a welcome in themselves, but he did the honours and shook hands all round. He had a brainwave. 'Why not do the last lap into Dingle with me? Johnny won't mind and we'll give the stationmaster a surprise. We're sure to find him on the job.[8]

So they did, and the stationmaster's family arrived in Dingle by train – possibly the first public passengers over the Dingle railway.

Another traveller in those construction days was John Adye Curran, KC who spent the 1880s as a judge in Kerry:

> I remember travelling to Dingle on this line, our carriage being a railway truck with a wooden rail round the edges, and chairs for our sitting accommodation. The line had not been finished, and we went off it several times during the trip. We, however, all arrived safely, and returned next day, having concluded the Sessions. [9]

For working trains, the main line was divided into three 'sections': Tralee-Lower Camp, Lower Camp-Annascaul and Annascaul-Dingle. It was at first operated on the single-engine-in-steam and manual-token system, but this was flexible and led to many breaches in practice, to the great detriment of safety, especially when special trains for cattle or fish traffic were required. Negligent operation of this type was directly responsible for a number of accidents, including the Curraduff bridge disaster of 1893. A proper block-system was begun but was not completed

5. TRALEE (Dingle) STATION in last days of passenger service, 1939, taken from yard entrance. Turntable pit on right. Coaches in siding are having batteries charged. *(A. W. Croughton)*

6. General view of Tralee NG yard in 1953. Loco shed in foreground (left) with derelict wagons alongside. In far distance gates to Ashe Street and on to Broad gauge yard are open. *(K. P. Seward)*

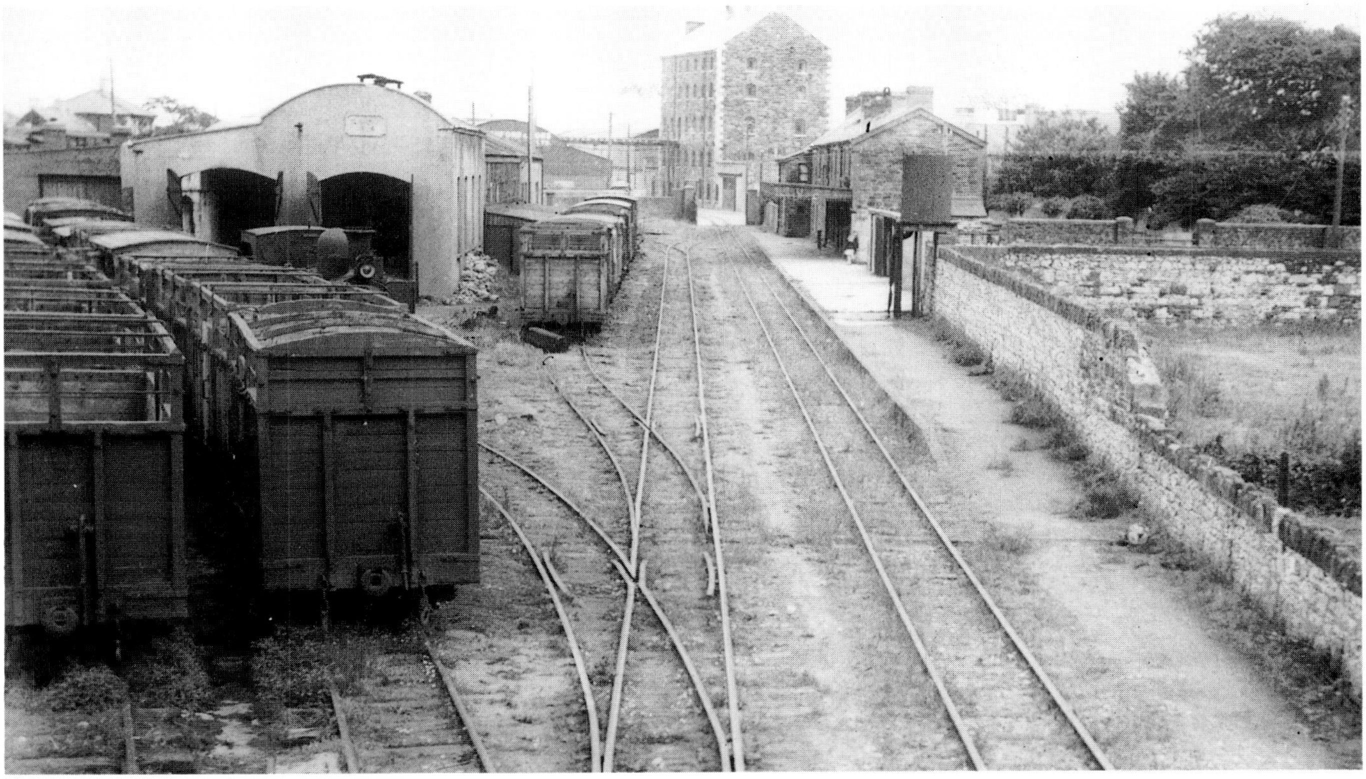

7 and 8. Two views of the yard in 1952 with rakes of wagons for cattle specials in front of loco shed – loco No. 2T just visible behind them (photo 7). A later 1952 photo (8) showing the carriage and wagon shops, different rakes of wagons in front of loco shed (closed) and gates to Ashe Street also closed. *(Both C. L. Fry)*

until 1898. Until 1895 there was no telephone communication between stations, and trains leaving Tralee or Dingle went into Limbo until their return.

A number of minor accidents occurred during construction, and a couple of potentially major ones, notably when a ballast train driven by Harry Quinn, loaded and assembled in breach of safety precautions ran away down Glenagalt bank. Control was regained at Skirlough before hitting the dangerous curves at Curraduff. At Deelis on the branch, a similar train pushed by its load part-derailed and damaged a nearby house. These incidents occurred because few of the wagons at the time were fitted for the much-safer vacuum-brake system. Only with the advent of the public service did full use of vacuum-brakes begin.

The much-maligned Board of Trade made its inspection once completion was in sight, but was too late to have any real effect. By then, the meagre capital and cheap construction had determined the pattern for years to come. General Hutchinson made his first visit of inspection in May 1890, while the company was appointing officials and staff. The wages and conditions of service were not then such as to retain men of top calibre, which is not to imply that the T&DLR did not have some good men in its employ. [10]

By November 1890 the line was virtually complete; Hutchinson's first official report was received on Christmas Eve. It was unfavourable and numerous items needed attention before a certificate could be given. In January 1891, Worthington suggested his paying £1,900 in lieu of maintenance and rolling stock not yet delivered.[11] By agreeing to this, the Company was given cash in hand for working the line. Before accepting from the contractor the rolling-stock obtained so far (much of which had been used in building the line) the Company had it inspected by H. A. Ivatt of the MGWR. His recommendations, however, were not fully carried out until mid-1892, due to lack of funds.

Hutchinson's second report (16 March 1891) was more favourable – what little could be done within the

9. DAILY GOODS working from Dingle. Loco No. 6T near Blennerville with the 12 noon ex Dingle. (The morning outgoing train was worked by 5T, see photo 23 also photo 37).
(J. G. Dewing)

financial constraint had been achieved and on March 28 final settlement was reached with the contractor. A special train opened the line on Monday 31 March 1891 and ordinary workings began next day.

The Company minute-books show clearly that from the outset, little could be achieved in the long-term; with restricted finances concern with day-to-day running was inevitable and the earnings did not at any time cover working expenses. 'Make do and mend' quickly gave way to 'make do'.[12] In addition there was friction, constant and acrimonious, with ratepayers whose pockets began immediately to feel the subsidies needed. A Board of Trade Enquiry was demanded of the Grand Jury by the public, and duly took place, with General Hutchinson presiding, at Tralee courthouse, 22 March 1893. This brought to light a number of malpractices; not the least being that one particular director profited if the railway failed because he was a collector of cess and had little interest in its success. Only injection of a large amount of capital could improve the situation.

To make matters worse, this was followed on 22 May 1893 by the Curraduff disaster (Chapter 2), which heightened the local disrepute of the Company, being a direct result of negligence, and lack of funds for maintenance.

Year by year the operating losses continued until by 1896 the sarcastic comments of the press were at their peak. One such ran as follows:

> *Our Dear Dingle Railway.* The Dingle Railway, which was put out to nurse for the first few years of its infancy, is to revert to the guardianship of the Kerry Grand Jury, according to our report of the proceedings of that body. There is something truly touching about this episode in the life of this infant phenomenon. Whether we regard it from the pathetic parting of the Directors with their charge or the paternal solicitude of the Grand Jurors for their offspring, the scene must be truly affecting. In fact the only parallel to it in modern days is the renunciation of the Catholic Faith in which he was baptised, and to be brought up, by Prince Boris of Roumania at the ripe age of two years. The little prince had as much voice in the solemn farce being pompously enacted in the name of religion as the ratepayers of Kerry have in the conversion of the Dingle Railway. But even the resumption of parental rights over this line by the Grand Jury is to be of a mere temporary character, and they are praying the Lord Lieutenant to allow them to push it out again to some other set of baby-farmers who may, it is hoped, deal better with it than the last. The reluctance of Colonel Rowan to part with his young and amiable charge does credit to his nursing qualities, but as he is himself a member of the Grand Jury, perhaps he may be rechosen for that dry nursing for which his fond heart seems aching. How conveniently the engineer, the manager and the secretary got their salaries raised before this touching incident in the life of the Dingle Railway. Alas for the future fate of the Dingle Railway. It may live and even thrive. But we fear its *caoine* like that of Con the Shaugrawn will tell us: 'The Ratepayers grew wake as the child grew strong'.[13]

How prophetic this was: On May 21, 1896, following an extraordinary general meeting of the Company at which the Incorporation Act's proviso was adopted, the Lord Lieutenant authorised the Grand Jury to appoint a Committee of Management. It was a change of name only, and not of personnel. Their first meeting (8 July) 1896 called on the Government to provide capital, blaming the previous Government for the penurious state and for agreeing to the line being operative.

This fell on deaf ears and in the first year of the Committee of Management, the ratepayers were drawn upon to the sum of £7,000 – a colossal amount (about £$^{1}/_{2}$ million by today's standards). However, in 1898, the Treasury did pay over £80,000 reducing the annual burden on the ratepayers by about £800. By now the redoubtable Tom O'Donnell, MP for West Kerry, was Chairman of the Management Committee.

Little change took place until 1907 when the Company through O'Donnell's efforts got a grant of £23,000 from the Inland Development Fund. This enabled the diversion long-needed at Curraduff to be put in hand, though it was 1908-9 before it was finished.[14] Also this year occurred the spectacular, but fortunately non-fatal, derailment at Lispole viaduct, poorly maintained track, acute curves and defective locomotive maintenance again being responsible.[15] Other benefits from the grant included installation of turntables at Lower Camp (opposite Crean's pub) and Castlegregory, machine tools for the workshops and rail and other permanent way material.

Still the management was unpopular with ratepayers and the service poor, so that when a Ratepayers Association was formed in Corkaguiny in 1910 to press for reform, the T&DLR was chief among its targets. The Company's accounting was highly suspect and arson at Tralee offices in December that year brought about an inquiry, which revealed serious deficiencies in the book-keeping.

From this point, the condition of the railway began to improve as a result of better management, and under Frith as locomotive superintendent real progress was made with arrears of maintenance.

In 1911 the Company issued an attractive brochure with coloured covers "Through Rare West Kerry", which was reprinted by *The Kerryman* in 1987 as part of the fund raising towards restoring locomotive No. 5T.

Therefore it is sad that the start of World War I and local political animosities should have led to an inevitable decline. High coal prices and shortages caused many train cancellations, while Government Control from 1916 and general wage increases accelerated the difficulties. Following the 1920-21 struggle with the Black and Tans and the 1922-3 Civil War, in which there was damage done to stock and buildings, the railway was closed for periods of some weeks. Bridges were blown up at Curraheen and Derrymore. There were several months in 1922 when

10. LAST PASSENGER WORKINGS. In the last week of the passenger service 1939 No. 8T (left) is at Lower Camp Junction with a train for Dingle. No. 6T has picked up the through coach for Castlegregory. *(G. J. Aston)*

11. DINGLE FAIR DAY, April 1953. No. 8T assembling the first (double headed) train out, prior to the arrival of the cattle from the Fair. Note the rarely-seen pillars of Dingle station at right. *(K. P. Seward)*

no trains at all ran, though this was the time of the historic "Flour Train" (see Chapter 8).

With the establishment of the Irish Free State it was decided to amalgamate all railways within the 26 counties to form the Great Southern Railways. This was first mooted in 1923, but the T&DLR had to hang on financially, by the skin of its teeth, until 1 January 1925 when it was taken over.

The GSR had its baptism of fire to the T&DLR on the very first day of operation, with an accident at Glenmore Crossing. It was faced with the task of maintaining the service as an important link for Corkaguiny – the roads were still unsuited to heavy traffic – yet doing so as economically as possible. Gradually the workshops at Tralee were run down and finally stripped of machinery in 1935 when the county subsidy finished. Heavy repairs to locomotives and stock were switched to Limerick or Dublin (Inchicore), day to day maintenance being done by GSR main-line staff and overall operating directives coming from Cork.

These were the years of the wholesale emigrations from the west of Kerry and the railway carried many emigrants on the first lap of their long journey. The echoing whistle of 'The Train' was a last recollection fondly carried by many of them. No one will need reminding of the account by Maurice O'Sullivan, but one brief quotation may be included:

> I caught up my bag and away with me. I had only gone a few steps when an echo came back from the whole town of Dingle with the whistle the train threw out, and as for myself, I was lifted clean from the ground. I looked round to see if anyone had noticed the start it took out of me, but nobody had. Everyone was inside the train but myself.[16]

O'Sullivan was en route to visit his English friend, the gaelic scholar, George Thompson.[17]

A great deal of revenue still came from excursion traffic, especially on the branch, and from 1926 the winter beet-traffic from Castlegregory, with the setting up of a sugar beet industry in Ireland.

The 1927 flooding of the Lee at the Basin breached its walls and thereafter Spring tides regularly flooded the railway, causing long delays.

During 1938-9 the Dingle road was completely resurfaced and metalled, making way for more bus and lorry competition. With the limitation and speed restrictions imposed on trains by the gradients and curves, journey times became excessive by comparison and on 17 April 1939 the passenger service was discontinued on the main line to Dingle and the branch closed to all traffic.

A daily goods train worked to Dingle and back until the fuel shortages of 1944, thereafter running only 'as required'. In 1945 the line, as part of the GSR, became the T&D section of Coras Iompair Éireann, and from 1947 onward only a monthly cattle-working took place in connection with Dingle Fair. This totally uneconomic working continued until 1953 when CIE gave notice of intent to close the section. Despite local attempts to press for retention of the service, it closed. The last cattle trains ran on 26/27 June 1953[18] and on July 22 a lone locomotive ran to Dingle to bring back wagons left there.

Two of the remaining locomotives went to Inchicore for scrapping, the other to Ennis (West Clare section). The wagons left at Tralee and not drafted to other CIE narrow-gauge lines, were broken up on 16 December 1953. A few bodies were sold locally as sheds. Some track was taken up in Tralee yard and on as far as Blennerville. The remainder of the line was torn up for scrap throughout 1955-6.

So came and went the Dingle railway and some people along the route had lived to see the Bianconi coach displaced by the train, only to see the train itself displaced by motor, lorry and bus. A chapter in the life of Corkaguiny was over.

1. On *public* lines the 3ft. gauge became extinct with closure of the West Clare Railway in 1961. A number of 'pleasure' lines used short sections of 3ft. gauge track. Following the successful reopening of a part of the T&D from Tralee to Blennerville, sections of the Cavan & Leitrim and County Donegal Railways are being constructed. Bord na Mona (Irish Turf Board) operates a large but contracting mileage of temporary and semi-permanent turf-carrying lines, mostly of 3ft. gauge.
2. Messrs Baddely and Ward *Guide to Ireland* (London, 1895).
3. £2,700 per mile – less than half the cost of most other Irish railways of the same decade.
4. Colonel Rowan, R. McCowen and M. McMahon.
5. Along Rock Street and Basin Road.
6. E. Blythe, *Farewell to Ulster* (Dublin 1970) 10-11.
7. J. M. Synge, *In West Kerry* (Dublin 1912) 60-61.
8. J. O'Connor, *Hostage To Fortune* (Dublin 1951), 5-8.
9. J. A. Curran, *Reminiscences* (London 1915), 219.
10. In 1890 Dingle stationmaster was paid £50 *per annum*, clerk to the manager at Tralee £60, ticket collector £30. Most serious of all, the locomotive engineer received only £120 (a six-day week) for looking after and repairing all locomotive and rolling stock of the Company and all other matters requiring repairs; to keep drivers' times and also an account of expenditure of oil, coals and loco stores of every description; to drive specials or take over another driver's place if necessary, or when called upon to do so'. There was no mention of any other maintenance staff until 1892.
11. By contract Worthington was to supply 4 locomotives and 70 carriages and wagons (total). In fact he supplied 4 locomotives and 47 vehicles of various kinds.
12. August 1891: Formal note from directors to general manager pointing out financial position and the need for severest economies.
13. *The Kerry Sentinel* 11 March 1896.
14. John Knightly of Killelton and a brother of the late Pat Connor of Camp who died in 1977 (lifelong servant of the railway) both worked on the Curraduff diversion as labourers. So did M. P. Griffin, who died in 1980.
15. *Cork Evening Echo* 30 January 1974.
16. M. O'Sullivan, *Twenty Years a-growing* (London 1931) 206-8.
17. *Cork Evening Echo* 17 August 1983.
18. A. J. Powell, *Trains and Railways* (London 1975) 157-162.

12. (Top) The wreckage on the Curraduff bridge and in the Finglas stream below. Note the curious 4-wheel brakevan hung on the parapet, which appears to have a cupola-style look-out; wagons smashed to matchwood and dead pigs everywhere. *(W. McCarthy or Daly of Tralee)*

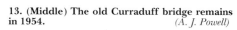

13. (Middle) The old Curraduff bridge remains in 1954. *(A. J. Powell)*

14. (Bottom) On the same occasion, the new diversion bridge over the Finglas. Both views looking towards Camp. *(A. J. Powell)*

Chapter 2
THREE MAJOR ACCIDENTS: THE CURRADUFF, BAUNOGUE AND LISPOLE DISASTERS

It was almost inevitable, given its cheap construction and lack of funds for proper maintenance, that the T&DLR would be accident-prone. Incidents with livestock and minor accidents were almost a daily occurrence throughout its working life, though surprisingly the latter days of once-monthly trains for Dingle Fair – although frequently hazardous and frightening – were free of any serious misadventure.

The railway came to the notice of the Board of Trade by way of three major accidents, early in its working life. However unhappy or serious the consequences for those involved, perhaps fatally, at the time, the historian can at least reflect philosophically how good can come from misfortune. The serious accidents ultimately drew Government grants, mostly thanks to the efforts of Tom O'Donnell MP, enabling safer trackbed diversions to be made; safety rules were tightened up: particularly in regard to the operation of block sections. Most important for the historians however, is that the three B.O.T. inquiries were extremely thorough and included a great deal of factual and technical information about the T&DLR at the times: data which would otherwise have been lost in the fire at the Company's offices in Tralee in 1910.

These reports are commended for their readability: especially the first one (1893) on the Curraduff disaster which, with its verbatim courtroom dramas, is almost like reading a novel. Copies can be consulted via the Dublin Library of the Irish Railway Record Society. There are a number of shorter, more popular accounts, mainly concerned with the Curraduff accident.[1]

THE CAMP VIADUCT (CURRADUFF) DISASTER OF 1893

The accident occurred on Whit Monday, May 22, 1893, which was the day of Dingle Pig Fair, when at Curraduff a special pig train with a coach carrying 38 pig buyers and representatives of Dennys and Lunhams factories crashed over the parapet of the viaduct, fell into the river below and killed the three members of the train crew aboard.

Just west of Camp the railway had to negotiate the steep climb up to the summit of Gleann na nGealt. This was the third highest station in all Ireland. The stiff upward climb in the westerly direction became, of course, a dangerously steep fall of line for over three miles on the homeward run, and at the bottom of this decline, below Camp village, was the very sharp curve (three chains radius at one spot) necessary to take the line across the Finglas valley. In the centre of that curve Camp Viaduct, or to give it its correct title Curraduff Bridge, was built by the contractor, Robert Worthington. Although it has not been in use since the diversion was completed in 1909, it still stands today, a mute reminder of a terrible tragedy that should never have happened.

On that day of Dingle Pig Fair in 1893 the railway was very busy, all its steam locomotives, coaches and wagons being pressed into full service to cater for the traffic. And its staff were so hard pressed that its recently-appointed Locomotive Inspector, Alfred Redshaw of Lancashire, was instructed to drive the Dingle pig special, although he was scarcely qualified to do so and was certainly a comparative stranger to the "road". He was fated to die in the crash, with his fireman Richard Dillon, and a permanent way inspector Bernard O'Loughlin.

There were many unusual circumstances leading up to the tragedy, some of which were never satisfactorily explained, although a lengthy inquest and a lengthier Board of Trade inquiry were held.

It seemed as if ill-luck were dogging the train from the moment it left Dingle with its line of seven wagons containing the pigs, one passenger coach and a brakevan. It got away at 1.30pm over half an hour late. At Lispole, the driver and the guard (Thomas O'Leary) had a loud argument as to whether the vacuum brake should be on or off. At Annascaul the train overshot the platform and had to reverse. It was when the steep ascent up the western slope of Gleann na nGealt started that the trouble really began. Whether it was that the load was too great or the engine in poor condition does not matter now, but the ascent took nearly two hours, with several stops. (A survivor stated: "We had a bad hill, a bad line, a bad engine and a bad driver.")

About 4.30pm the train reached the summit, and Redshaw who had been looking very fatigued and worried at the last stop evidently lost his head. Guard O'Leary later swore that the vacuum brake was on, but at any rate the train careered down towards Camp, throwing the pig buyers from side to side in the carriage, and in the guard's van at the rear, where nine of them were travelling against Company rules. O'Leary shouted the train was a runaway and there was immediate panic. One young man named Power jumped out half a mile from the bridge and miraculously escaped. From a distant field a man named Darcy saw the train rush down the slope towards the curving bridge and the next moment saw the tangled mass of steel and timber and dying pigs in the river below.

The engine hit the parapet, crashed through it and toppled into the valley, hauling all the pig wagons with it. Redshaw was shot into the air and hurled into a mass of debris. Dillon, who was a Corkman on loan from the Great Southern and Western Railway, was found dying underneath the engine, and the body of O'Loughlin, a native of Limerick, was found several yards away. Upwards of 100 pigs were killed. The passenger coach hung precariously over the edge but did not fall into the valley. Thirteen were seriously injured, others bruised and shocked.

Despite the terrible scene of horror all around him, Thomas O'Leary, who was not badly hurt, realised with great presence of mind that the passenger train from Dingle was due in a very short time. He immediately rushed back along the line and met the oncoming train only a short distance away. He succeeded in stopping it. O'Leary, whose son was later stationmaster at Castlegregory Junction for many years, received great praise for his action. The fact that two trains could be in the one "section" of line at all was something which could never have happened in later years, and was a sign of the slipshod signalling and operational procedure allowed in the early days of the Dingle railway.

There were great scenes of anguish and excitement after the crash. It was stated that when news reached Tralee over a thousand people gathered in the station there. Redshaw's English wife and two children presented a pitiable sight.[2] The injured pig buyers were brought back to Tralee by the Castlegregory branch train.

There was a great wave of public indignation against the unfortunate directors of the line (of whom Lt. Col. William Rowan, J.P., was chairman) and the police had to be called to prevent deeds of violence. At the official inquiry this indignation was increased by a representative of the Company foolishly hinting that the accident might have been caused by residents of Camp putting soap on the line and thus preventing the wheels from gripping. Mr Harrington, Solicitor (for Tralee Town Council) said: "The people of Camp can't buy soap to wash themselves, not to mind putting it on a railway." (laughter).

In due course the nine days wonder abated and the resentment died down. But special care had to be taken between Glean na nGealt and Camp where every train had to stop dead, before re-starting slowly around the curve. Yet this did not satisfy the engineers and after the turn of the century a lengthy deviation of the line was made. This started west of Camp village. The line went further up the valley, a new iron viaduct was built quarter of a mile southwards (it still survives) and much less severe gradients and curves were obtained.

The last train ran over the newer viaduct in July 1953, and now the shells of both survive as mute reminders of a very colourful and interesting railway, and a very dreadful accident.[2]

A gruesome footnote

To some, the most gruesome aftermath of the tragedy lay in the survival of six uninjured pigs who were then shipped to the slaughterhouse. *The Irish Times* of 26th May 1893 reported: "A consignment of six uninjured pigs, survivors of the dread crash at Camp on Monday, was today received in the Cork Bacon Factory of Messrs Lunhams."

THE BAUNOGUE ACCIDENT OF 1898

One of the bleaker and more exposed parts of the system was at Baunogue, the second summit of the line (450ft), near mile post 24 (from Tralee that is). From the lonely platform at Garrynadur the climb at 1 in 60 Eastwards was far from the road and the furthest from the linesman's cottage at Ballinclare. Here on 24th November 1898 the 7.35am train from Dingle was partly overturned. Several passengers were injured, one of whom died from the injuries later that day. The train comprised locomotive No. 6T, then almost new but due to deficiencies of maintenance among the other engines, having to carry the brunt of the workings, a covered van and three coaches.

Jamesie Moriarty, an original employee of the Company, who had worked on the construction of the line for one shilling (i.e. 5p) from 6am to 6pm each day, in a taped interview with Fr. McKenna in 1960, remembered it as a very blustery, showery day.

At the Board of Trade Inquiry, conducted by Lt. Col. Addison, the crew suggested that a sudden squall of wind had overturned the last coach on that exposed section of the line. The Official verdict confirmed this supposition but Colonel Addison's report also implied that the state of the permanent way was far from satisfactory. The damaged section had been repaired well, but elsewhere there were loose fittings and rotten sleepers. It was clearly the expert view that a roll on the poor track by the last vehicle had coincided with a gust of wind that overturned the last coach, which in turn pulled over the other two coaches before the coupling broke. The van and locomotive remained on the track.

15. Scene of the Baunogue disaster. In this view from September 1952, No. 2T on a relief special has halted for attention to the cowcatcher (pilot) which has fouled the track. *(B. C. Johns)*

16. NINE DAYS WONDER: Scene of the Lispole disaster, with Loco No. 6 having rolled down the bank from the curve, below St. John's chapel. Note the men standing in the cab, and the detached chimney far right. The man near the chimney and holding on to the fence is Tom Francis Sr, father of one of this book's authors, and at that time stationmaster at Castlegregory Junction. *(W. McCarthy)*

THE LISPOLE DERAILMENT OF 1907

This accident was fortunately free from fatalities but was nevertheless a very alarming derailment. The following details are from the subsequent Board of Trade inquiry.

The accident occurred on March 1, 1907, and the train involved was a special goods from Tralee to Dingle, hauled by engine No. 6 (built in 1897 by the Hunslet Engine Co. of Leeds at a cash price of £1,735 payment spread over three years). Beyond Garrynadur at the bottom of a steep gradient it met disaster at the approach to Lispole Viaduct. The engine jumped the rails and turned over twice before coming to rest on the grassy slope.

Driver Patrick Counihan told the inquiry (presided over by Major J. W. Pringle) that he applied his vacuum brake soon after passing through Garrynadur station to steady the train and then released it. He did this a second time and then told his fireman to apply his hand brake down the bank. He did so and the driver heard a crash under the engine as if something had broken and the speed begin to increase. He had no brake power left on the engine. He then whistled for the guard to apply his hand brake (back in the guard's van). The speed did not reduce. It continued to increase until the engine left the rails. He was thrown with the engine, first on its left side, then on its right. He crawled out of the cab close to the bridge. He had not "reversed" the engine and applied steam because he was afraid to do so on account of the sharp curves at that stretch of the line.

The train guard, Mike Foley, said that after Annascaul the train consisted of two cattle wagons (containing ordinary goods not livestock) and four covered goods wagons. When he heard the three whistles for the hand brake he applied it but the speed increased. He saw the fireman jump off the engine and then he was knocked over by the derailment. When his van came to a standstill he got out and saw the driver coming up the bank. He was bleeding from the mouth. The driver told him that the connecting rod of the hand brake broke on the engine and was useless. He (witness) could see that the vacuum brake on the wagons was working properly.

John Mullins, a cleaner and acting fireman, said that when he applied the brake something broke underneath. "She was going very quick then, about 30 to 35 miles an hour and I thought it was best to jump off."

John Donohue, permanent way inspector; Michael Jansen, ganger, and Edward Kiely Carey, locomotive superintendent, also gave evidence, mainly about the check-rails at the sharp curves near the scene.

Major Pringle himself had visited the scene 12 days after the crash. The engine was still where it had come to grief. He examined the broken brake rod and had no hesitation in saying that the two ends, a knuckle joint and screw, had been welded together with a scarf joint, and the weld showed very inferior workmanship.

In his report the Major said that from Inspector Donohue's evidence it was clear that it was not uncommon for drivers to disregard the limits of speed prescribed by the regulations: "The fatal accident which occurred near Curraduff Viaduct in May, 1893, showed the danger of high speeds on such severe gradients and sharp curves as are common on this railway. It is to be hoped that with this second derailment before them, the staff of the line will not content themselves by noting disobedience of the speed regulations, but will take action to prevent such infractions by reporting them to the traffic manager."

Another extract from the Major's lengthy findings reads as follows: "The advisability of a deviation to improve the gradient and curvature on the Curraduff incline was pointed out by the late Sir Francis Marindin in his report on the accident of 1893. The Lispole bank is another place where an improvement in alignment is much to be desired."

The directors took the latter warning to heart and a few years later (as soon as their finances would allow it) lengthy deviations of the line were made at both Camp and Lispole.

1. W. McGrath: Address to Kerry Archaeological and Historical Society, 1972; *Cuisle na tire* (CIE) No. 3, 1950; *Cork Evening Echo,* 27th May 1950; 30th January 1974; 25 September 1981.

   H. Gunston: The Camp Disaster: 90 Years On: *Llanfair Railway Journal,* No. 88, 1983, pp. 13-15.

2. Mr J. Edwards of Tralee has a set of tools stamped "A. Redshaw". After the 1893 crash, Redshaw's widow was almost penniless and had to sell all her husband's effects. Mr Edwards' father purchased the tools from her before she left Tralee.

   In the Protestant section of Tralee Burial Ground there is a headstone, extant in 1993, recording the following information:

   "Erected by Mary Redshaw in loving memory of her husband, Alfred Thomas Redshaw, killed at Camp Disaster, 22nd May, 1893, aged 27 years."

Chapter 3
THE ROUTE DESCRIBED

As a most interesting and erudite complement to the train journey Tralee-Dingle, the reader is recommended to T. F. O'Sullivan's book "Romantic Hidden Kerry", Tralee, 1931.

Setting out from the 'Dingle' station in Tralee, the line edged away from the broad gauge lines to Fenit and Limerick and followed the North Circular Road, crossing Rock Street by way of a signalled crossing after about 300 yards. Originally, the line might have extended along Rock Street itself, but the wiser counsel of Worthington prevailed. Passing the bacon factory on the right and hugging the curve of the circular road for a further 300 yards, it crossed Pembroke Street on the level, with the keeper's cottage to the left and a group of schools to the right. Proceeding past the gasworks, cemetery and nursing home to the left, trains came to an obligatory stand for the signalled crossing at the junction of Strand Street and Spa Road (3/4 miles). The keeper, whose house adjoined, would open the gates and precede the train with a flag or lamp. Originally, there was also a whistle instruction to the driver. A further 400 yards brought the Basin Road crossing, kept by a cottager, and the line proceeded south, with the boot factory and old canal basin on the right. Here, at the 1 milepost there was a stone-faced platform for Basin Halt, with a small corrugated iron building (later stone) with an awning, adjoining the boat houses on the quays and within sight of the offices of the Limerick Steamship Co. The station building became a private residence and was subsequently demolished. From this point to Blennerville, now described, is the section restored under the auspices of Tralee UDC and the Tralee-Dingle Steam Railway Company.

Immediately beyond the halt the line crossed the Dingle Road, and then crossed the River Lee by a standard steel girder bridge and continued on its own embankment across the Ballyard salt marshes of the estuary, as it left the urban area of Tralee for Blennerville and Annagh, a region frequently under water, particularly when the spring tides hit the estuary. A regular nuisance to permanent way staff, the sleepers were almost always wet, with pools of water making the trackbed spongy and in frequent need of reballasting. In latter years trains rolled badly on this section. At particularly high tides, trains might have to wait several hours for the floods to subside; local passenger timetables carrying a footnote to this effect. Impatient crews might find themselves well and truly stranded with their fires out.

From here the line ran south-west for about 3/4 miles, with views of the Slieve Marsh mountains directly ahead and the sweep of Tralee bay to the right. Then it took a sharp curve to the right across a tributary of the Lee at Hilliard's (Ballydunlea) Bridge, and joined a minor road to Blennerville. Blennerville itself could be seen ahead as the line ran on its own right-of-way adjacent to the road. Keeping to the right of this road, the line came to Blennerville station, a single platform to the right of the line, with an attractive stone building and awning, this being about 2 1/2 miles out of Tralee. Here, the restored section of line ends.

The company's rule book denoted the crossing over the Dingle Road as 'ungated', but originally gates were fitted, although the crossing was not signalled. From the crossing, and leaving the canal swing bridge and hump-backed bridge over the river on the right, the line ran, tramway style, up a narrow side lane between houses and past a now fully restored corn windmill, a landmark for miles across this flat terrain, before turning left to join the Dingle road.

Just before reaching the hamlet of Tonevane, the rails swung across the road to the left hand side, over a stream, and made a broad sweeping turn at Tonevane cross, to remain on the left side of the Dingle road. Here, as further on, the local practice of covering the heads of donkeys was prevalent, to hide from them the alarming spectacle of the on-coming train. The trains seldom slackened speed and road users, particularly cyclists and motorists in latter days, had to keep a sharp look out. Early timetables list Tonevane as an official stopping place.

Still at the left of the road it remained until approaching Curraheen, as Tralee water works with its whitewashed walls came alongside on the left, whereupon the line crossed the road and took an independent course for some 3/4 mile, on which Curraheen platform – no shelter – was situated at a crossing that served a nearby farm. On rejoining the road, it remained on the right, until both road and rail crossed the stream at Clasheen bridge, when the line curved back to the Bay for a brief stretch. After crossing another stream it passed Derrymore platform – Derry Quay to railwaymen – some 7 1/2 miles out of Tralee and another ruined mill, on the left. At this point the view had opened out, with Tralee Bay, Derrymore Strand and the distant Maharees prominent on the right, and with the Slieve Mish foothills closing in on the left. This was once a favourite spot for excursionists by train, since pathways gave good access to the sandy beach of the bay.

Rejoining the road for a few hundred yards, the line wandered away again through a couple of fields to avoid steep road inclines, and returned to the roadside close to the 'Old Green Way' at the little settlement of Killelton, with its prehistoric oratory – a link with the dawning of Christianity in Kerry. Here too, the outline of the brooding Slieve Mish range with Gearhane (2,423ft.) rose clearly to the south, while the Knockglassbeg River flowed down Glountrim to the sea.

Shortly after crossing the Knockglas estuary with its steep cliffs and inlet from the bay, a small cart track joined the road, and the train was supposed to slow to a statutory 5mph as it crossed the road and passed the outer home signal of Castlegregory Junction, $9^3/4$ miles from Tralee, the most elaborate system of tracks on the line.

This too, was once a favourite alighting point for excursionists. Fitzgerald's Bar was just across the road at the right, and Crean's a few yards down the road, opposite the branch turntable. Westbound trains for Dingle used the side platform with the main, corrugated iron and wooden buildings, while those eastbound used the island platform. Some trains from the Castlegregory branch ran through to Tralee and vice-versa but most ran into the bay siding, alongside the road, where the locomotive would run round its train and maybe attach any through coaches or wagons to the rear of main line trains. The entire track was renewed in 1933 using rails from other Irish narrow gauge lines and the two pairs of beautiful and impressive double-gantry signals were removed on closure of the branch in 1939, as was the turntable. Originally a wooden signal box stood opposite the island platform, containing eighteen levers and the electric tablet machinery. This was seemingly demolished in the 'troubles' and replaced by a ground frame on the island platform. The station house, occupied by the signalman for many years, stood across the road close by Fitzgerald's. A little lamp store close to the station building was removed in 1951.

The Junction Bar (Fitzgerald's) today preserves the memory of the Dingle Railway in a selection of framed photographs; some of the seating is made from T&DLR sleepers and the bar footrail is a length of the original 1889 rail. The site of the former station has been levelled and partly obliterated by road widening, but the Kerry Archaeological & Historical Society were instrumental in the fixing of a commemorative plaque, to the old stone water tower that remains at the roadside. This was unveiled in November 1978 by Mrs Molly O'Leary of Camp, wife of the last stationmaster at the Junction and daughter-in-law of Guard O'Leary who was commended for his actions during the Curraduff disaster.

Now just ahead on the Dingle line lay the worst and most prolonged gradient anywhere in Ireland or Britain. To the south, the hilly slopes of Knockglassmore rose steeply past the Glandine ridge to the peak of Gearhane, source of the Finglas, the white stream of Blanaid and Cuchullin in the Táin. On nearby Caherconree (2,713ft) is the fabled fort which Cuchullin carried in order to gain his love. On a fine day, an observer on the slopes of Caherconree could watch the smoke of a train all the way from Blennerville to Lispole, even though the line between Camp and Driscoll's Cottage is obscured by an intervening hill!

Into the foothills, steeped in legend, the railway climbs on its way to Dingle, curving broadly south, away from the branch line to Castlegregory (described later) which descended to road level and runs along the coast of the bay.

After a few hundred yards through scrubby fields, the main line adjoined the Dingle road on the right, though considerably lower, and crossed a trackway leading to a cluster of dwellings, via a standard steel girder bridge. Here the climb began in earnest, at 1 in 35 alongside the road, crossing the Finglas by a steel bridge and passing the original outer distant signal for the junction. Here there were views of successive waterfalls of the Finglas in a gorge below which flowed into a millpond that once served the disused Bunowa mill. The branch line crossed this same stream lower down. The course of the appalling curve (nominal 3 chains radius) across the original stone viaduct at

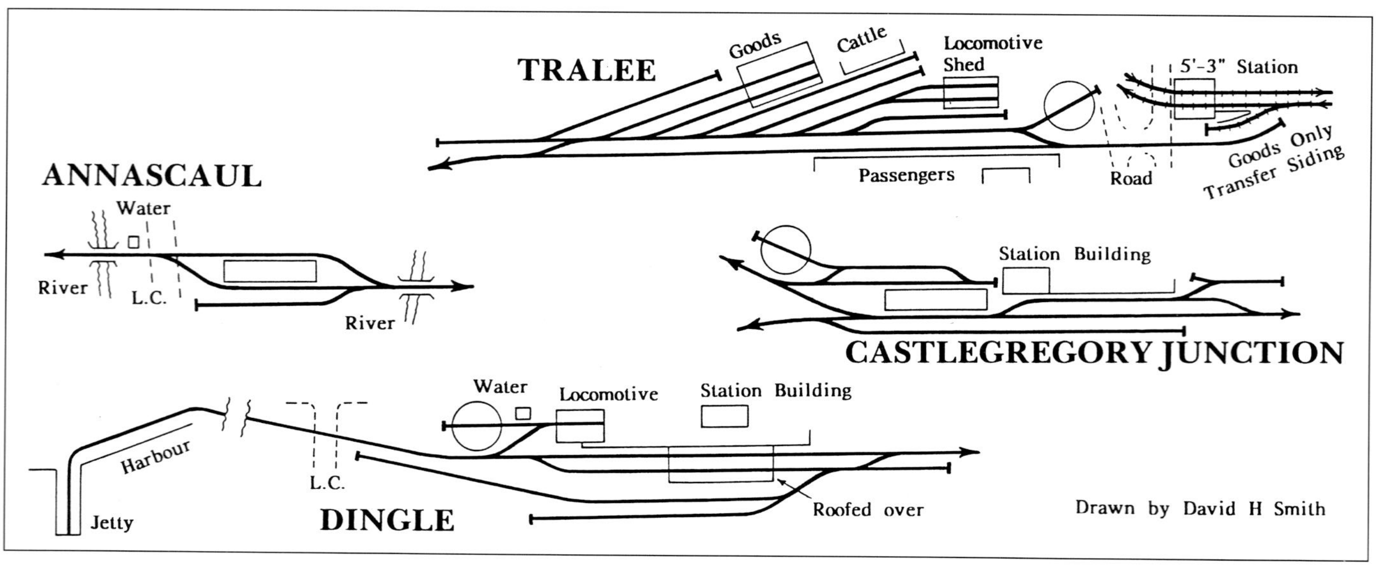

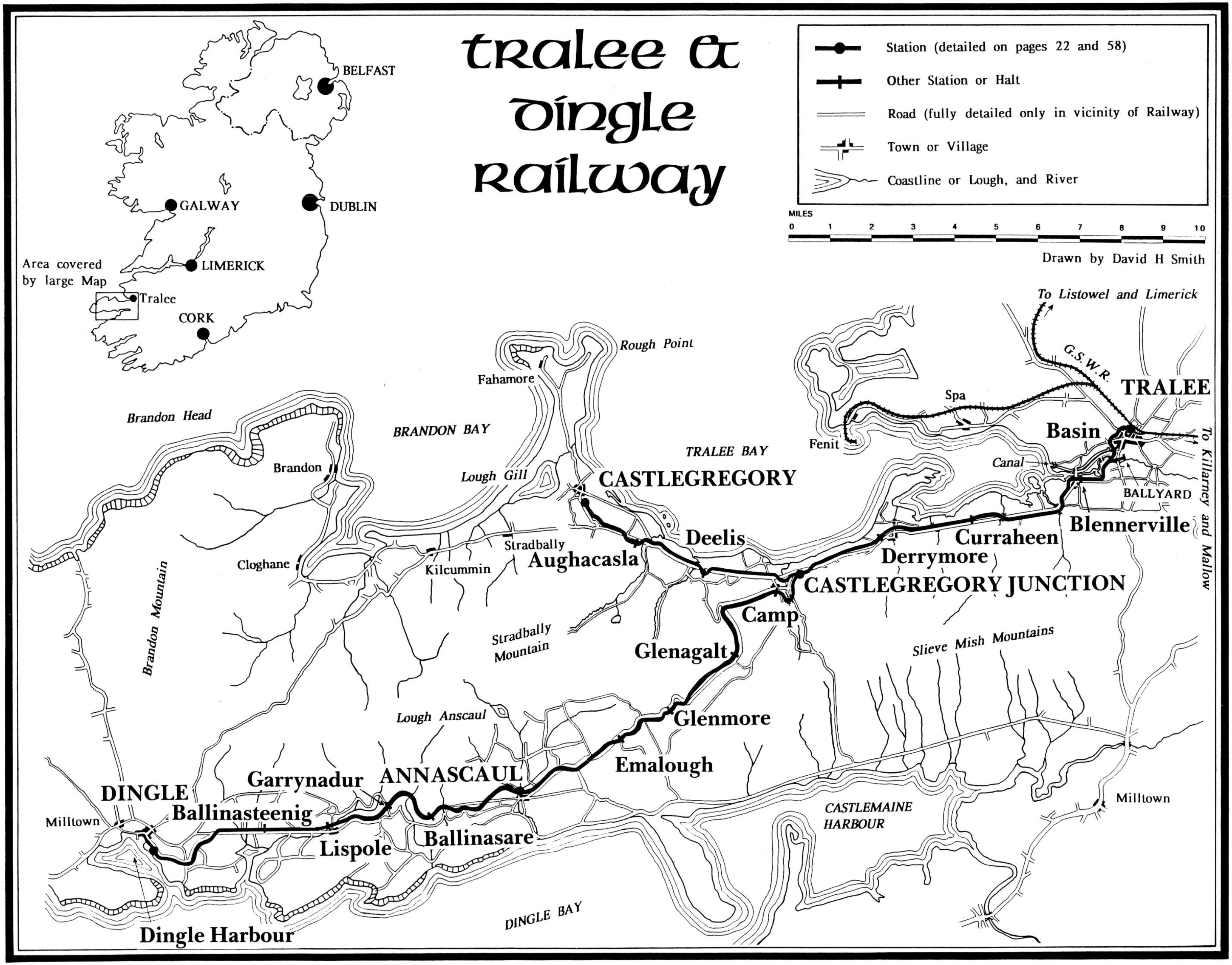
tralee & dingle railway
Station (detailed on pages 22 and 58)
Other Station or Halt
Road (fully detailed only in vicinity of Railway)
Town or Village
Coastline or Lough, and River
MILES
0 1 2 3 4 5 6 7 8 9 10
Drawn by David H Smith
BELFAST
GALWAY
DUBLIN
LIMERICK
Area covered by large Map
Tralee
CORK
To Listowel and Limerick
G.S.W.R.
TRALEE
To Killarney and Mallow
Spa
Fenit
Basin
Canal
BALLYARD
Blennerville
Curraheen
Derrymore
CASTLEGREGORY JUNCTION
TRALEE BAY
Rough Point
Fahamore
BRANDON BAY
Brandon Head
Brandon
Lough Gill
CASTLEGREGORY
Deelis
Stradbally
Aughacasla
Kilcummin
Cloghane
Brandon Mountain
Camp
Stradbally Mountain
Glenagalt
Slieve Mish Mountains
Glenmore
Lough Anscaul
Emalough
ANNASCAUL
Garrynadur
DINGLE
Ballinasteenig
Milltown
Lispole
Ballinasare
CASTLEMAINE HARBOUR
Milltown
DINGLE BAY
Dingle Harbour

Curraduff could be seen: a U-turn in the hillside, above the road and 30ft above the river gorge. This was the scene of the notorious pig special disaster of 1893. The diversion of 1907-8 took an easier curve, passing beneath a concrete over-bridge and crossing the river on a standard steel bridge, only a short distance from the reputed 'Faisi's grave' with its ogham inscriptions. Passing the site of Camp castle, the grassy platform of Camp village was gained on an easier slope at 1 in 50, with school and church close by. Tralee-bound trains had a compulsory stop here for brake adjustments before the final descent on to the Curraduff curves which were still sharp by any standards even after the diversion. After Camp, the climb stiffened with a steep pull of 1 in 28 up to the $11^1/_2$ mile point, then easing slightly to 1 in 30 for the next mile.

On the right, passengers had superb glimpses of Tralee bay, way out to Carrigaha. In days when the Castlegregory branch train was running, the connecting service from the junction could be seen speeding through the fields to Deelis.

Just past the 12 mile point, the line curved south again quite sharply, preparatory to crossing the central spine of the mountains. The road was crossed on this curve, at Scrallaghbeg gate (Skirlough crossing) where there was a gatekeeper's lodge, called Driscoll's Cottage after the two sisters who lived there. Their lemonade made with water from the glen (Tobernagalt) was famous locally. The crossing was signalled with double semaphore arms on the single pole. This was one of the loneliest cottages on the system. Today it is the property of Padraig Kennelly and an ideal place from which to view the panorama. There was a 5mph speed limit in force here, though descending trains often exceeded it and the crossing gates were demolished more than once. Ascending trains were often at walking pace or less by the time they reached Glenagalt bank beyond this crossing. The crossing was also protected by a short stone wall, built against the funnelling winds from the bay, after a train was blown off the rails in a gale on Christmas Eve 1912.

The line proceeded slightly below the roadway to its left, following the contour of the hillside for $1^3/_4$ miles at 1 in 31 up Glenagalt bank, crossing small streams that fed Glenagalt stream in the picturesque valley below. Sheep were always a nuisance on this part of the line, hindering the struggling trains upwards. In the valley stood the farmhouse and spring of Tobernagalt whose waters have mystical healing properties attributed to them.

The line had now gained its highest point and, rounding a curve at the head of the valley reached the platform at Glenagalt bridge halt and entered a short cutting shortly before the 14 mile point. Here trains in both directions were supposed to halt for attention to brakes and to ensure enough steam pressure for the vacuum. Glenagalt was one of the bleakest, loneliest spots on the line. Even on a fine day, the valley was always hushed and quiet. Just beyond the platform, a bridge crossed the railway carrying a track down into the valley, joined by a path from the platform itself. At one time the halt had a tin-roofed shelter. Another bridge was passed a few yards further on and the train began the descent at 1 in 30 for a continuous 2 miles.

There were no longer views of Tralee bay to the north, for the mountains had been crossed. Now there were occasional glimpses of Dingle bay to the south and west. A very brief respite came in the levelling at milepost 15 then, if the rule book was being observed, speed was reduced for the sharp reverse curves approaching Glenmore over the next mile or so.

Swinging across the road and then the stream by a neat little stone bridge, there was a brief rise of 1 in 29 to Glenmore platform and crossing. An old resident of the district avers that trains ceased to stop at the bridge after a few years and instead halted westward at Lougher, which the railwaymen then called Glenmore Halt. The crossing at Glenmore was blind for both road and rail and probably the most dangerous on the entire system. It was the scene of many accidents and near misses. Eastbound trains usually stopped for a breather and to blow up steam pressure before the final slog up to Glenagalt summit. Westward, the run to Emalough was one of continuous switchback, with rising pitches of 1 in 37 and some atrociously sharp curves which hugged the course of the road, except for a short deviation to the south at milepost 16, passing Lougher, where there was no platform but courtesy stops in passenger days. The rise continued up to the 17 milepost with brief levelling before a further climb at 1 in 37 up to Emalough platform, with shelter and the road crossing at Gortbreagogue whence came a final levelling before the helter-skelter descent started in earnest. The station here was known as Emalough Cross in T&DLR days and shown as such on their tickets. The descent was continuous at 1 in 29, alongside the road, with the majesty of Flemingstown mountain, Killduff mounds and Glan Lough to the north, and picturesque Dingle bay to the south west. Just before milepost 18 the line crossed the road again to enter Gleann an Scail, and the legendary site of Cuchullin's fight with the giant. The beauty of this district and its heroic and literary residents has been vividly described by James Lyons. Sheep were again a hazard on this stretch of line. The trains seldom gave other travellers any warning or slackened their speed downwards over the many road crossings. Close to the settlement of Mall, another courtesy stopping place, there was a short level stretch while road and rail parted company to avoid some bluffs in the hillside. Rejoining the road and crossing a stream by a steel bridge, the line crossed the old path to the derelict Ballintermon House, and another to the Manor House, scene of one of William Hope Hodgson's novels. The descent west resumed at 1 in 29-33, providing a formidable task for loaded trains coming east from Annascaul and the cause of much stopping, restarting and delay with cattle trains.

The rails kept north of the road until they passed the

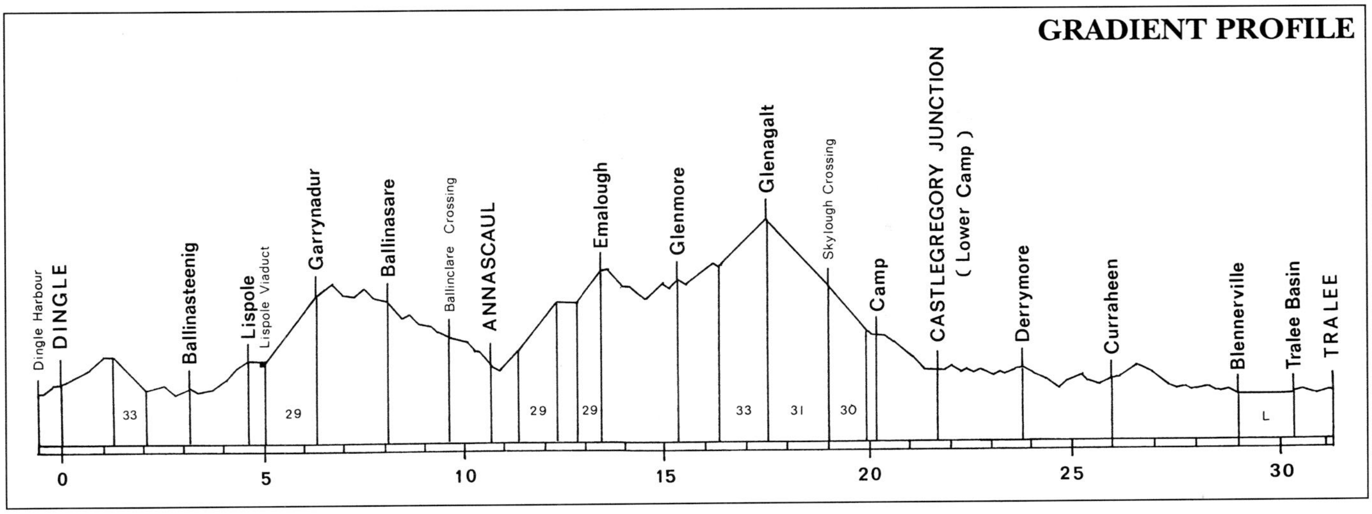

school, diverging on their own right of way, and ran north of the South Pole Inn on the left with its many memories of Tom Crean, Antarctic explorer. Crean used to walk down to the station at Annascaul every evening, in the years 1920-38 to collect his daily paper sent out from Tralee. The line crossed a tributary of the Owenascaul just above the village. Beneath an arch of trees that fringed a brief cutting, the line crossed the main stream of the Owenascaul, and entered Annascaul station, immediately north of the village.

The track layout was simple but effective here, with passing loop and goods bay, corrugated iron buildings and stone water towers at either end of the yard. As at Lower Camp, one of the towers, had been out of use for many years, and was replaced by a standpipe. There was also a standpipe beside the buffer stop in the goods bay. The west tower stood close by the station house, just beyond the road crossing. A pleasant feature of the station in summer, as with many of the hedgerows of the trip, was the bank of red fuchsias on the north side. Today the site is almost covered with housing, though the water towers remain.

Sean Kennedy has told us how fishermen from the Blasket islands came across to Dingle each year and thence travelled by train to Annascaul. This was a regular expedition to gather tree branches, sally reeds and willow canes in order to repair their lobster pots for the year ahead. Annascaul was their nearest source of trees. Maurice Keane (1870-1961) has confirmed this in his autobiography *On Land and Sea* published posthumously in 1990 from a phonograph recording of his reminiscences.

Straight off the platform edge, the climb up to a second summit began. The line crossed another branch of the Owenascaul just beyond the water tower and entered a cutting. Rising steepily at 1 in 32, the line veered momentarily north, on the longest stretch away from the road, in order to avoid some acute curves and bluffs.

Up the scrubby slopes at Ballynacourty, the climb had eased to 1 in 39 past milepost 21, and the train would whistle for Ballinclare gate where there was a stone cottage and double signal. The pathway from the crossing led to the Fair Green, where the famous spring and autumn Ballinclare Fairs were held. Extra trains were run for this occasion, in shuttle from Annascaul and Dingle. One of the line's gangers lived here for many years, and permanent way and fencing materials were frequently unloaded. As at Skirlough, it was a very isolated spot. Over the road, the line swung south and past the townland of Farrannacorrigan and milepoint 22. After an occupational crossing, the line veered further south to avoid contours before turning north to cross the road again at Gortacurraun gate on a sharp curve, and almost immediately, Ballinacourty gate, where there was a cottage for the keeper, but no signal.

From this point the up-grade stiffened, turning south at 1 in 30, skirting Ballinvogig past milepoint 23 and up to Ballinasare platform beside the crossing for Ballynasare bridge. Continuing its winding course, the line turned north once again to cross a trackway at Ballynasare Beg and climbing at 1 in 40-50 up through Baunogue South to milepoint 24 at the apex of a sweeping curve which turned south once again. The second summit of the line was gained just beyond milepoint 24 and was on a very open, scrubby section, exposed to the fierce winds that swept the mountainside. Several incidents of trains being blown off the rails occurred at this point; that of 1898 involving a passenger fatality. After milepoint 24, the descent resembled that from Emalough, and was continuous at 1 in 60 past a corner of Puckisland townland to Garrynadur platform, where a pathway to the Dingle road was crossed.

The descent was now very steep, at 1 in 29 for almost a mile, rejoining the Dingle road, close to milepoint 25, with the Owenalondrig river slightly to the north. In the north-east towered Slievenagower (1803ft), Benoskee (2713ft) and Knockmulanane (1913 ft). Road and rail were briefly together for the descent as far as St John's chapel, where the railway diverged on to the acute curves approaching Lispole viaduct, still at 1 in 29, scene of the 1907 derailment which resulted in a safer diversion being built in 1909. The descent actually finished in the middle of the viaduct spans, a fact which is obvious on viewing the line from the side. There was a 10mph speed restriction over the curves and viaduct but this was often exceeded by locomotives pushed downhill from the summit by their heavy trains.

In the 1920s, the civil engineer expressed concern at the condition of Lispole viaduct and put an absolute ban on double-heading of locomotives over the spans. This was seldom observed, however, for two practical reasons – descending trains, as we have mentioned, were often pushed down by their weight and stopping to uncouple locos was out of the question; ascending trains were too concerned about climbing the bank at all to risk stopping and not being able to re-start on the 1 in 29 up! The viaduct was an elegant structure of two 50ft. steel spans approached by stone arches. It is still standing in 1996.

The Dingle road was rejoined by the railway close by Lispole smithy, where the Long Straight – 2 miles through Ballinasteenig and more or less on the level – began. Lispole station was at the occupational crossing by milepoint 26; Churchfield was to the north, and the ruined site of St Martin's Church. In the goods only days of the 1940s, quite lengthy stops were scheduled here in both directions, indicating considerable freight traffic and there was a short siding into which wagons were shunted. Turf (peat) specials were run from Annascaul bogs to Lispole and 2 or 3 wagon-loads left in the siding for farmers and householders to purchase direct from the trucks. The last "Station Master" (i.e. halt keeper) at Lispole was a Miss Mary O'Sullivan who has many memories of the railway goods traffic to her community.

Passing through Cloonacurran on the level, trains could accelerate here, though the proximity of the road made it a dangerous spot for cyclists and pedestrians (often 'herds' with their animals). Passing Whitepound bridge and fording the river at Emlagh bridge where there was a crossing, the line passed Ballinasteening platform with a shelter at one time, near to milepoint 28.

There was a short rise over the Garfinny river, but still on the straight, with the woollen mill and Flemingstown to the north, and the line continued alongside a low stone wall for a full half mile through Ballineetig, sometimes marshy at times of spring tides, until the road split into two, both bound for Dingle. The railway line swung very sharply across the road into a narrow passage between stone walls, dividing the road and hedges, and taking the south side of the lower road past milepoint 29, climbing now at 1 in 33 for about a mile due south to Ballintaggart and the site of the old church, from where there are clear views across to and beyond Beenbane Head to Valentia and Cahirciveen. The summit was at milepoint 30, close to Ballintaggart Lodge, reputed to be haunted! This short level stretch crossed the pathway to Beenbane as the descent began alongside the road to Lough Lodge, where views across to Reen were to be had. Still on the falling grade at the roadside, the Dingle racecourse was passed and the whole town of Dingle was to be seen spread out below, the railway station being prominently above the town, with its barn-like over-roof and guardian signals, immediately north of the old coastguard station.

The station yard at Dingle was quite comprehensive for a narrow gauge line. Passing the outer signal to enter the yard, there was a farmhouse on the left, behind the cattle pens, and a goods loading-bay with crane and corrugated-iron-roofed concrete store. Over the passenger lines, the over-roof of wood stretched from the station building alongside the single platform, was the stationmaster's house, now demolished. From the end of the platform, three steps led down to the back door of the single-road locomotive shed, a stone building dated 1914, which replaced an earlier timber structure destroyed by fire during the "troubles." The stationmaster's house was altered at the same time, and the station building and over-roof were rebuilt in the early 1920s after damage during 'The Troubles'. Behind the locomotive shed was the stone water tower (same pattern as at Annascaul and Lower Camp) with hand-pump for raising water, and two permanent way huts, one originally a lampshed. These were close by the stone-built whitewashed keeper's cottage, beside the gates at the west end of the yard, where a single track led down to the harbour in the town below. By a curious coincidence both terminal stations at Tralee and Dingle are now in use as funeral parlours.

The extension to the pier was out of use from the 1930s onwards. It descended very steeply at 1 in 29 in a cutting alongside the road, through another pair of gates at the path to Emlagh cottages, which were on the left. Here road and rail finally diverged, the road continuing to Bridge Street or The Mall, the railway crossing the stream on a small timber decked bridge (still in existence) more or less on the level, a section that was frequently flooded during high tides. The line followed the curve of the harbour, and the platform of the little station, designated 'Pier' although short of it, was on the right, usually festooned in fishing nets, with the corrugated-iron covered building, locally named 'The Red Shed' just behind. The line continued along its alleyway until this opened into Quay Street and close by the harbour office, it diverged briefly on to the quay itself. The railway line on to the quay had the distinction of being the most westerly rails in Europe!

A most interesting account of walking the trackbed in the opposite Dingle-Tralee direction, was given by David Foster in the *Cork Holly Bough* 1990, pages 22 and 27. Mr Foster's account was re-presented with many interesting photos in colour as "Through Rare West Kerry" in the tourist magazine *Ireland of the Welcomes* Vol. 42 (No.3), 1993.

The text continues, after the photographic coverage of the route, on page 58.

TRALEE

17. No. 8T having collected brakevans from the Main Line yard, and filled the 3-plank open wagon with coal for the round trip to Dingle (as well as stacking extra briquettes between the toolboxes), moves out of the yard and down the street tramway (Ashe Street) to the Narrow Gauge terminus, June 1950. *(Ivo Peters, copyright Julian Peters)*

18. It is Fair Day Eve, July 1951, and 2T reverses after No. 1T (in distance) down Ashe Street and past Latchford's Mill, to coal-up in the Broad Gauge yard. Note the month's accumulation of dirt gouged from the flangeway. *(E. S. Russell)*

19. Inspector Crowe walks alongside No. 1T as she returns to the NG yard, after coaling – note the stacked briquettes; July 1951. *(E. S. Russell)*

TRALEE

20. After marshalling the train, No. 1T (in better condition) awaits the arrival of 2T to become train engine on the cattle special. Meantime the fireman redistributes briquettes, while a group of staff collect their pay (right). *(E. S. Russell)*

21. No. 2T now in place as train engine, the ensemble is ready to leave – almost! No. 1T develops an injector fault and the whole train has to reverse from alongside the carriage works to give 1T access to the loco shed/workshop. *(E. S. Russell)*

22. No. 1T is now "on shed". The CIE Inspectors are looking after her. Note that the reversed train is only just inside the yard gates. Note 5T's old toolbox in use on 2T as extra sandbox. *(E. S. Russell)*

TRALEE

23. IN GOODS ONLY DAYS. Early morning at Tralee. No. 5T is at right, on the 7.30am daily freight working to Dingle (return trip 12 noon ex-Dingle). No. 3T on shed, shortly to be drafted to the Cavan & Leitrim section, while those coaches will go to the West Clare. It is 11th April 1940. *(D. W. K. Jones)*

24. The building (1918) replaced an earlier wooden shed that was burned down. Here in July 1950, Nos. 6T (L) and 1T (R) are on shed. Note water tower inside shed door (L). *(T. J. Edgington)*

25. The shed line ran back at raised level into the loco workshop for maintenance access. Well-equipped until the 1930s, the shops had to make-do-and-mend after that: hacksaws and hammers being popular tools. The shed had lifting gantry and sheerlegs. Here No. 8T rests between duties on the monthly specials, still looking in remarkably good external condition. *(T. J. Edgington)*

26. (Above) Tralee Basin Quay in the 1890s, with the course of the railway running in the rear distance. *(Lawrence Collection, Dublin)*

BASIN HALT

27. A rare view of the stone building at Tralee Basin Halt, derelict at the time of this 1950s view. It replaced an earlier corrugated iron hut, but was later demolished. *(Author's Collection)*

BASIN – BLENNERVILLE

28. EN ROUTE TO BASIN: No. 6T with the 8.30am mixed train for Dingle (and through coach for Castlegregory) has just crossed Strand Street, Tralee. It is the last days of independence, 1924, and the T&DLR, though impoverished, is at its zenith. *(LCGB: K. A. C. R. Nunn)*

29. Nos. 8T and 1T are beyond Basin and en route to Hillyards Bridge and Blennerville in this view taken from the brakevan of an empty cattle working to Dingle, June 1952. *(H. S. Orbach)*

30. Nos. 1T and 2T with cattle empties for Dingle, June 1951, cross the Ballyard salt marshes and approach the Blennerville road, near Hillyard's bridge.
(Ivo Peters, copyright Julian Peters)

BLENNERVILLE

31. NOT QUITE "THE FLOATING TRAIN", No. 6T halted with the daily goods for Dingle, waits alongside the road for the floods to subside, in the spring of 1949. Blennerville is in the far distance.
(Rev. Shirehampton)

32. Blennerville in the 1890s, showing the windmill disused in those days too! Blennerville station is to the left of the mill tower. *(Lawrence Collection, Dublin)*

33. The railway crossed the main street of Blennerville and here in 1931 a passenger train working through to Tralee from the Castlegregory branch, crosses behind loco 6T. *(Courtesy Padraig Kennelly)*

BLENNERVILLE

34. Here in April 1952 8T and 1T draw up to Blennerville station with a fully loaded cattle train from Dingle Fair. Note the disused and derelict windmill tower, a landmark for miles around. *(C. L. Fry)*

35. Almost the same spot as 34, taken during track lifting in 1954 and showing sleepers and rail stacked on the old platform. *(A. J. Powell)*

36. Almost 40 years later, tracklaying in progress on the new site of Blennerville station. Note the splendidly refurbished windmill.

BLENNERVILLE – LOWER CAMP

37. The daily goods working (12 noon ex-Dingle) has stopped and ultimately passed one cow, only to encounter another. No. 6T at Curraheen in April 1940 has cows fore and aft of her train. *(D. W. K. Jones)*

38. Driver Paddy Martin on train engine No. 1T looks out as they cross the road at Curraheen en route to Dingle with cattle empties on the last Fair workings, June 1953. The train comprised the entire stock left in running order: 6 wagons and brakevan 5T. Note 1T's cracked spectacle glass. Taken from the pilot loco, 8T. *(H. S. Orbach)*

39. Site of Curraheen crossing in 1992, with tramway rails still visible. *(D. H. Smith)*

40. AT SPEED: making good pace on the straight, Nos. 1T and 2T pass Ivo Peters' famous Bentley, close by milepost 8 at Derrymore Bridge, June 1951. *(Ivo Peters, copyright Julian Peters)*

41. No. 5T pilots 8T on a cattle working from Dingle in 1943, leaving the railway's own right of way, and rejoining the road *(Fr. F. Browne SJ)*

CASTLEGREGORY JUNCTION

42. HIGH DAYS AND HOLIDAYS: An excursion from Dingle to Derrymore strand in 1912 has paused at the island platform to pick up more excursionists. Note the signal box at right. Photographed from the signal ladder, looking East toward Derrymore. Although this old print is rather faded, it is of value in being one of only two known views of the signal box. *(W. McCarthy)*

43. DUAL LANGUAGE: Looking west from the island platform in 1932, at a somewhat indecisive gantry signal. The photographer is standing in the branch bay. Centre left the line climbs away to Camp and Dingle; centre, the branch drops down to the Castlegregory road, and at right is the short spur up to the turntable (used by the branch engine). Crean's pub (Aunty's) at right. *(James Fisher)*

44. Late afternoon July 1951 and a loaded cattle train returns from Dingle Fair behind 1T and 2T. The train is at about the same spot as that in picture No. 42. Note the branch tracks lifted from the bay and the ground frame (left) that replaced the former signal box.
(T. O'Brien, Cork Examiner)

CASTLEGREGORY JUNCTION

45. Close up of the Ground frame, 1954. *(A. J. Powell)*

46. Castlegregory Junction, 1939 in the last week of passenger operations. Left distance. "main" line to Dingle; centre distance, the branch to Castlegregory; right, the slope up to the turntable. *(G. J. Aston)*

47. The outgoing special of empty cattle trucks for Dingle, July 1951 behind 1T and 2T, taking water at the standpipe. The stone water tower visible behind the train (centre) had been out of use for many years. *(E. S. Russell)*

48. (Top) **COMMEMORATION:** The derelict water tower was the only surviving relic of the station site at the junction after road widening in 1978. Here, at the instigation of the Kerry Archaeological and Historical Society, a plaque commemorating the railway was unveiled by Mrs Molly O'Leary, widow of the last stationmaster at the Junction, and daughter-in-law of the guard of the Curraduff disaster train.
(Author's Collection)

49. (Middle) **THROUGH TRAFFIC:** In April 1938, No. 6T, the branch engine, is seen attaching the coach from Castlegregory and bogie bolster No. 77T, to the rear of the 2.30pm mixed train from Dingle to Tralee. *(W. A. Camwell)*

50. (Bottom) Adjustment to the motion of No. 1T while No. 2T takes water from the standpipe. C/f photo 47. July 1951. Empty cattle working for Dingle. Note the number of running wagons (plus a further 8 on a "relief" working the same day) compared to the final working in 1953 (photo 38).
(E. S. Russell)

51. (Top) STEEPED IN LEGEND. In this 1977 view one of the authors (Walter McGrath) is pointing out the Ogham stone at the alleged Faisi's grave, near Camp, to Stephen Coughlan (News Editor, Cork Examiner). In the background are BOTH Curraduff bridges over the Finglas: top left the original 1891 and centre right the diversion.

52. (Middle) MODERN IMAGE? A slotted concrete signal post at Camp in 1954. *(A. J. Powell)*

53. (Bottom) CAMP: Looking West at the platform close by St. Mary's church and school. Alongside is the field donated to the school by Great Southern Railways. *(J. M. Jarvis)*

54. Just past Curraduff and climbing to Camp, Nos. 1T and 2T head west in June 1951. The cottage, centre (just above 1T's cab) belonged to M. P. Griffin who worked on the Curraduff diversion.
(Ivo Peters, copyright Julian Peters)

55. BETWEEN CAMP AND SKIRLOUGH: Beginning to climb in earnest, Nos. 8T and 1T in June 1952 with empty wagons for Dingle Fair. Tralee Bay in the background, Castlegregory and the Maharees at Left. *(H. S. Orbach)*

56. SKYLOUGH (SKIRLOUGH) CROSSING: Ivo Peters' Bentley waits as the train behind 1T and 2T crosses the road to begin the climb of Glenagalt Bank proper, at 1 in 29: the stiffest (and longest!) bank on any railway in these islands. The Crossing keeper's cottage (Driscoll's) is just above the bank on the right. *(Ivo Peters, copyright Julian Peters)*

GLENAGALT BANK

57. GLENAGALT BANK: Nos. 1T and 2T begin the long slog up to Glenagalt summit, June 1951. Driscoll's Cottage is just visible in centre background, above the train.
(Ivo Peters, copyright Julian Peters)

58. At almost the same spot as 57, 1T and 2T plod upward in July 1951. *(E. S. Russell)*

59. HEAD OF THE VALLEY: Rounding the curve 1T and 2T are drawing near to the summit of the bank and a welcome rest at Glenagalt Halt, July 1951. *(E. S. Russell)*

GLENAGALT SUMMIT

60. GLENAGALT PLATFORM: The outgoing LRTL/IRRS "Last Passenger" special behind loco No. 8T pauses for a blow-up alongside the abandoned platform. The concrete slab (left) marks the former shelter. Taken from the overbridge.
(D. G. Coakham)

61. The "Relief" working for Dingle Fair, June 1951 behind 8T, pauses at Glenagalt platform. Note loco stacked with briquettes even though an additional coal wagon accompanies the train. *(W. A. Camwell)*

GLENAGALT – ANNASCAUL

62. 8T with "Relief" special for Dingle Fair, June 1951, pauses in the cutting just behind Glenagalt platform to pin down brakes for the helter-skelter descent to Annascaul.
(W. A. Camwell)

63. Rushing downhill from Glenagalt, Nos. 1T and 2T approach the road crossing at Glenmore, the most dangerous on the line and scene of numerous scrapes and near-misses, June 1951.
(Ivo Peters, copyright Julian Peters)

64. Still coasting downhill this Dingle-bound special is approaching Emalough crossing. Pat Whitehouse's head just visible behind the driver in the cab of 1T, June 1952. *(H. S. Orbach)*

ANNASCAUL

65. June 1951 Annascaul and 8T on early "relief" working is taking water, while Willie Garratt's fitter from Tralee tinkers – here seen at the toolbox.
(Ivo Peters, copyright Julian Peters)

66. A few minutes later 8T eases forward to clear the water tower for the out-going double-header behind 1T and 2T. Michael Davies in front of 8T.
(Ivo Peters, copyright Julian Peters)

67. Returning fully loaded from Dingle Fair, No. 8T is taking water at the West end of Annascaul yard. No. 1T is standing on the little bridge over the Owenascaul stream that makes an island of the site. Both locos will fill left hand tanks here, then move up-yard to the standpipe to fill the right hand tanks, June 1952. . . . . *(H. S. Orbach*

68. . . . . which they have just finished doing here, as the train prepares to start the long switch-back section up to Glenmore and Glenagalt, June 1952.
(H. S. Orbach)

69. The out-going train of empties to Dingle, June 1952 has watered engines at both ends of the station and has reversed back to the platform to clear the level crossing and release traffic. Bill Hanlon in the cab of 8T (pilot), John Powell walking back along platform, beside 1T.
(H. S. Orbach)

70 & 71. Two views of the July 1951 working of empties to Dingle behind 1T and 2T. Note the party of Scouts (from Caherconree) among whom was one of the authors (W. McGrath). *(E. S. Russell)*

72. NEAR THE SECOND SUMMIT: No. 2T pauses with a "relief" special in September 1952, to unload fencing posts for the ganger who lived in the cottage here — that of the Crossing Keeper at Ballinaclare. *(R. N. Clements)*

73. GARRYNADUR: The returning LRTL/IRRS Last Passenger special, June 1953, halts at Garrynadur in the evening sun, behind loco 8T. Framed in the cab is Fireman Bill Lynch and Guard Casey in the door of the brakevan. *(J. C. Gillham)*

74. LISPOLE VIADUCT. A lovely panoramic view of the empty cattle wagon special for Dingle Fair in June 1951, behind 1T and 2T. Note no question of uncoupling the pilot!
(Ivo Peters, copyright Julian Peters)

75. LISPOLE VIADUCT. The out-going LRTL/IRRS Special, June 1953, pauses on the decking of the viaduct, close by St. John's chapel – compare with the accident picture (No. 16). *(C. L. Fry)*

76. The same train, broadside. *(J. C. Houlihan)*

77. LISPOLE STATION. Rather a dark print but an important one, being the only view we know of Lispole station. Note the corrugated iron shelter and goods store, the oil lamp on pole and the glimpse of the goods siding at left of picture. No. 8T is bound for Dingle with the afternoon mixed train, in 1935. *(F. Le Manquais, per T. Middlemas)*

78. Ballinasteenig platform in 1949, without shelter any longer (note concrete base), but still with dual-language name-board. The "Long Straight" heads toward Dingle in the distance. *(Rev. Shirehampton)*

79. June 1951 and the outgoing train of empty cattle wagons has the end of its journey to Dingle in sight as it passes Ballinasteenig on the "Long Straight".

(Ivo Peters, copyright Julian Peters)

DINGLE

80. Dingle station, No. 1T with a late-evening relief special (late due to steaming problems) draws alongside the stationmaster's house in August 1951. *(Author's Collection)*

81. A view of the over-roof and cattle pens at Dingle in between monthly specials, 1950. *(C. L. Fry)*

82. A rare view of the pillars of Dingle station, not often captured by photographers. Here the LRTL/IRRS Special of June 1953 is departing from the station, giving a short ride to the schoolchildren of Dingle who had gathered to sing a song of welcome on this historic occasion. *(D. G. Coakham)*

DINGLE

83. A general view from the West end of Dingle yard, looking East in July 1952. No. 8T is on shed and 1T alongside the turntable (centre left). *(H.S. Orbach)*

84. The West end of Dingle yard and the old Crossing keeper's cottage. In later years Driver Jack Cotter lived in this house and as you see he has parked his engine overnight, quite convenient for the morning! The track going through the gates at the left is the disused harbour branch, or Pier extension, as the Railway Company called it. This scene is in August 1951. *(Author's Collection)*

85. A view of the Pier extension/harbour branch with the overgrown track still in situ (left). In the distance is Dingle town. *(Author's Collection)*

86. A splendid "railway" view of Dingle, showing the station centre left, the harbour (pier) extension centre and parallel with the thicket of shrubs, the "Pier" station and the pier itself, early 1900s. *(Lawrence, Dublin)*

CASTLEGREGORY BRANCH

87. OVERVIEW (from signal post) of Castlegregory terminus. Lamp huts and Stationmaster's house (similar to that at Dingle) at left, with station building (corrugated iron) beyond. Coach for the 3.35pm to the Junction awaits at platform, this will be added to the rear of the 2.30pm ex-Dingle (see 49). Branch loco 6T on shed centre, goods bay at right, April 1938. *(W. A. Camwell)*

88. In this scene of 1935, No. 3T is branch loco. This train had worked through from Tralee at 11.55am, arriving at Castlegregory 1.20pm. On the return working (3.55pm) the coach would be added to the 2.30pm ex-Dingle and 3T would remain at the junction to take the branch coach from the 5.30pm ex-Tralee. This would reach Castlegregory about 7pm. The only through working from Castlegregory to Tralee was the 8.10am (school) train, arriving at Tralee 8.46. It ran an hour and a half later on Saturdays. Note boxes of shellfish at right of train, waiting to be loaded and the glimpse of the station building. *(F. Le Manquais, per T. Middlemas)*

89. **THE LAST TRAIN OUT:** Staff and locals pose for the last time with branch loco No. 6T, April 1939. The lady in the long coat standing in front of 6T's chimney is Molly O'Leary who, 40 years later, was to unveil the plaque at Castlegregory Junction (see photo 48). Her husband, Jack O'Leary, stationmaster at Castlegregory Junction is at right, standing on the rail in front of 6T's cowcatcher.
(Author's Collection)

90. Autumn 1939 and the branch is being lifted. In this scene below Bunowa, near the Junction, local boys have commandeered a trolley used by the demolition gangs. Second from left is Tom Quilter of San Francisco, who sent us the photo. *(T. Quilter)*

CASTLEGREGORY BRANCH

On leaving the junction at Lower Camp, the branch line for Castlegregory descended quickly to road level, passing the branch locomotive's turntable opposite Crean's pub, and immediately crossing the Dingle road which turned off left. The branch left the road briefly to pursue a separate way round a sharp curve beside the smithy at Bunowa bridge. Here the line spanned the Finglas river by one of the standard steel bridges (now demolished), the stone-faced road bridge (now widened) being some thirty yards to the right. Today the old Bunowa mill is partly refurbished as a summer residence. Within about a hundred yards the road was rejoined and the rails immediately crossed over to the right hand side, by Garrahies House. Keeping along this side, the minor road from Camp village to Tonakilly was crossed as it intersected the main road, and Kilgobbin Church of Ireland and the rectory could be seen across the fields toward the sea, which was only about a third of a mile away. Part of the stretch of railway between Bunowa and Carrigaha was liable to flooding, though there are no records of delays to trains from this cause, and certainly after 1926 no extensive maintenance to the trackbed was necessary.

Passing the 1 milepost from the junction, Glenfield House, with its gate-lodge, came up on the left, with the house hidden by trees, as road and rail threaded past Ballygarrett and Cappaclough East after a level crossing at Barnagh bridge, where the creamery now stands. A further half-mile brought the meeting point with the road from Skirlough (Schrallaghbag) to the sea west of Tonakilly and Cunnagharoe, where another level crossing was made. Continuing alongside boggy marshes which stretched down to the beach on the right, the line which bridged the Glenagalt stream near milepost 2, on its final course to the sea, swung sharply across the road to diverge left for the approach to Deelis platform, which was across the road from a group of cottages. This halt also served Meenascorthy, one of the largest farms in the district, and the many other nearby dwellings. The strand reaching round to Carrigaha point provided very safe bathing and cliff caves, near where kelp was burned in former times for medicinal purposes: hence the plot called Garran-na-Ceilp, on Meenascorthy farm.

This boggy area was noted as a botanist's paradise and is given extensive coverage by Praeger in his book "The Botanist in Ireland" (London, 1937).

Back to the road again, the rails crossed immediately to the right hand side and ran between the hayfields and turf marshes of Meenascorthy and on to Carrigaha, crossing another little road to the beach and yet again, close to milepost 3, crossing minor roads at the forge in Carrigaha and, after Lisnagree, at Aughacasla school. The line continued on the right of the roadway, now within 500 yards of the coast, and crossed the old lower road to Castlegregory which branched to the right. After a further level crossing the Aughacasla river was crossed by a stone road and rail bridge. Very soon the line crossed the road to the left, reaching the platform at Aughacasla halt, on the 4 milepost.

After the halt, the railway and road ran parallel but with a hundred yards or so between them, for about half-a-mile, until the railway turned back to the road and immediately crossed again to the right hand verge and over the Owneamallaght river, again by a dual-purpose stone bridge (Cloughanesheskeen bridge). At milepost 5, the line veered away from the road to the right and, continuing through the townland of Cloughanesheskeen, crossing minor farm entrances parallel to the roadway, climbed easily to Kelly's Height.

From this small hilltop there was a sharp descent through a short cutting, and from here the downgrade was continuous into Castlegregory station. Shortly after Kelly's Height, the roads forked, straight on for Brandon and Connor Pass and right for Castlegregory. The road was regained at the Drehidnamaud crossing and the rails took the right hand side of the road for the last half mile to the platform of Castlegregory terminus at the 6 milepost.

Here, as at Dingle, the station was a little outside the village, and the facilities were similar and adequate. There was a stone-built stationmaster's house, identical with that at Dingle, both being roughcast, run-round loop, turntable, cattle pens, goods shed and loco shed. The station building itself was of corrugated iron. From outside the yard, the main road continued into Castlegregory, giving the option of a left-hand turn up Main Street or straight along Strand Street to the fascinating sandy Maharees Peninsula.

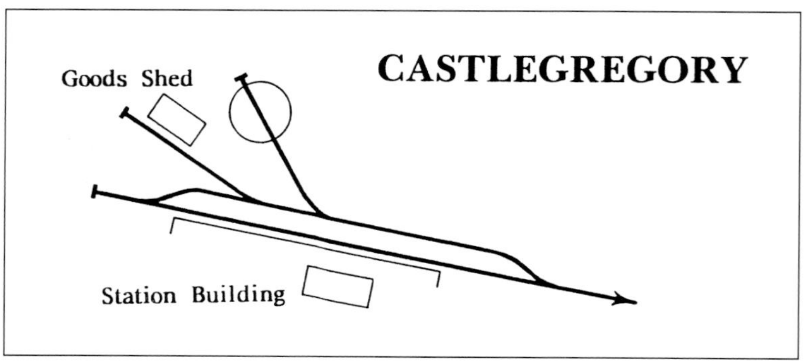

Chapter 4
THE PHOTOGRAPHIC RECORD AND 'RAILFAN' VISITORS

Almost every month of the years 1950-53, Irish and English railway enthusiasts, plus a few from the USA and elsewhere, descended on Tralee's "Dingle Railway" station to make the round trip westward, travelling either on, or alongside, the only train of the month: the special cattle working which ran to serve Dingle Fair. Some of the most celebrated personalities among railway historians, voyageurs and photographers who included both professional and amateur railwaymen, made this pilgrimage, often returning two or three times to renew the thrilling experience. In so doing, the Dingle railway earned a reputation for adventure and interest unrivalled by any other in the world, and since most of these visitors wrote about their experiences, and took numerous photographs, they have left an important legacy of factual matter on record. The cataloguing of this record has been an important task for the present writers and it can confidently be asserted that this is to date the only complete survey of the material available.[1]

The following extracts give a clear impression of why these visitors came to ride the Dingle railway.

> . . . There are many reasons, each of which must be peculiar to the individual, but perhaps it was the ever-present spirit of adventure, never lacking on this unique line of railway which was the greatest attraction.[2]
>
> . . . The journey was perhaps the last piece of adventurous railroading to be found in these islands . . . A ride on the footplate of the leading engine was probably the most worthwhile experience any amateur could have.[3]
>
> . . . There followed a long, exciting grind along the verge of the road – collar work all the way . . . there was never anything like this on any narrow-gauge line in England and Wales.[4]
>
> . . . Undoubtedly the most remote and spectacular railway byway in the British Isles and in many respects the most extraordinary – the Tralee and Dingle . . . I experienced a feeling of excitement and suspense such as I had never known before on rails . . . the feeling that anything might happen before the journey was over.[5]
>
> . . . We chose the double-headed train which pulled twenty wagons over the hills and we made it in about 5 hours for the 30 miles. I cannot remember when I enjoyed a journey more.[6]

That this spirit of adventure persisted right to the end, was confirmed by A. J. Powell's account of the very last train from Dingle Fair, on 27 June 1953 which had to leave minus a fireman, and whose absence caused difficulties until he finally caught up with the train two miles out of Dingle, having taken the post lorry![7]

Perhaps the earliest mention of the unusual attractions of this line in a railway enthusiasts' journal and certainly some of the earliest and most interesting photographs, were featured in an article by T. J. Goodlake in 1898.

> Nothing strikes a Sassenach visitor to Ireland more than to meet on a public highway perhaps two locomotives drawing a miscellaneous collection of bogie carriages and trucks to the number of twenty or more. Yet such an apparition is often to be met with on the road that runs from Tralee, the far-off capital of Kerry, to the prehistoric town of Dingle.[8]

Among his interesting photographs are scenes of Curraduff viaduct (after the accident but before the diversion), Emalough platform showing the little shelter once a feature of all the halts, a cattle-grid (to prevent cattle straying on the then unfenced sections), locomotive number 1 as rebuilt after Curraduff, and a coach, showing the hitherto unsuspected feature of two end-observation windows; all-in-all a precious set of period photographs.

Did this article perhaps prompt H. L. Hopwood, a professional railwayman from England's Great Northern, to visit Tralee in September 1901 while touring other Irish lines? He photographed engine No. 2 majestically heading a train of coaches and improvised cattle wagons converted from low-sided trucks.[9]

Photography in those early days was only for the strong. Not only had a large and cumbersome camera plus tripod to be carried, but also the heavy glass plates for exposure. This physical limitation, plus the fact that unless one had business in fish, the line was situated well off the beaten track, may account for the fact that few photographs survive prior to these views. There are the maker's photos of the locomotives numbers 1-6 (1889-98),[10] a re-touched proof 'pull' from *The Kerryman* of an early train at Tralee, now believed to be a field trip by the Cambrian Archaeological Society in 1891 and dramatic prints of the wreckage at Curraduff (1893) and Lispole (1907).[11]

These last two are thought to have been the work of Bill McCarthy of Ballymullen, though there is some doubt about the Curraduff one (*Kerry Sentinel* 27 May 1893) which has been attributed to Messrs Daly & Sons of Nelson St Tralee. These were first used by Edmond O'Flaherty, railways manager CIE who has lectured several times in recent years on the railways of his native Kerry. Both photos were preserved by Tom Francis, son of Camp stationmaster and thanks to his acumen, two further McCarthy photos from this era have been published by Padraig Kennelly, both of supreme interest.[12] One of an excursion group at Camp, shows a number of railway personnel including Driver Quinn, John Baker, Inspector Murphy of Dingle, and Tom Francis Snr., stationmaster at the Junction; the other

91. The very last cattle special to run on the T&D Section laboriously climbs out of Annascaul, being overtaken by two cyclists, watched by John Powell from pilot 8T's cab. The train was moving so slowly that photographer Henry Orbach was able to climb down from the pilot, take his photo and climb back aboard with plenty of time. Train loco is No. 1T on her last run. *(H. S. Orbach)*

92. No. 2 at Tralee in 1901 when loco maintenance was at an all-time low. Note square spectacles, loss of condenser pipes and lifting jacks on tank tops, and removal of crosshead pump and rear cowcatcher. Cab steps have been fitted (they were initially lost when motion skirts removed). Note first wagon which has lift-off sides fitted to a 2-plank open truck, for cattle traffic. Lining-out just discernible on tank sides and oil lamp, but not on tool boxes. *(LCGB Collection: H. L. Hopwood)*

93. Champion Rail Traveller T. R. Perkins took this shot of No. 3T on the morning train out of Castlegregory, in 1929. *(T. R. Perkins)*

94. A very rare shot indeed: locomotive No. 4T (originally No. 8) actually captured AT WORK on the Tralee & Dingle . . . all other photos show her out of use. Here she is attaching the through coach from Castlegregory to the rear of the afternoon train from Dingle to Tralee, which is alongside the island platform. Note No. 4 carries the handsome brass number/works plate formerly carried by the original No. 4. The year is 1932. *(James Fisher)*

shows the Junction and an excursion train. Most importantly it shows the original signal box built at the Junction, of which it was thought for many years that no photograph had survived.

Tom Francis Jnr. preserved several photos of this period, including one of his father sitting on barrels outside Fitzgerald's Bar at the Junction. An 1899 photo by John Wills – noted for his connection with the firm of Bassett-Lowke and of the Ravenglass & Eskdale and Fairbourne Railways – shows three T&D wagons on the pier extension at Dingle; the only known view of the extension in use. (*Cork Evening Echo,* 30th April, 1982).

In 1904, the T&D locomotive superintendent P. Higgins, who had come from the Dublin, Wicklow and Wexford railway, and who had accomplished a great deal towards overcoming the bad maintenance and low staff morale at Tralee, submitted with justifiable pride an article to Britain's *Locomotive Magazine,* on new carriage and wagon stock built in the T&D workshops. This, together with two excellent photographs of the vehicles, was published in 1905.[13]

In 1907 Harold Fayle of Clonmel carried his plate camera to Tralee and on to Dingle taking a series of remarkable scenes, the negatives being preserved by the Irish Railway Record Society.[14] Fayle was to become a celebrated historian of Irish railways, founder of *Fayles Bulletin* (compendium of Irish railway practice and forerunner of the Irish Railway Record Society Journal) and founder member of the Irish Railway Record Society.

Perhaps the biggest disappointment from those far-off days is the paucity of T&D material in the celebrated Lawrence collection of glass negatives (c 1875-1925), preserved in the National Library – and which contains many interesting scenes of other Irish lines.[15]

In 1914 H. L. Hopwood returned to Tralee in company of another railwayman, a world-famous recorder of the railway scene, K. A. C. R. Nunn of the Great Eastern Railway, whose collection of negatives[16] is for the enthusiast one of the most interesting and historic. This was a particularly interesting period of the railway's history, as mentioned earlier and these photographs show clearly the great improvements wrought.[17]

An interesting photo of 1922 shows the chassis and engine of the little 4-wheel railcar at Tralee, prior to the fitting of a body by the C&W Department.

Ten years later, with 'The Troubles' over, Nunn was back in Tralee and Dingle, accompanied by another renowned railway photographer, A. W. Croughton, also from the Great Eastern. They set up tripods at Dingle and at Castlegregory Junction, so taking some of the last photos of the independent regime, before the GSR took over. In these pictures [18] the locomotives are shown at their best – clean, freshly-painted and lined out.

In 1929, T. R. Perkins visited the line as part-fulfilment of his ambition in life to travel every mile of the tens of thousands of miles of public railway then operating in Britain and Ireland. For the record he achieved this ambition, so far as is known unequalled by any other rail-traveller, in 1932. He left a full and complete record of his two visits to the T&D section of GSR (1929, 1932) and these were published quite recently.[19]

By the 1930s, cameras were becoming more portable, thanks to roll-film. Two Irish enthusiasts destined to achieve prominence in Irish rail matters first focused their cameras on the line at this time, R. N. Clements, locomotive archivist and sometime editor of the Irish Railway Record Society Journal, and C. L. Fry, doyen of Irish railway modellers whose Irish International Railway and Tramway System was to achieve truly international fame.

H. R. Norman was at Tralee in 1931 taking photographs. In 1932, James Fisher of London was touring the peninsula with his wife. They secured a very rare scene at Castlegregory Junction: locomotive No. 4T on a branch train. We do not know of any other photograph of this locomotive *working* on the T&D. Then in July 1934, as part of a far-ranging tour of Irish railways begun in the late 1920s, came Henry C. Casserley, perhaps the most renowned of all railway photographers and certainly the most prolific in print. He travelled to Dingle and back, making the first comprehensive round trip coverage on record.[20] In Fr. Senan Moynihan's article *In Kerry Long Ago,*[21] he mentioned the breathtaking view from the line near Skirlough. Casserley was to capture this splendidly, including the distant smoke of a train on the Castlegregory branch, on his 1934 visit. He was sufficiently persuasive to have the locomotives not in use pulled out of Tralee shed for his camera. Harold Fayle had similar success when he revisited Tralee a little later,[22] while continuing research for his book on the Irish narrow gauge railways.[23]

In 1935 Fred Le Manquais visited the railway and took some most interesting views of operations, including a scene at Lispole showing the siding used for local peat sales and produce. Happily his negatives have been preserved by Tom Middlemass who has written a number of excellent railway books, and who featured some of Le Manquais' work in the 1988 *Cork Holly Bough.*

Walter McGrath of the *Cork Examiner* made his first trip on 'The Dingle' in 1937, at the age of 15, travelling to Camp Junction en route to the scout camp in the shadow of Caherconree, a district whose wild beauty and historical curiosities have beckoned him back many times since.[24] It is significant that his first exercise in writing[25] should have concerned the Dingle train.

Also in 1937 came a far-sighted pioneer in publishing books and monographs on light and narrow gauge railway matters for the enthusiast, Roger W. Kidner, on a fact-finding and photographic mission for his forthcoming handbook.[26]

W. Edwards of Tralee took photographs on the branch in the late 1930s, one of which showing a beet(?) train on Bunowa bridge near Camp was published in the 1976 *Cork Holly Bough.*

95. DURING THE WAR: Fuel shortages and other restrictions in force still allowed priority to be given to the Fair Day cattle workings from Dingle. In this April 1943 view a special, heavily loaded with cattle for the factories in Tralee, is just leaving the railway's own right of way at Annascaul and joining the public road; the locos are 8T and 5T. A nice view of Bristol covered goods 23T with drop ventilators added for cattle workings. *(Fr. Frank Browne SJ)*

In 1938, the photographic pattern for the future was set by the two visits of Birmingham banker, W. Arthur Camwell, noted photographer of the rural rail scene and editor of the *Stephenson Locomotive Society Journal.* During these visits, the latter of which coincided with Dingle Fair, Camwell not only managed to capture the most comprehensive record of workings on the railway up to that time, including the long-neglected Castlegregory branch, but managed to locate the entire locomotive stock about its duties, the first time a photographer had done so. It was a fortunate visit, since little time remained for the branch.

More branch scenes and a few elsewhere were secured by A. W. Croughton, back in 1939 for an extensive tour of Irish railways after his 1920s visit.[27] In the very last week of passenger services, April 1939, Gerald J. Aston of the LMS, later line traffic manager of British Rail (LM region) took a comprehensive series of views of fair day workings from Dingle to Tralee.[28] So, luckily for posterity, the passenger services on the T&D received fair coverage shortly before withdrawal. Unfortunately no movie film of this period is known to survive.

Before leaving the 1930s, mention must be made of a most interesting set of box-camera snapshots taken, probably in 1931, but locomotive details suggest possibly as late as 1937, by an unknown photographer, and featured in *Kerry's Eye,* by Padraig Kennelly.[29] These show a train halted by floods at Blennerville; the same train passing under the occupational bridge on the diversion at Camp; a train crossing the road at Blennerville and a branch train entering the bay platform at the Junction.

To stimulate wider interest among enthusiasts came an article by C. Mytton-Davies in the *Railway Magazine,*[30] suitably illustrated with some of the best Camwell photos.

The Second World War put paid to intended visits, though a few snatched brief glimpses. One such was J. G. Dewing of London, a well-known railway photographer. He chased the daily goods train by bicycle and secured a fine photograph near the Basin.

Frank Kelland Jones was there at the same time and took a number of excellent scenes, including the early morning departure of the daily goods and a lovely view of the train halted by a cow. This was a regular occurrence, but rarely captured on film. These views were featured in the 1987 *Cork Holly Bough.*

In July 1943 the celebrated photographer, Fr Frank Browne SJ, took a series of photos of a returning cattle special, leaving the private right of way just East of Annascaul and joining the public road.

Despite decreased workings due to fuel shortages, publication of Harold Fayles' definitive book on the Irish narrow gauge railways in 1946 stimulated much interest. It is still a recognised classic reference text, and the photograph section on the T&D, using Camwell and Fayle material, is excellent. Happily it has been reprinted. Roger Kidner's *Light Railways in Eire* was also available by this time.

During these latter days of freight operations, Dublin photographer and archivist of express locomotive performance, Sean Kennedy, began visits to Tralee in company with the well-known modeller of Irish Railways and exponent of spring drive (Clockwork), (An)Drew Donaldson. Kennedy's photos are of the finest quality, in a technical sense, to be taken of the T&D.

It was 1950 before the first wave of enthusiasts appeared to ride the cattle trains each month. A lot of credit for the existence of a very comprehensive record of these working is due to CIE who gave them permission to photograph on the railway property and to ride these unusual workings. Walter McGrath travelled to Tralee for the monthly train in January 1950 but just missed it, consoling himself with photographs of the Curraduff bridge which were duly published.[31] A significant visitor arrived in May 1950 when P. B. Whitehouse of Birmingham was holidaying with his wife in Ireland. In addition to his still camera, which he used to great advantage, he also had a movie camera. The Dingle made a vivid impression on him and he was to write extensively about it in years to come.[32] June that year saw Cyril Fry and Ivo Peters both at Tralee taking photographs; most of this material has been published.[33]

In September 1950, the celebrated historian James Boyd, noted for his many authoritative and painstakingly researched histories of Welsh and Manx narrow-gauge railways, travelled to Dingle with a party touring other Irish narrow gauge lines. He wrote of these travels in *Railway World* [34] – an account that formed a model for subsequent versions. Mr Boyd's ciné film of the T&D taken 1950-3 has been released on videotape recently. It includes interesting sequences showing the derelict Curraduff viaduct seen from an ascending train, and a long interlude at Lispole station, awaiting the return of the train crew who had gone into the village to hear "The Oaks" (horse race!) commentary on the radio.[34]

By 1951, the pattern was well-established and the fame of the monthly specials had spread. Some enthusiasts were contacting CIE and arranging visits to the T&D a year ahead! Every party travelling with the special no liability tickets charged at road bus fare from CIE had some unusual adventure to recount, from brake failure or lack of water, to arguments with cars parked thoughtlessly across the apparently abandoned track. Few narrow gauge railwaymen can have achieved the fame of Billy Hanlon and Jack Cotter of Dingle and Paddy Martin of Tralee who carried some notable personages both officially and unofficially in the cabs of their locomotives, ranging from Derby-trained professional locomotive engineer A. J. Powell to L. T. C. Rolt, general manager of the Talyllyn Railway in Wales, or the Chairman of I.C.I., Sir Peter Allen. Walter McGrath travelled as far as Glenmore in February 1951 only to have his adventure in the form of a wagon derailment, which he duly photographed and reported in *Fayle's Bulletin.*[35]

96. No. 3T is branch engine for the day and is standing at the Junction with the daily through-working from Tralee to Castlegregory in 1935.
(Fred Le Manquais, courtesy T. Middlemas)

97. Dingle in 1938 and a Fair Day afternoon. No. 1T at the platform heads the 2.30pm for Tralee while at left, Nos. 2T and 5T are waiting with an assembled cattle special working that will follow when it has a cleared path.
(W. A. Camwell)

98. Dingle, 1939 and in the last week of workings, No. 1T is piloting the morning mixed working (10.50am) from Dingle, headed by No. 3T. This was because No. 1 was to remain at Annascaul and pick up wagons from the Fair at Ballinaclare. *(G. J. Aston)*

99. Still 1939 and this shows No. 8T as branch engine for the day, with the 11.55am through working for the Castlegregory branch. *(A. W. Croughton)*

100. June 1950 and 8T has coaled up in the main line yard, run along Ashe Street and is about to re-enter the narrow gauge yard. Cyril Fry is on the footplate with Driver Cotter. *(Ivo Peters, copyright Julian Peters)*

101. Annascaul June 1951 and the outgoing double header, behind 1T and 2T is running along the island platform to wait until 8T has cleared the crossing and water tower at the Dingle end. (See frontispiece). On the platform are "Cam" Camwell and Michael Davies. *(C. H. S. Owen)*

June 1951 saw a real enthusiasts' reunion at Annascaul! A party organised by Arthur Camwell had proceeded to Dingle with driver Bill Hanlon, including several noted railway personalities such as Cedric Owen, Peter Bowles and Michael Davies, savouring the delights of The Dingle for the first time. Mr Davies' account of this trip was featured in the *IRRS Journal* for February 1987.

Meantime a double-headed train also left, with a contingent of passengers aboard, being met at conveniently photogenic spots by Ivo Peters. The two trains crossed at Annascaul – a long stop because one guard at least had adjourned to the village bar – and many friends met together and many feet of film were exposed on the manoeuvres of the trains in passing. Ivo Peters' brother-in-law, Peter Girdlestone was present, taking movie film; indeed one of the most atmospheric films to be made on the line, with a very exciting sequence of the car overtaking the train on the long straight at Ballinasteenig.[36] Arthur Camwell was also taking movie film including a spectacular sequence of the train re-starting on the Curraduff diversion.[37] Ivo Peters followed his train down to Dingle, securing an entrancing series of photographs virtually all of which are beautifully reprinted in his book, *The Narrow Gauge Charm of Yesterday*.[38]

In July Mr and Mrs Whitehouse returned with Eric Russell. Again, still and ciné were taken and a fine movie sequence was made of the climbing of Glenagalt bank. The still cameras captured drama at Lispole as Jack Cotter's train all but ran away down the steep descent from Garrynadur.[39] The return special next day was met by Tommy O'Brien of the *Cork Examiner*, who took several fine photographs at Castlegregory Junction.

In August, Sir Peter Allen travelled to a holiday in Dingle with his two daughters in the company of a party of enthusiasts, one of whom wrote a gripping account of the two-way trip for *Trains Illustrated*.[40] Between them, Sir Peter and his daughters took some one hundred and twenty photographs of T&D interest, surely the most comprehensive record of such a trip? They covered not only the journey but Dingle harbour station and the fair as well. Their enjoyment of the trip was recorded in *On the Old Lines*.[41]

Inevitably, since Tralee station offices kept no visitors book, it has not proved possible to trace all the visitors to the line who took photographs. There is one gap between September 1951 and June 1952. There are scenes by an unidentified photographer taken on a visit in early 1952[42] and *Country Life* magazine in 1952 showed a train halted by Blennerville floods taken in the spring of that year by a Rev. Shirehampton.

In June 1952, Pat Whitehouse was back for his last visit to 'the Dingle'. Also there were Ian Allan, celebrated publisher of railway books, and A. J. Powell, together with an American friend Henry S. Orbach. The friendly atmosphere of 'the Dingle' cemented many friendships but none happier than that of Whitehouse and Powell who together, with the help of most of the enthusiasts named in this chapter, wrote the story of the Tralee and Dingle railway. Despite its modest appearance, this little book, which contains some of the best photographs by Fayle, Camwell and Peters, is a model of what such a book ought to be: a mine of information, thanks to dedicated and careful research among the official records held by CIE. The stock list in particular is a monumental piece of detective work, painstakingly compiled by deductions made from derelict vehicles at Tralee and such meagre official records as could be tallied. Happily, too, despite his involvement in many other world-famous railway projects, not least the establishment of the Colourviews archive of railway pictures in Birmingham, Whitehouse found time to edit his movie film into a comprehensive whole. *Fair Days Only* is presented as a trip from Tralee to Dingle and back to Annascaul on one of the monthly specials. Actually, with cinematic licence, it shows scenes taken in 1950, 1951 and 1952.[43]

In July 1952 film was taken on the line by Richard Kehm of the USA, an IRRS member. He was accompanied by R. N. Clements, also taking photographs. They were followed in September by C. L. Fry.[44] All made excellent coverage of the journeys and inevitable incidents. Also on that September trip were B. C. Johns and members of the Cambridge University Railway Society. Their excitement came when locomotive No. 2's cowcatcher came adrift near Ballinasare and caught in the track. Two of Johns' photos were published.[45]

Another gap in record occurs until the visit of Ian Duncan of Derby in March 1953. Some photos taken on this trip, which included an unusually short train of single goods van and brakevan worked to Dingle by two locomotives because the stock was already at Dingle, following a breakdown there in February, were printed in *Kerry's Eye*,[46] as was a most valuable scene of the assembled staff at Dingle in April 1953 taken along with several other interesting views by Mr K. P. Seward of Pontesbury. This included two ex-T&DLR drivers, Hanlon and Martin, whose service spanned most of the life of the line.

In June 1953 J. H. Price, of Cook's Continental Timetable fame, arranged an extensive tour of Irish tramways and narrow gauge railways for the Light Railway Transport League, in association with the IRRS. A party of 45 set out from Tralee on 11 June 1953 behind Billy Hanlon and locomotive No. 8 which was carrying the League's new headboard. Plenty of stops were made for photographers, who included R. Hosford, a Cork master baker, who took some movie film of the event, as did J. H. Roberts.[47] Canon Lyne, Rev. Mr McCann and Dingle schoolchildren formed a reception committee at Dingle for this first passenger train into Dingle for many years. The song of welcome from the children was remembered by many of the visitors and the children themselves doubtless remembered their short ride on the train. J. H. Price wrote a colourful account of the trip for *Modern*

102. In July 1951 Nos. 1T and 2T are caught in full flight, down from Garrynadur and about to "hit" Lispole viaduct at speed in breach of regulations. There was no question of stopping! The train was being pushed by the near-runaway wagons. So much for uncoupling the pilot! *(E. S. Russell)*

103. Some of the Junction staff outside that other building at Lower Camp, Fitzgerald's Bar. At left is Kathleen Spillane (later Mrs Keane of Curraheen), her father, signalman Tim Spillane, and Stationmaster Tom Francis Sr, circa 1910. *(W. McCarthy)*

104. STAFF POSED AT DINGLE on one of the last cattle workings, 1953: L-R: Inspector Crowe, P. O'Connor (loader), A. Lynan (Inspector), Paddy Kennedy (fitter) and Paddy McWilliams (Guard).
(K. P. Seward)

105. MEMBERS OF THE LIGHT RAILWAY TRANSPORT LEAGUE and THE IRISH RAILWAY RECORD SOCIETY participating in the last (special) passenger train to run on the Tralee & Dingle, section, June 1953, identified as follows: In brakevan doorway: G. A. Wigham; In loco cab: Billy Hanlon, W. Lynch; Alongside train below L-R: W. McGrath (author), R. Meadowcroft, Dingle Garda, D. G. Coakham, B. Miller, G. R. Mahon, J. A. Cadisch, R. G. Jarvis, F. G. Boyle, C. A. Mayou, ———, C. L. Fry, ———, J. H. Roberts, Christian Brothers' Superior, J. M. Wiseman, J. H. Price (organiser), Canon Lyne, Rev. McCann, W. K. Jenkins, L. Hyland, ———, V. Goldberg.
(J. C. Houlihan)

Tramway.[48] Among the celebrated railway enthusiasts present were the Jarvis brothers, R. G. and J. M., the latter taking the only set of colour transparencies known of the line, and Messrs V. Goldberg, J. C. Gillham, W. McGrath, D. G. Coakham, L. Hyland, G. R. Mahon, G. A. Wigham, J. B. Hollingsworth and many others all of whom had their cameras busy. Also on board that day was barrister Dermot P. Kinlen, grandson of Tom O'Donnell MP who had been intimately connected with the line (1900-18). On June 26 came the very last working for Dingle Fair. A. J. Powell and H. S. Orbach rode down on the footplate. While on the job, they made an invaluable photographic record of the surviving stock at Tralee and Dingle, and filled a notebook with their measurements.

Then finally came the fateful July 23 when Billy Hanlon made the last trip to Dingle with a brakevan to collect the few wagons left there. Padraig Kennelly recorded the melancholy departure from Tralee, posing the staff beside the engine. So passed the Tralee and Dingle into railway legend; but it will never be forgotten as we have this amazing legacy of photographic records, thanks entirely to the unique character and adventure of The Dingle Train.

An interesting publication by Tom Fox of The Mall, Dingle, is DINGLE DOWN THE YEARS: A Collection of old photographs (1993). This includes a section on The Dingle Train and among pictures of interest that have not previously been published are an 1890s study of guard Jim Sullivan in a completely different (in terms of braid and adornment) uniform to that worn by guard Jim Ashe at much the same period. There is a view of the harbour extension in the streets of Dingle, a family group by the name-board at Ballinasteenig platform and a scene of track relaying on the Castlegregory branch.

1. This present chapter is an extensive updating of our article *Cork Holly Bough* for 1974.
2. P. B. Whitehouse & A. J. Powell, *op. cit.* 3.
3. P. B. Whitehouse, *On The Narrow Gauge* (London 1964) 45-55.
4. J. I. C. Boyd, *Railway World* (London 1951).
5. L. T. C. Rolt & P. B. Whitehouse, *Lines of Character* (London 1976), 174-183.
6. P. C. Allen, *On The Old Lines* (London 1957). 48.
7. A. J. Powell, *Trains & Railways* (London 1975), 157-162.
8. T. J. Goodlake, *Railway Magazine* (London 1898). 441-6.
9. Locomotive Club of Great Britain, negative no. H. 737.
10. Hunslet Holdings Ltd., Leeds, England.
11. *Cork Evening Echo,* 30 January 1974; *Kerry's Eye,* 23 December 1976.
12. *Kerry's Eye,* 23 December 1976.
13. *The Locomotive Magazine* 5 (London 1905).
14. The Irish Railway Record Society (Dublin), negatives Nos. 51, 54, 58, 60, 61.
15. The National Library, Dublin, plates Nos. 4052, 4053, 6659, 6667, 1047.
16. Now held by the Locomotive Club of Great Britain, 11 Braywood Avenue, Egham, Surrey.
17. Negative Nos. H738, H2204-5, 1853-6.
18. Negative Nos. 4057-62 (Nunn); Croughton Plates held by Colourviews Ltd., Birmingham.
19. T. R. Perkins, *Journal of Stephenson Locomotive Society* (Birmingham 1975).
20. Many of the H. C. Casserley photographs reproduced, in Rowlands' book.
21. Fr S. Moynihan, *Cork Holly Bough* 1969.
22. The Irish Railway Record Society (Dublin), negative Nos. 794-9.
23. H. Fayle, *Narrow Gauge Railways of Ireland* (London 1946) (Reprinted 1970).
24. Lecture to Kerry Archaeological and Historical Society. 20/8/1972.
25. W. McGrath *Scout Annual 1941* (Cork 1942) 1-4.
26. R. W. Kidner; *Light Railway Handbook* (London 1939).
27. Real Photographs Ltd., now owned by Ian Allan Ltd. Neg. nos. X6358, 6362 and 6364-70.
28. G. J. Aston's photographs are part of the Locomotive & General Publishing Co.'s stock, though they do not know the identity of the photographer; negative Nos. 6282-93. Also now owned by Ian Allan Ltd.
29. *Kerry's Eye,* 18 December 1975.
30. *The Railway Magazine* 5 (1939), 337.
31. W. McGrath, *Cuisle na tire* 3 (1950) 11-15.
32. All P. B. Whitehouse material available through Millbrook House Ltd., Birmingham.
33. Several photographs by C. L. Fry and Ivo Peters, in Rowlands' book. Most of Ivo Peters' material is in I. Peters, *The Narrow Gauge Charm of Yesterday* (Oxford 1976); a few additional photographs in I. Peters, *Somewhere Along The Lines* (Oxford 1977).
34. J. I. C. Boyd *Railway World* 1952; Videotape: "Manx & Irish Lines Remembered", Railfilms, 1992.
35. W. McGrath, *Fayle's Bulletin* 3 (1951). (Files of *Fayle's Bulletin* are held by The Irish Railway Record Society, Dublin).
36. A print of this film is held by D. G. Rowlands, 16mm silent.
37. This film is in Mr W. A. Camwell's archive. It is shown regularly at railway meetings.
38. I. Peters, *The Narrow Gauge Charm of Yesterday* (Oxford 1976). Photos 10-36.
39. Several of E. Russell's photographs reproduced in Rowlands' book.
40. F. N. Swift, *Trains Illustrated* 5 (1952).
41. P. C. Allen: *On The Old Lines* (London, 1957).
42. The Narrow Gauge Railway Society archive. An extensive Tralee & Dingle file is held by the Librarian, The Sycamores, Church Street, Golcar, Huddersfield, Yorkshire and is loanable to members.
43. *Fair Days Only,* 16mm silent film. Colour or B&W prints formerly available from Colourviews Ltd., Birmingham (also on 8mm). A few rental film libraries hold copies for hire.
44. Certain of the Clements and Fry photographs are reproduced in Rowlands' book. Kehm's film has not so far been traced. It was shown to the Dublin Irish Railway Record Society in 1953.
45. *The Railway Magazine* 1 (1953).
46. *Kerry's Eye,* 18 December 1975.
47. This print is still in possession of the Hosford family, Cork. J. H. Roberts's footage is released as part of the Midland Publishing "On Line" Video: "Irish Railways Vol. 3, 1994".
48. *The Modern Tramway* 8 (London 1953).

106. Locomotive No. 1 seen at Dingle as rebuilt after the Curraduff disaster. (For near original condition, see photo No. 1). She carries simplified lining out and an acetylene headlamp replaces the oil lamp on the heavy bracket. Note square spectacles and triple-light back sheet, Pearson lubricator on dome and handrail round smokebox sides. Note too the bogie van (fish traffic) at rear just behind loco. 1907

(H. Fayle)

Chapter 5
LOCOMOTIVES

The T&D had nine locomotives, plus the little 4-wheeled railcar assembled at Tralee in 1922. Seven were from the Hunslet Engine Company of Leeds and two from Messrs Kerr, Stuart & Co. (later absorbed into Hunslet's). All were sturdy, reliable locos if given reasonable maintenance. But that is what they did NOT get! Routine maintenance was abysmal in the years 1891-1903, mainly due to lack of funds. When new locomotives were desperately required in 1892 and 1898 they had to be paid for in instalments. Company cheques were dishonoured and raw materials, spares and equipment lacking. The problems of cashflow were not resolved until the Chairmanship of Tom O'Donnell MP who had the necessary political "clout" in England, and were not fully addressed until the GSR amalgamation in 1925.

For example, locomotive No. 1 was not repaired until 18 months after the Curraduff accident. On Fair Day November 1901, three locomotives failed in service and it was then that the Company purchased a pony and trap to ensure continuance of the Mail Contract! No. 2 spent three years in Tralee yard awaiting major overhaul with permanent firebox troubles until reboilered in 1903. In June 1902 No. 6 was the only usable locomotive: a situation that lasted until the new Kerr, Stuart No. 7 was assembled and put into service. No. 6 was then promptly stopped for repairs and No. 7 carried on alone until No. 5 returned to work.

If the early history of the locomotives was determined by penury, it was also affected by the competence or otherwise of the Loco Foremen, who at times came and went with astonishing rapidity. No less than 14 men held the post between 1891 and 1925 when the GSR took over, some lasting but a few days and one appointee never arriving.

It cannot have been easy when Reports to the Board by the Foremen, of shortage of stores and raw material, incompetent staff, and urgent major work required were constantly met with put-offs and economies, until the 1907-14 period when Chairman O'Donnell obtained Government funding for various improvements. The Foremen, too, were not unaware of the various malpractices and dishonesty of Board Members. It is worth mentioning that Foremen Tompkins (1893-5), Higgins (1903-4), Carey (1904-8) and O'Gorman (1914-25) achieved a great deal with the odds stacked against them. Alfred Redshaw who replaced the first Foreman Graves, in 1892, had but a few months in which he could make little impact, as he died in the Curraduff bridge disaster in 1893.

One of the most distinctive features of the T&D locomotives were the wooden toolboxes carried on the front platforms from 1890. When T&D locos were transferred elsewhere, these were the first items to go, and immediately imparted a "non-T&D" look!

All nine locos had bells mounted on top of the firebox. On the first Hunslets, these were linked to the Motion and rang continuously when the loco was in motion! This was rapidly altered to manual control by the contractors. Later locos came provided with manual operation only.

As supplied, all locos were lined out in the pattern shown in photographic grey in the Hunslet Works Photos, even the Kerr, Stuarts: this included lining on tank ends, a complex design around number plates and even on cylinder covers and tool boxes. This vanished under grime and neglect but was revived by Carey as locos went through the works and were repainted. It can be seen on some of the 1907 photos by Harold Fayle. A somewhat simpler lining was adopted during O'Gorman's regime, as in the photos of Hopwood, Nunn and others.

All nine locos had cowcatchers of the distinctive pattern supplied by Hunslets on the original 4 locos. This became recognisable as the "T&D style" and was perpetrated on the Kerr, Stuart locos as well.

The Hunslets had attractive oval brass number and makers' plates combined, whereas the Kerr, Stuarts had a more functional oblong numberplate and a smaller oval brass maker's plate. All were affixed to the side tanks.

THE HUNSLETS

In all, the Railway had five 2-6-0Ts (Nos. 1, 2, 3, 6, 8) provided by the Hunslet Engine Company to a standard (and highly effective) design; one 0-4-2T (No. 4) (for the Branch) and a 2-6-2T (No. 5).

The 2-6-0s had 13 x 18in. cylinders, 3ft $0^1/_2$ in. diameter driving and 2ft diameter pony wheels, with a 6ft 10in. - 4ft 3in. - 4ft 6in. wheelbase; the centre drivers were flangeless. The two-ring telescopic boilers were 3ft $5^1/_8$ in. int. diameter by 8ft barrel, working pressures 140lb/sq. in. (Nos. 1-3) until reboilered when 150lb/sq. in. became the norm. The boilers had a single flood-type injector (Nos. 1, 2, 3) and crosshead feed pump and were fitted with condensing gear. A Pearson-type lubricator was fitted to the dome. These were removed circa 1900. Nos. 6 and 8 were supplied with an improved boiler, with 124 tubes of $1^3/_4$" dia, later fitted to 1, 2 and 3, at 150lb/sq. in. working pressure, two lifting injectors and without the condensing gear, which had been removed from the original engines at the time the line was opened. The tube heating surfaces were 494 sq. ft. and the firebox 66sq. ft., the casing being 6ft. 2in. long with a sloping, non-drop grate of 9.7sq. ft. area. The locos had outside Walschaerts valve gear and working weight was about 31 tons. The water tank capacity was

107 & 108. Two 1924 views of No. 1 in the final T&DLR livery carried up to amalgamation within the GSR. Note railway crest on side panel, just in front of cab: the two white blobs are the castles with crown and legend above. Note that lining on back sheet, also that there are now two square rear windows, but cab front specs are round. Handrail gone from around smokebox. Taken alongside goods bay in Tralee yard.

(LCGB: K. A. C. R. Nunn)

109. No. 1T at Inchicore during her last major overhaul. Note how standardised Inchicore fittings (chimney, smokebox, numberplate) have replaced the Hunslet originals and the fresh new battleship grey paintwork. She ran in this condition until the last cattle special of 1953, when she was withdrawn from service – she lasted the whole history of the Tralee & Dingle as a working railway. *H. C. Casserley)*

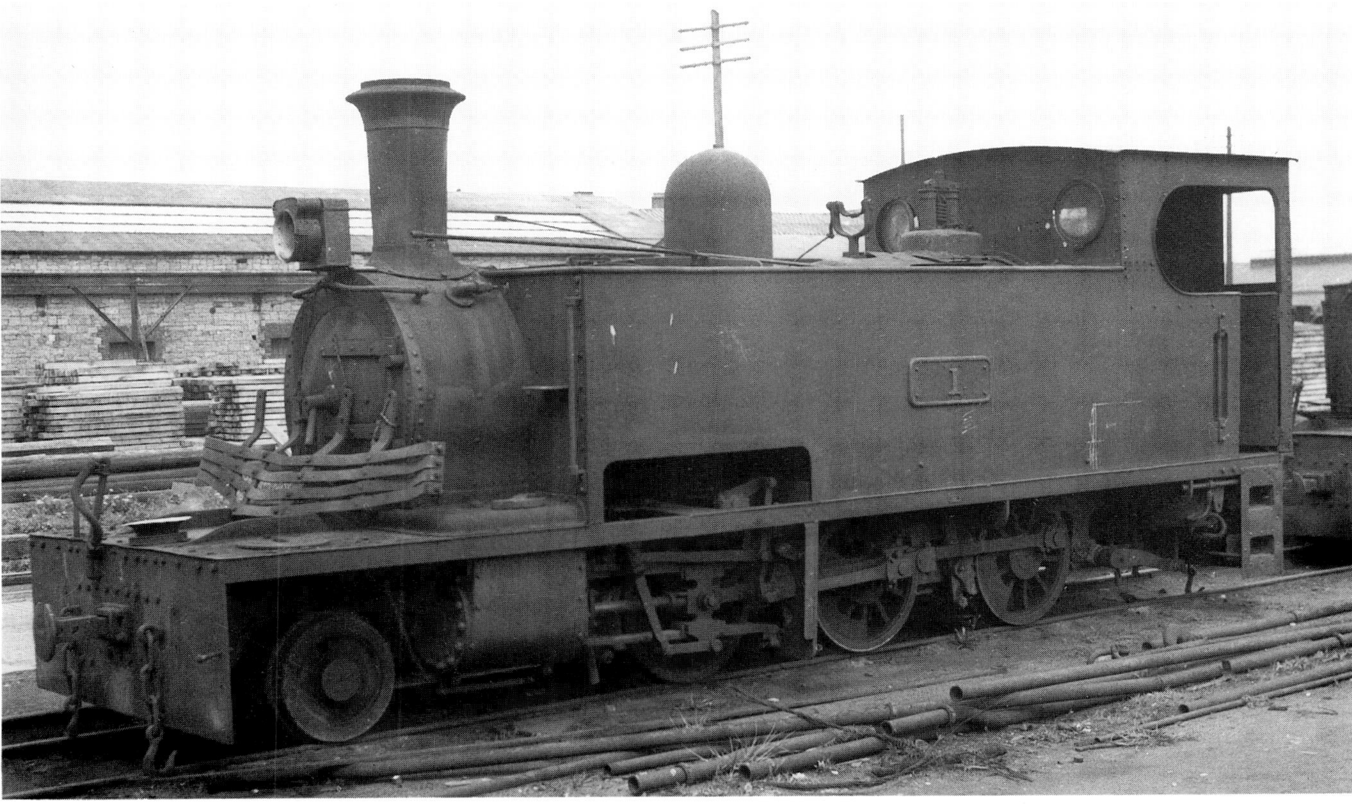

110. And 20 years later, awaiting her fate at Inchicore, just in front of her old mate, 2T. Note bell removed for Nigeria. *(K. P. Seward)*

750 gallons (Nos. 2 and 3) and 730 gallons (Nos. 1, 6, 8), coal capacity 30cu. ft. or 15cwt. Nos. 1, 2 and 3 were fitted with side skirts to protect the motion, and cowcatchers/pilots at both front and rear. The skirts and rear pilots were removed well before the line opened, as were the speedometers. Removal of the skirts left the locos without cab steps initially, and portable steps were used until proper cab steps were fitted.

It has been said that the original locos ALL came with cabs and driving gear at both ends, but this was not the case: only No. 4 was so fitted. The long front platform gave rise to this notion. Originally all the locos had square spectacle windows and there might be double or triple square windows on the rear cab sheet. Round cab front windows came in from 1910 onward. Sliding glass windows were fitted to the rear sheet around 1930.

Nos. 6 and 8 were supplied without skirts or speedometers. All had lever reverse until the 1920s, when screw reversing was fitted, except No. 6 which was not converted to screw until 1957.

Oil headlamps were fitted from new, and changed to acetylene, around 1910-12.

Nos. 1-3 had sandboxes on top of the boiler, behind the chimney though No. 1 lost hers in rebuilding after Curraduff. Nos. 6 and 8 (and the rebuilt No. 1) had individual sandboxes in front of the water compartments of the side tanks.

Nos. 1-3 were supplied in 1889, No. 6 in 1898 and No. 8 in 1910. Maker's numbers being: 477-9, 677 and 1051.

The branch engine, 0-4-2T No. 4, Maker's No. 514, supplied in 1890, was fitted with a cab and driving controls at both ends of the footplating in accordance with the then Tramway Regulations, since there were no turntables at either the Junction or at Castlegregory until O'Donnell's cash windfalls. She also had the condensing gear, speedometer and motion skirts, all of which (like Nos. 1-3) were removed by 1891. The cab at the chimney end remained until 1898. The single injector and cross-head pump were retained throughout her short life – she was never reboilered.

Again, Walschaerts valve gear was employed. Driving wheels were identical to those of the moguls, but the pony truck wheels were 1ft. 10in. dia. The cylinders were 11in. x 18in., working pressure of the boiler, 140lb/sq. in. and the tube area was 359sq. ft. The firebox surface was 45sq.ft. and the grate area 6.3sq.ft. Coal capacity was 29cu.ft./14cwt. and water capacity 500 gallons.

The larger (and surviving today!) loco, 2-6-2T No. 5, Maker's No. 555, supplied in 1892 was externally similar to the moguls, and was the last to be supplied with motion skirts, crosshead pump and single injector. However the condensing gear and speedo were omitted. It was fitted with Holden's patent oil-firing equipment. It differed from the 2-6-0s in having a longer boiler and firebox and of course in having the trailing bissel truck. Wheel diameters were identical to the moguls. Cylinders were 13.5in. x 18in., wheelbase: 6ft. 11in. - 4ft. 6in. - 4ft. 6in., two-ring telescopic boiler same diameter as the moguls but 9in. longer, working pressure was again 140lb./sq. in., increased to 150lb. on reboilering. The firebox was 6ft. 7in. long and the grate area was 10.6sq. ft., heating surfaces: boiler (138 tubes of $1^{5}/_{8}$in. dia.) 531sq. ft., firebox 70sq. ft. Coal capacity (after removal of the Holden oil firing equipment, c. 1904) was 34cu. ft./17cwt. – it had originally been only 17cu. ft., the oil tank accommodating 106 galls. of oil. Water capacity was 780 galls.

Cab layout (and in particular bunker access) was restricted and rather poor on all the Hunslet locos, by comparison with the two Kerr, Stuart locos: yet the Hunslets were universally preferred by the railwaymen, who cursed the small fireboxes, inaccessability of the inside Stephenson link motion and poor brakes of the Kerr, Stuarts.

THE KERR, STUARTS

It is not now known how or why the first Kerr, Stuart 2-6-0T, No. 7 was "sold" to Loco Foreman Litton in 1902; but he was responsible for the ordering of both. Nominally more powerful than the Hunslets (in tractive effort terms) they were always inferior in performance, and in braking. No. 7 was Maker's No. 800 and No. 8 (later 4 – after 1907 when the Hunslet 0-4-2 was scrapped) was Maker's No. 836 and supplied in 1903.

No. 7 was assembled in some haste at Tralee for of the other six locos on the T&D's books only No. 6 was available in service and was being worked to death. During this time the branch services were worked by pony and trap and there was only one return Tralee-Dingle journey per day!

The two Kerr, Stuart locos were a standard design and stood somewhat higher than the Hunslets. They had single slide bars and outside cylinders with inside Stephenson's link motion. Wheel diameters were 3ft. and 2ft. with wheelbase: 6ft.-4ft. $6^{1}/_{2}$in. - 4ft. $6^{1}/_{2}$in. Boilers 3ft. 3in. internal diameter with 8ft. 7in. barrel; working pressure 160lbs./sq. in., the cylinders were 12.5in. x 20in. Boiler tubes: 107 of $1^{3}/_{4}$in. dia., firebox 4ft. 7in. long, area 47sq. ft., tube area 431sq. ft. and grate area $7^{1}/_{2}$sq. ft. They weighed 31 tons and coal capacity was 45cu. ft./1 ton; water capacity 750 galls.

THE BETTER YEARS

During Mr O'Gorman's time as Loco Foreman, the locos were well maintained and turned out in the original T&DLR livery of dark green lined out in red (between two lines of cream), with crest on tanks. Locos lost handrails around the smokeboxes, oil lamp brackets and external whistle pipes in this period.

Following the GSR takeover in 1925, Inchicore-type oblong number plates were fitted in place of the T&DLR brass ones, and the suffix "T" added to each number. The 2-6-0s were classified Class KN1 and the

2-6-2T PN2. Locos were sent to Limerick or Inchicore for heavy repairs and gradually received standard Inchicore-pattern chimneys, smoke-boxes etc. Paintwork was battleship grey and (later) black with red buffer beams.

In latter (CIE) days, there were no coaling facilities other than from trucks in Tralee Main Yard and locos on the once-monthly Fair workings had to take along enough briquettes in an open wagon, or stacked all over the loco itself, for the round trip to Dingle.

All the locos had shallow ash pans which were fine for good quality (low ash) coal but troublesome with poor fuel (as found on the Cavan and Leitrim section). Peat firing was tried during the fuel shortages of the '40s, with disastrous results.

111. No. 1T at Dingle (with Paddy Martin in the cab) still in good shape four years after her major overhaul. Note missing safety valve cover and loss of cab vent with fitting of new sheet in 1934. This was 1938.
(W. A. Camwell)

112. No. 1T sandwiched between 8T and 2T in Tralee shed where the lines run back through to the workshop area. Note here cylinder top cover removed and No. 5T's toolbox on front plate.
(Ivo Peters, copyright Julian Peters)

113. No. 2T at Dingle, 1938, in very fair condition considering a major overhaul (1940 – her last) was approaching. She had single-hole cab steps and shorter version of the Inchicore chimney from 1935 at which time the short handrail round smokebox was fitted. Note original sandbox behind chimney. *(W. A. Camwell)*

114. Maker's photo of No. 2 – note condenser pipes (removed before line opened) and crosshead-drive pump. Pearson lubricator on dome. *(Hunslet Holdings)*

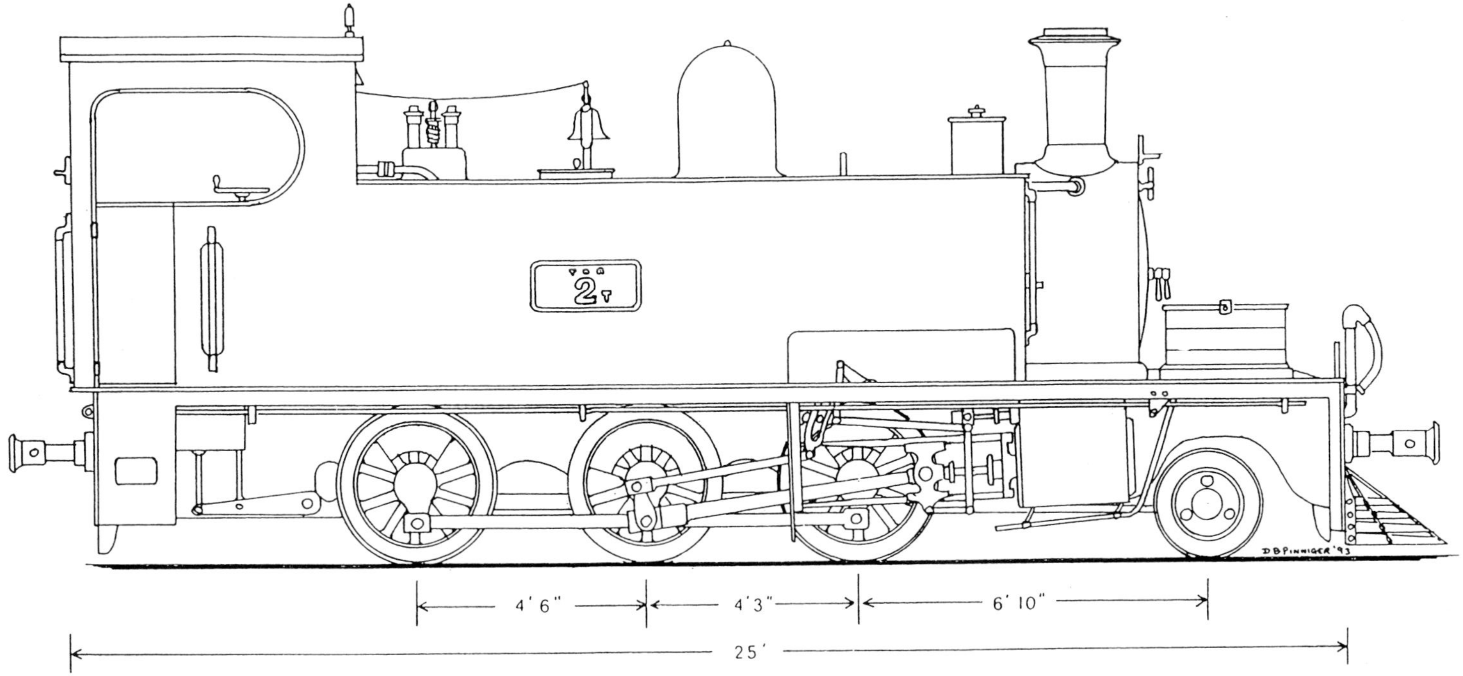

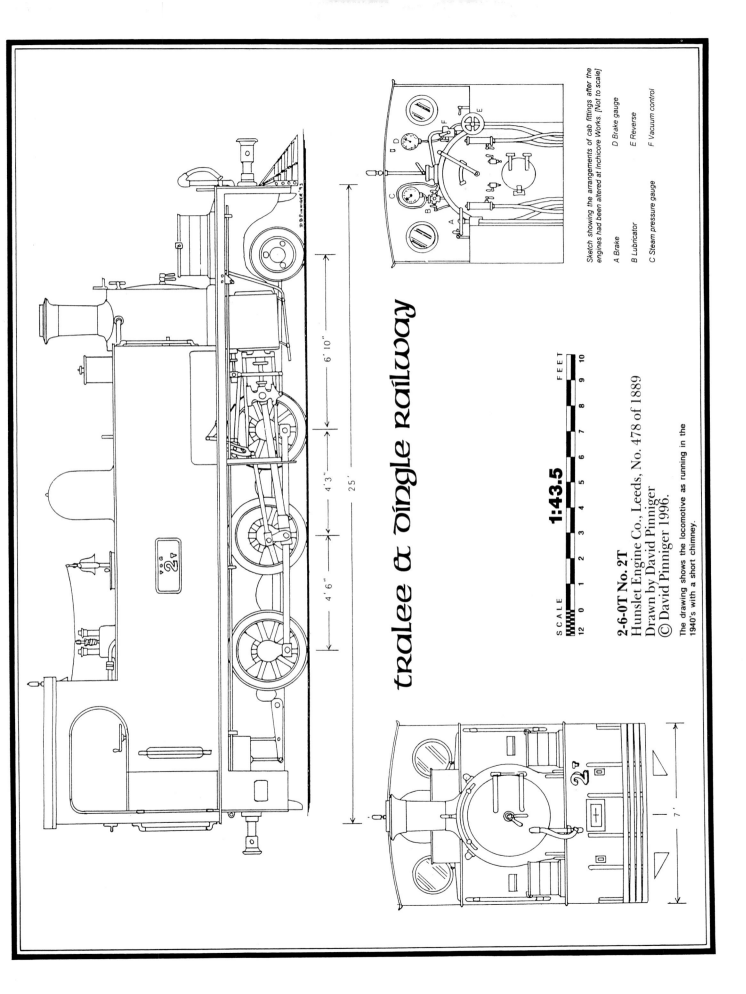

Tralee & Dingle Railway

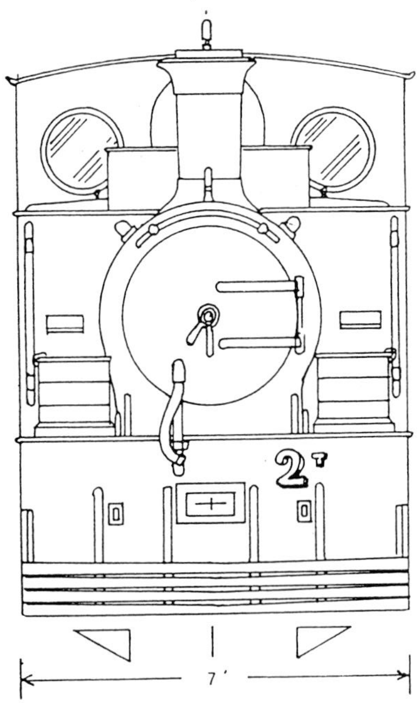

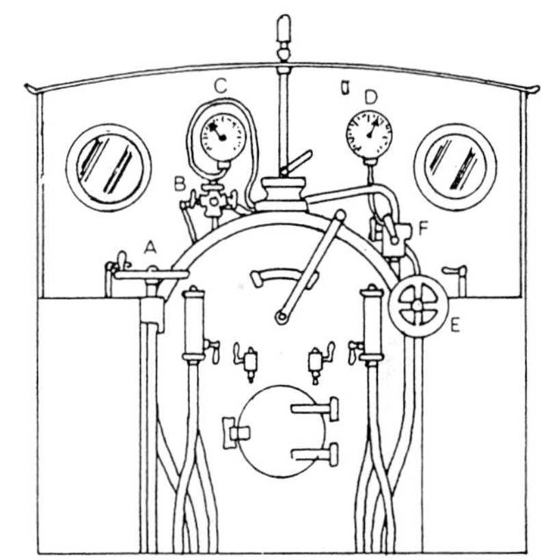

Sketch showing the arrangements of cab fittings after the engines had been altered at Inchicore Works. [Not to scale]

A Brake

B Lubricator

C Steam pressure gauge

D Brake gauge

E Reverse

F Vacuum control

1:43.5

2-6-0T No. 2T
Hunslet Engine Co., Leeds, No. 478 of 1889
Drawn by David Pinniger

The drawing shows the locomotive as running in the 1940's with a short chimney.

115. No. 3 of the original locomotives supplied and in very similar condition and fitting-out to No. 2, here seen at Annascaul with that mysterious bogie van (79T) behind. She had only three more years of work on "The Dingle" before going to the Cavan & Leitrim section. *(W. A. Camwell)*

116. The original No. 4, as supplied for the Castlegregory branch trains, with cab at both ends (no turntables). She was the earliest victim of neglect, ill-treatment and prejudice; withdrawn in 1902 and scrapped in 1907. *(Hunslet Holdings Ltd.)*

117. No. 4T out of service (as usual!) at Tralee in 1934. Note brass number plate (ex-original 4) on tank side, works plate removed to lubricator. *(H. C. Casserley)*

118. No. 4T (the original No. 8) at Inchicore in 1938, where she was undergoing a major overhaul. Note the standard Inchicore fittings (and replacement of that spurious "No. 4" brass plate). She was very unpopular with T&D locomen, mainly on account of her poor brakes, and they contrived to keep her out of service for most of the time until her transfer to the Cavan & Leitrim in 1941. Unlike the Hunslets she was not missed! *(W. A. Camwell)*

NOTES ON INDIVIDUAL LOCOMOTIVES

Hunslet No. 1 (T)

Some further detail on this loco up to the time of the Curraduff bridge disaster of 1893 was given in the Board of Trade Accident Report, and is reproduced verbatim below:–

Description of Engine

The engine was built by the Hunslet Engine Company at Leeds, was used by the contractors when constructing the line, and was handed over to the Company in 1891.

It is an eight-wheeled tank-engine, with six wheels coupled, and a leading two-wheeled bogie pony truck. The centre pair of the coupled-wheels are not flanged.

The wheel-base is as follows:–

	Ft.	In.
Bogie-wheels to leading-wheels	6	10
Leading-wheels to driving-wheels	4	3
Driving-wheels to trailing-wheels	4	6

The estimated weights on the different pairs of wheels, with tanks and bunker full, are:–

		Tons
On bogie-wheels	—	$6^3/4$
On leading-wheels	—	$7^3/4$
On driving-wheels	—	$7^3/4$
On trailing-wheels	—	$8^1/2$
Total		$30^3/4$

The diameter of the coupled wheels is 3ft. $^1/2$in., and that of the bogie-wheels is 2ft.

The diameter of the cylinders is 1ft. 1in., and the length of stroke is 1ft. 6ins.

The repair books in the shops do not seem to have been very carefully kept, but, as far as can be gathered from the evidence, this engine was put into a proper state of repair when it was first acquired by the Company, and was last thoroughly repaired in November 1892, since which time it has run 8,695 miles. It was also in the shops for repairs on 14th February, 18th March, 24th to 26th March, and 20th to 22nd May. Upon this last occasion a new right-hand side trailing-spring was put in, and the brake-blocks were adjusted, and it was stated in evidence that it was in good running order when it left the shops.

The following are the weights and lengths over the buffers of the different vehicles composing the Curraduff accident train:–

	Weight		Length over Buffers	
	Tons	Cwts	Ft.	In.
Engine (with tank and bunker half full)	28	0	28	11
Cattle wagon	2	15	16	1
Third-class carriage	3	10	29	1
Guard's van	2	15	16	1

The passenger carriage had two four-wheeled bogies, and the cattle waggons and the guard's van were four-wheeled vehicles.

The total length of the train, including the engine, was 186ft. 8ins., and the total weight, including the weight of the engine, and the weight of the passengers and the livestock (estimated at $2^1/3$ tons, and 14 tons respectively), was 70 tons.

The whole train, including the cattle waggons, was fitted with the automatic vacuum-brake, capable of being applied by the driver, or by the guard if necessary, and working blocks upon every wheel on the train, except the bogie-wheels of the engine, so that, out of the total weight of 70 tons, $63^1/2$ tons were upon braked wheels.

In addition to this there were ordinary screw hand-brakes upon the engine and the guard's van, and side levers for working the blocks on one pair of wheels of each of the cattle-waggons.

She was rebuilt completely in 1894-5, losing the boiler-top sandbox and gaining a triple rear window and two-hole cab steps. A lifting jack was substituted for the nearside toolbox for a few years. She was reboilered twice in 1902 and in 1920 and had a final major overhaul at Inchicore in 1934-5, gaining the GSR chimney. She worked on all the Fair Day Specials until closure of the line in 1953, and was considered worked out. She was sent to Inchicore and condemned, being cut up there in 1955. Her bell survives in Nigeria!

Hunslet No. 2 (T)

Suffered firebox trouble (bad workmanship) from 1892 onward and in 1901 was stopped for "general repairs" for no less than 3 years: a record even for "The Dingle". She was reboilered in 1903, and had her last major overhaul at Inchicore in 1940, receiving GSR-style smokebox and a rather shorter GSR-style chimney than any of the other T&D locos. When 5T went to Inchicore in 1949, she left behind her metal toolboxes. No. 2T acquired one of these as an extra sandbox throughout the '50s. In 1952 she lost her chimney while working a cattle special and it was replaced with a "standard" one for her last few months of work. She failed in service November 1952 and was stored derelict among the rolling stock taken out of use in Tralee Main yard. On closure of the T&D section in 1953, she went to Inchicore for scrapping and was cut up with 1T in 1955. Her bell was presented to Mr Cyril Fry and saw regular use as his house bell.

Hunslet No. 3 (T)

She also suffered from arrears of maintenance until reboilered in 1902. On closure of the T&D passenger services in 1939, she was transferred to the Cavan & Leitrim section by GSR, being overhauled at Inchicore en route, and not arriving there until 1941. There she retained all her "Dingle" fittings except her wooden toolboxes, but numberplates, cowcatcher, bell etc. were gradually removed. She was worked hard on the "Cavan" – particularly on Arigna coal trains – and used on lifting the Belturbet section of the C&L, being cut up in the exchange sidings there along with the Kerr, Stuart 4T in August 1959.

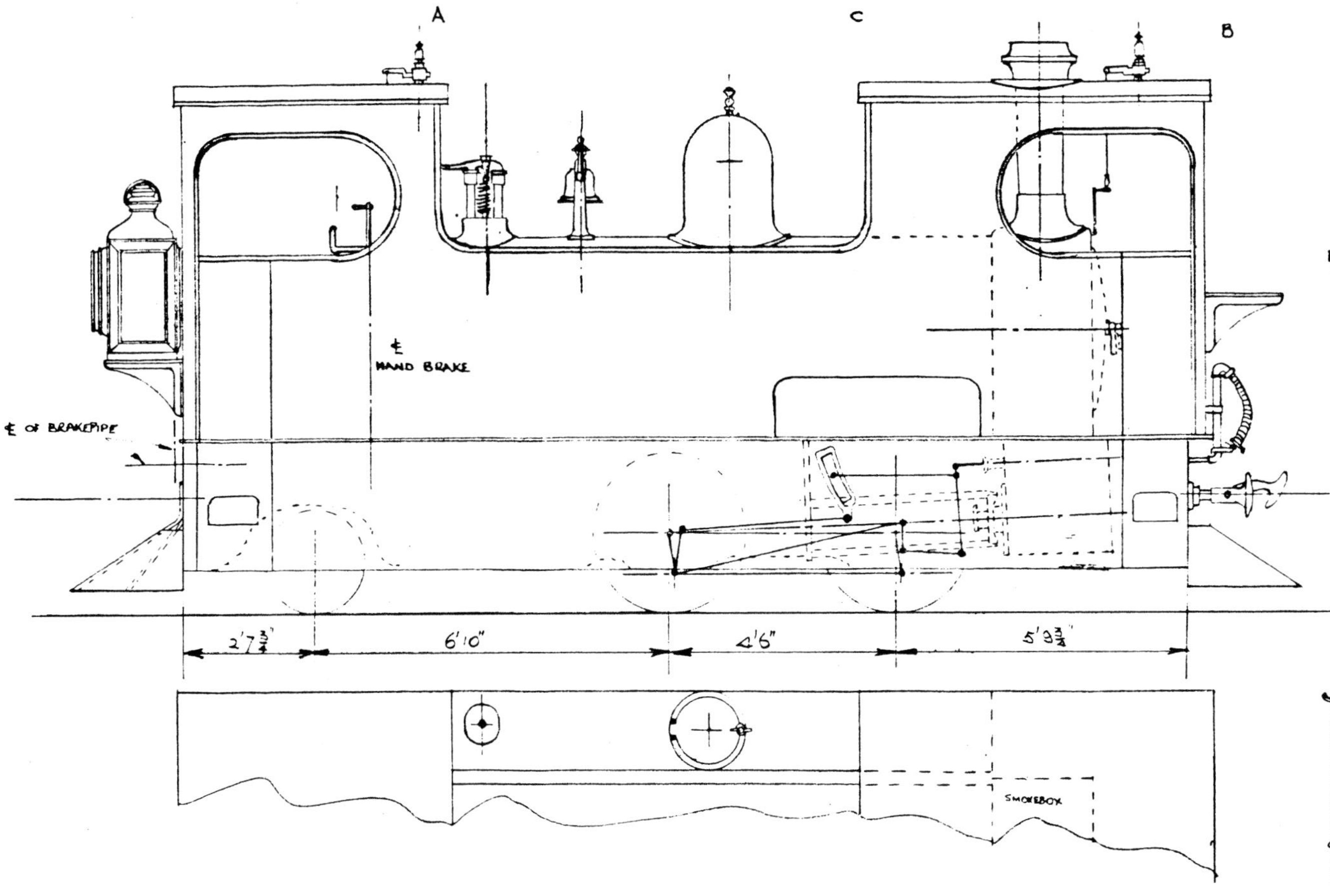

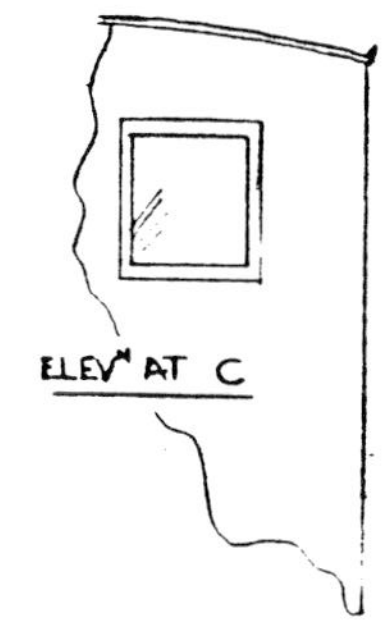

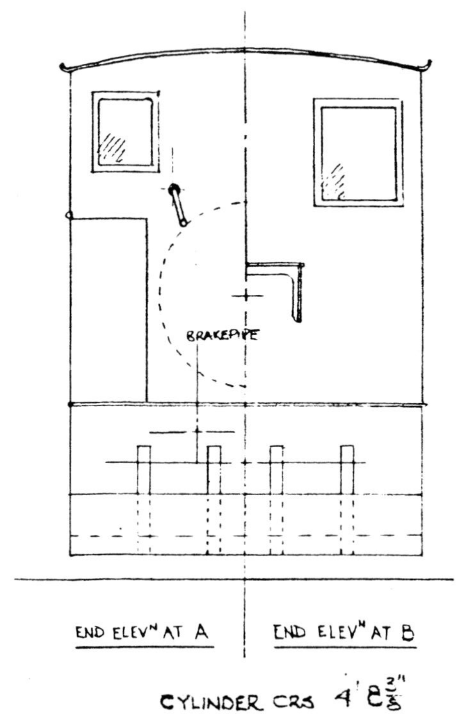

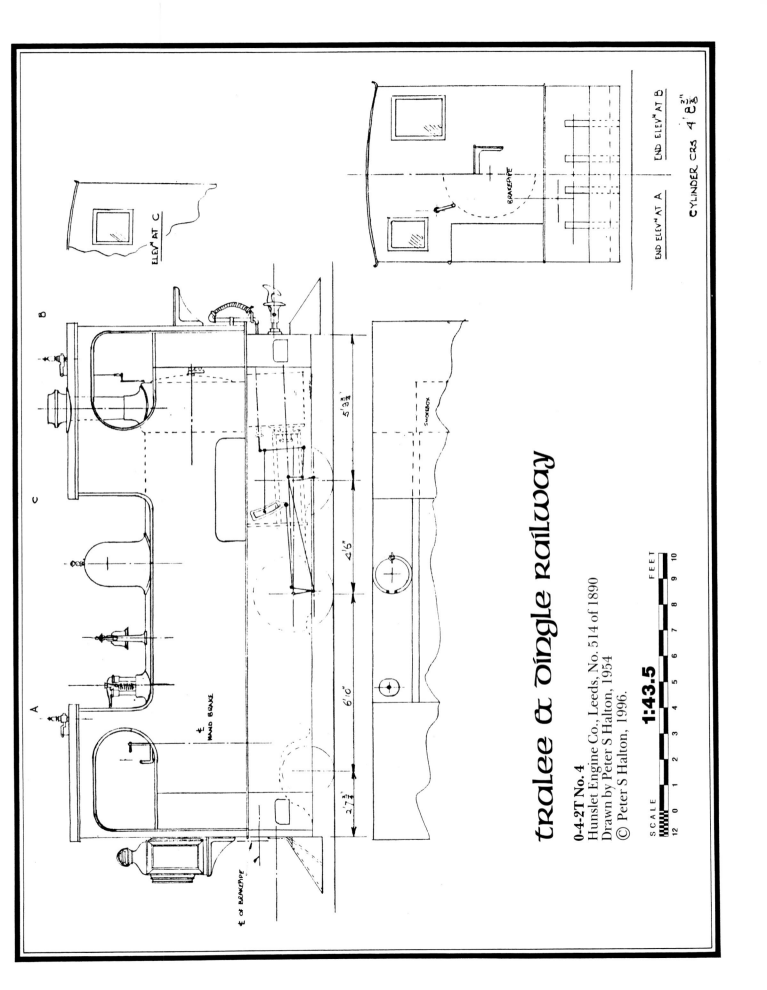

tralee & dingle railway

0-4-2T No. 4
Hunslet Engine Co., Leeds, No. 514 of 1890
Drawn by Peter S Halton, 1954

SCALE **1:43.5** FEET
12 0 1 2 3 4 5 6 7 8 9 10

119. No. 5 as supplied in 1892, fitted with motion skirts but without the steam condensing gear of the original three 2-6-0s. Note the absence of toolboxes and the lifting jack on the running plate, Pearson lubricator on dome, triple-light rear window and square front specs. Note also that there is no heavy oil lamp bracket at that time.
(Hunslet Holdings Ltd.)

120. Removal of the motion skirts on No. 5 initially meant loss of cab steps. Note now the crosshead-driven water pump. As supplied she was, of course, oil fired using Holden's patent apparatus.
(Hunslet Holdings Ltd.)

121. No. 5T at Dingle in 1938 during a period when she was worked very hard. Note the patch on the side-tanks and the metal toolboxes. She was taken out of service in 1949 but of course, amazingly and wonderfully survives today. *(W. A. Camwell)*

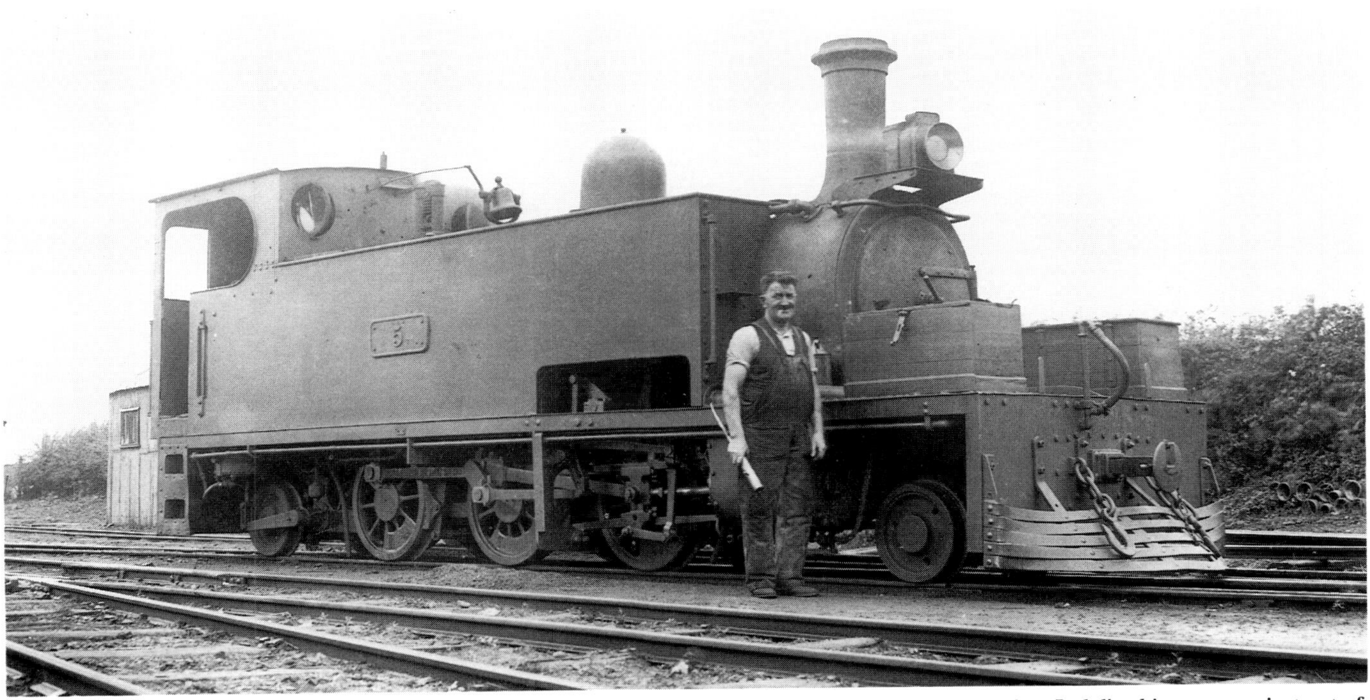

122. No. 5T seen here at Dingle in 1931 as Driver Jack Cotter paused in his oiling round for the photographer. Jack lived in a cottage just out of the left of the picture. Note that she still had her wooden toolboxes, Hunslet chimney and handrail missing from smokebox (but see photo 123). Inchicore-type number plates fitted. *(W. H. C. Kelland: Bournemouth Loco Club)*

123. A close fit on Tralee Turntable! Note handrail still round right hand side of smokebox. (1931.) *(R. N. Clements)*

124. The 5.15pm to Dingle at Tralee, ready to come forward and then reverse into the passenger platform on the foreground line: seven bogies plus three wagons, including coach for Castlegregory. *(R. N. Clements)*

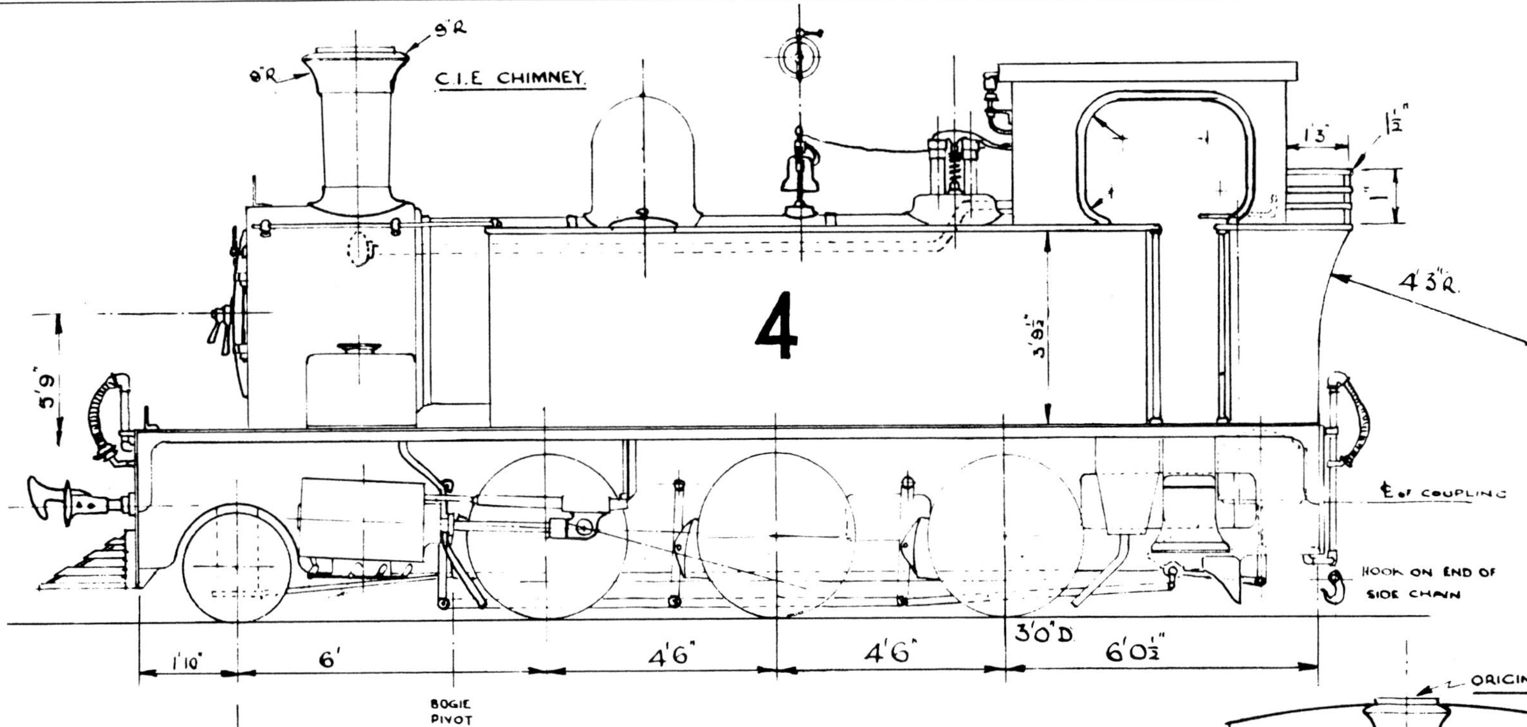

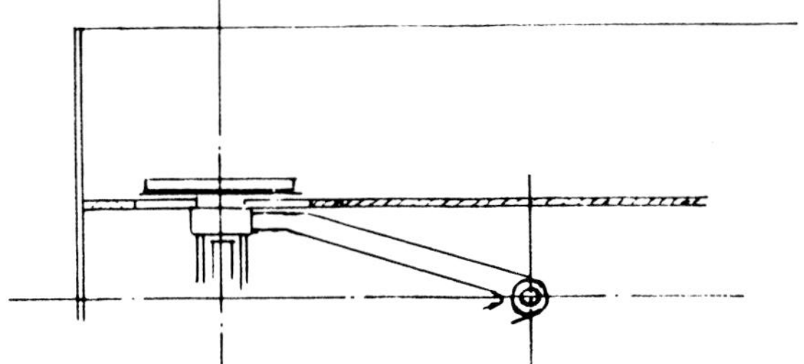

PONY TRUCK DETAIL.

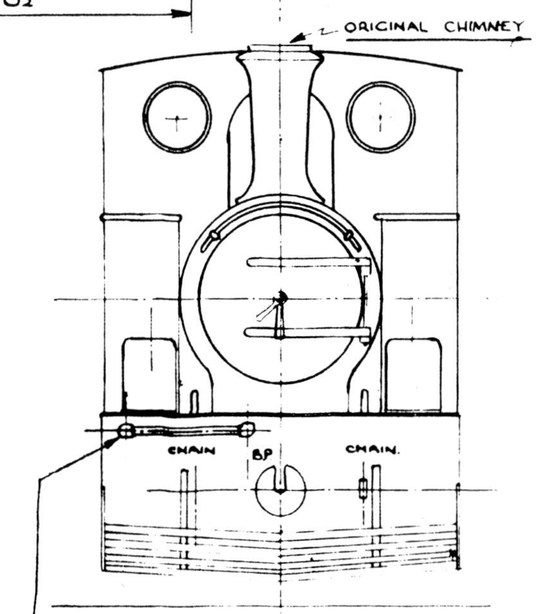

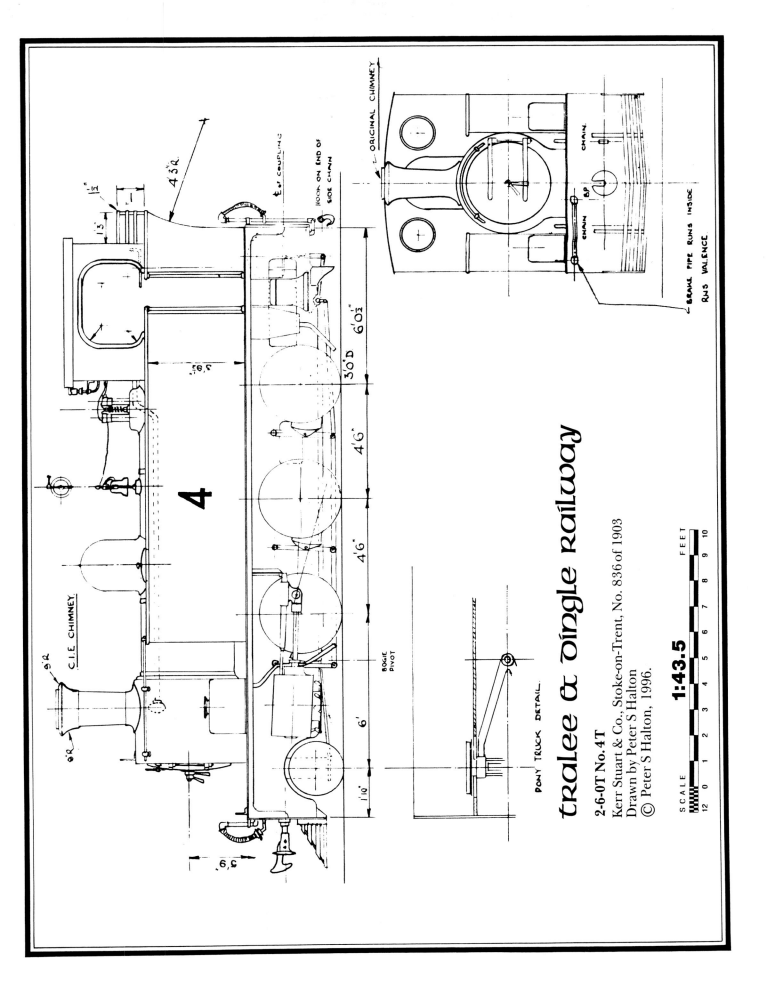

Tralee & Dingle Railway

2-6-0T No. 4T

Kerr Stuart & Co., Stoke-on-Trent, No. 836 of 1903
Drawn by Peter S Halton

SCALE **1:43.5** FEET

12 0 1 2 3 4 5 6 7 8 9 10

Hunslet No. 4

This loco suffered neglect even earlier than the other locos, partly due to being shedded away at Castlegregory and to being underpowered for the level of service that the branch traffic required – i.e. not worth tinkering with. Heavy repairs (firebox again) were required by 1898 and she was mainly used as standby – for which role the cab and regulator were removed from the chimney end. Homespun and dangerous repairs to the firebox were noted by Mr Cusack of the MGWR, brought in to inspect the condition of the locos in 1902, and he recommended withdrawal pending a complete overhaul. In the event she was dumped in the spare wagon siding at Tralee and remained there until sold for scrap in 1907.

Hunslet No. 5 (T)

The only loco to survive today, she was ordered in April 1891 and paid for in instalments over three years. She was the first inside-framed 2-6-2T built for a British NG line, and proved so economical and impressive as an oil burner, that further sets of the Holden apparatus were ordered for the 2-6-0s, though fitting was not implemented, and indeed No. 5 was converted to coal firing in 1893. As part of his very thorough investigation of the Curraduff disaster in that same year, Major Marinden had a train made up to the same weight as that in the accident and travelled with it – behind loco No. 5: the only one available! – down a number of the gradients, including that on to Curraduff viaduct. Since No. 5 is still extant today, it is of interest to quote from his account of the tests.

> In order to ascertain what would be the effect of the application of the vacuum-brake upon a train of nine vehicles, running at different speeds, upon inclines of 1 in 32 and 1 in 30, I arranged to travel up from Dingle on a train made up exactly in the same order as that to which the accident happened, and, although it was not practicable to have the train loaded in a similar manner, and the rails were in very good condition, instead of being very greasy as upon the afternoon of the accident, the experiments, while they cannot be taken as an absolute indication of what probably happened upon that occasion, were not without value.
>
> The total weight of the train was 25 tons 10cwt., or 55 tons 10cwt. including the engine, but excluding the weight of the few people who were travelling in it, while the engine, the only one available, weighed about 2 tons more than the No. 1 engine, the one which was wrecked by the accident.
>
> I found that with 120lbs. of steam the vacuum could be blown up to 20 inches in 15 seconds, by the use of the large ejector, but that a vacuum of only 11ins. could be obtained by the small ejector in four minutes; that when the valve in the guard's van was fully open, after applying the brake, a vacuum of 15 inches could be obtained by the use of the large ejector, but that the brake-blocks remained on upon half the train; that when the brakes were applied, and both ejectors shut, the brakes leaked off all the vehicles except the engine and four waggons, in $7^1/_2$ minutes, and off the whole train in 9 minutes; that when the small ejector was not kept running the vacuum sank to 5ins. in $^3/_4$ minute, and to zero in $2^1/_2$ minutes; and that with 79lbs. of steam it was possible to obtain a vacuum of 15ins., but no more.
>
> One of the washers on a connecting hose-pipe had been found to be defective, and was replaced, but it was evident from the above results that there was a leak in some other place which could not be detected, and this was also shown by the fact that, when running, the vacuum could not be maintained above 15ins., and the large ejector had to be used to blow up the vacuum before applying the brake. The following were among the stops I made on the journey:–
>
> 1. Gradient, falling 1 in 30; speed, 24 miles an hour; 20 inches of vacuum.
>   Stopped in 120 yards by use of the vacuum-brake only.
> 2. Gradient, falling 1 in 32; speed, 25 miles an hour; 17 inches of vacuum.
>   Stopped in 156 yards by use of the vacuum-brake only.
> 3. Gradient, falling 1 in 32; 17 inches of vacuum; started as sharply as possible from rest; vacuum-brake applied after running 50 yards. Stopped train in 50 yards.
>
> In coming down the incline to Curraduff with the waggon-brakes pinned down, the engine hand-brake on, and the guards-brake rubbing, the speed never exceeded seven miles an hour, although the vacuum-brake was only once momentarily applied.
>
> The result of these experiments certainly confirmed my opinion, that, if proper care be used, the brake power available on these trains is ample to enable a driver to keep control over his train on the incline of 1 in 30, even if the brakes are in a somewhat leaky condition, as was the case in the train by which I travelled.

She was worked extremely hard in the period 1896-8 and was – together with the newly rebuilt No. 1 – frequently the only loco available.

By 1901 she was in poor condition, particularly boiler and firebox, but underwent effective general repairs in 1902 that kept her in service until reboilering in 1906.

Again, she was worked intensively during the '30s and early '40s being the engine favoured for the daily goods. Her wooden toolboxes were replaced by unique and distinctive metal ones in 1936. Her side tanks were patched in 1934. She was also the loco used for the unsuccessful experiments with turf-burning in 1944. However the decreasing maintenance during those troubled years took their toll and by 1948 she was at the back of Tralee shed "Not Movable" awaiting general overhaul. The story of her last run on the T&D is told in Chapter 9.

125. No. 6T at Castlegregory in 1938. The most accident-prone of all the Dingle locos, she retained lever reverse and only had a sliding panel fitted to the cab backsheet in 1945. She went to Inchicore in 1950 and was needed back on the T&DLR, but authority decided otherwise and she went first to the West Clare, then to the Cavan & Leitrim. *(W. A. Camwell)*

126. No. 7 of which photos are few and far between, this being at Tralee in 1907 – note the wooden and corrugated iron loco shed (replaced in 1918). You may be able to discern the lining out on the toolbox and around the numberplate. The works plate (oval) was removed to the right-hand side lubricator during the early 1920s. (No. 8/4's went on the left side lubricator). There is lining along the frame edge and footplating too. *(H. Fayle: IRRS)*

She was then pushed to the exchange sidings (by 2T) until the Limerick Steam crane came along to lift her on to a transporter wagon for Dublin.

She spent almost a year outdoors at Inchicore, before being completely overhauled and sent to the Cavan & Leitrim section in the wake of 3T and 4T. Her toolboxes remained at Tralee, and her numberplates were removed in Dublin, but at first on the C&L section she kept her bell, lamp bracket and cowcatcher. They were successively removed in the following years of intensive use, working out of Ballinamore. On closure of the C&L section in 1959, she was still in reasonable working order and was even – unlikely though it seems – considered for use on the Isle of Man railway before being sold and shipped to the USA. The story of which is recounted in Chapter 10.

Hunslet No. 6 (T)

As indicated above, this locomotive was used intensively right from her arrival at Tralee. She was worked-out and badly in need of general repairs by 1903. In the event these took some 9 months to complete. She had her revenge for the cavalier treatment by being involved in many accidents, including the Banogue derailment of Chapter 2, this being in her first few months on the T&DLR. A pattern was set and she was considered accident prone. Certainly she featured in more GSR Accident reports than all the other T&D locos together! Some of the more spectacular being the Lispole derailment of 1907 (Chapter 2), the Glenmore fracas with a car on the first day of GSR "ownership" (Chapter 7) and the Circus crash of 1940 (Chapter 8).

Her regular driver of the '30s and '40s, Tom Cournane, was not without a dry sense of humour and some of his Report Forms make entertaining reading today, however unhappy they may have been for the victims.

A typical one, an encounter with a cow near Garrynadur, ran as follows:

GREAT SOUTHERN RAILWAYS
Locomotive Department
OBSTRUCTION REPORT FORM

1. **Date of obstruction:** 15.8.41. **2. Nature:** 1 cow.
3: **Place (Give nearest mp):** 24 3/4. **4. Train time:** 8am; **Class:** Goods; **From:** Tralee. **To:** Dingle; **Time of occurrence:** 12.20pm.
5. **Driver:** Cournane. **Fireman:** McMaher. **Loco:** 6T.
6. **Composition of Train:** 6 wagons, 1 van.

Note. Particulars required where Trespassers, Animals or other obstructions are found on the line.

7. **Answer queries 5 to 16 on Clause 2, also the following:**
8. **Distance obstruction seen from footplate:** About 40 yds.
9. **Name of trespasser or owner:** Cannot say.
10. **What steps were taken for removal of obstruction?:** Pushed clear of line.
11. **Are there accommodation/farm gates near?:** Farm gates.
12. **Were they open or closed?:** One open.
13. **On which side of line was obstruction observed?:** Left.
14. **In what direction was it moving?:** Standing.
15. **What condition were fences in the vicinity?:** Good wire.
16. **In case of lorries on line or delays due to relaying state if Rules 250, 251 and 252 were carried out:**
17. **Was previous train flagged?**

General Remarks: Reported to Stationmaster Dingle at 1.30pm.

No 6T worked cattle trains up to 1950 then, badly in need of general overhaul, Foreman Garrett of Tralee sent her to Inchicore for repair, since she was needed for the monthly cattle specials which really required four locos (i.e. two double headed trains); particularly after 5T went to the C&L instead of returning to Tralee. Without No. 6, there were only Nos. 1, 2 and 8T left on the T&D.

Instead No. 6 remained a long time at Inchicore, despite Garrett's requests for her urgent return; then she was overhauled at last and sent to the West Clare section in 1953, losing her bell, number plate and cowcatcher. She retained her number 6 on the Clare and also on the C&L. When the Clare was dieselised in 1955, she returned to Inchicore for scrapping, but was reprieved and renovated in 1957 to deal with emergency coal traffic on the Cavan & Leitrim, where she worked a prodigious mileage until closure in 1959. She worked on the Dromod section demolition and was cut up there in February 1960.

Kerr, Stuart No. 7 (T)

Little is recorded of this locomotive which arrived and was erected on the T&D to enter immediate and intensive service. Despite nominal superiority in tractive effort over the Hunslet locos, it was inferior in performance and frequently relegated to the Castlegregory Branch in the years 1903 onward, turn about with No. 8. Neither loco was used unless unavoidable for cattle specials or heavy mixed trains.

It was, however, quite economical on fuel compared to the Hunslets.

Photos of her in 1924 show her fitted with a non-T&D style cowcatcher.

In an attempt to increase power, Mr Carey had the cylinders bored out to 13.5in. diameter and increased the working pressure to 160lbs./sq. in., but it made little difference and the alteration was not made on No. 8.

She became No. 7T on absorption into the GSR in 1925, and – as with No. 4 (ex 8) her maker's plates were transferred from side tanks to the sandboxes on the front footplating. She was however largely worked out and confined to light duties. She needed reboilering, new tyres and firebox. It was suggested that a larger boiler be tried, but in the event she was condemned in 1928 and scrapped at Limerick.

Kerr, Stuart No. 8; later No. 4 (T)

Just why the T&D ordered another Kerr, Stuart loco is not clear, but it may have been linked to the fuel economies noted with No. 7 or the fact that financial credibility with the Hunslet Company was at an all-time low. Whatever the reason, No. 8 arrived in 1903 and was erected in the shops at Tralee.

Alas she proved no more popular with crews than her sister; due mainly to her weak braking power: a disastrous shortcoming on the T&D.

When the Hunslet 0-4-2T No. 4 was scrapped in 1907, her handsome brass numberplate was transferred to No. 8, which thus became No. 4 in the T&D stock list. The maker's name on the plate was filled out.

In the '20s she was mainly on the Castlegregory branch. The locomen found ways of keeping her out of service during most of the '30s, and neglect compounded other problems and she went to Inchicore in 1938 for a general overhaul. There she received new GSR numberplate, chimney and dome and returned bravely to Tralee. However the locomen had their say, and visitors during 1939 noted that she was constantly out of service at the back of the loco shed. Withdrawal of the passenger service and closure of the branch (where she theoretically operated) caused a re-think, and she was drafted to the Cavan & Leitrim section in 1941. We only know of one photo that shows her working a T&D train: in all the others she is out of use!

Problems in firing her with Arigna coal kept her out of service on the C&L too for a while. However she was necessarily pressed into use and, once familiar to the C&L men, she became quite a popular loco and was used intensively on passenger services. She survived to work demolition trains on the Belturbet section and was cut up there in 1959.

Hunslet No. 8 (T)

This, the last loco built for the T&D, was one of the most successful and gave the least trouble. She was the last T&D loco to retain her original fittings, as she did not go into Inchicore shops for a major overhaul until 1937-8. Of the locos left at Tralee in the '40s, she was in the best condition and bore the brunt of the latter-day monthly cattle trains. On one such working she notched up more than 160 miles on a nominal 63 mile return trip (see Chapter 8). She was normally the first loco in steam at the weekend, being used to haul the other two/three out of the shed.

On closure of the T&D section, despite considerable wear in her motion, it was felt that there was still useful life in her, and she was part-dismantled and sent to the West Clare section in January 1954. The authors have yet to meet anyone who saw her in service on that line and she does not appear to have been photographed at work there. On dieselisation of the Clare in 1955 she was condemned and sent to Inchicore where she was scrapped in 1956.

No. "9T"

A number of reference books on Irish NG railways (e.g. Newham, Fayle and Kidner) note that ex-Cork and Muskerry loco No. 5K built by Thomas Green & Co. in 1892 was transferred to the T&D section in 1935-6. In fact parts of No. 5 were put into the rebuilding of No. 6K (an identical sister loco of 1893) at Inchicore in 1935. Mr Clements is of the firm conviction that No. 6K was the intended loco and almost certainly with the Castlegregory Branch in mind. However by this time GSR were trying to close the Branch (only Katty Breen's spirited championship of the line kept it open until her death!) and in the event No. 6K went to the Schull & Skibereen in 1938. She did little there as the line closed in 1946 and possibly her last steaming was for Cyril Fry's benefit when she pulled out the surviving S&S stock for him to measure in 1950. A proposal to send her to the Cavan & Leitrim came to naught as the more suitable 5T became available instead.

LIVERY & FITTINGS

Until GSR days (1925) the locomotives were painted in the Company's livery: dark green; lined out on tanks, backsheet, toolboxes, cab doors and cylinders with three bands: cream-red-cream. As locos went into GSR shops at Inchicore or Limerick for major overhauls, they emerged in plain battleship grey, to be followed (late 1930s) by plain black with red front and rear beams. The individual maker's fittings gave way to those standardised by GSR (Inchicore) for their narrow-gauge locos: chimneys, smoke-boxes, cab-fittings etc., and the original oval brass numberplates were replaced by oblong cast-iron ones.

INSPECTION RAILCAR

In 1922 the T&DLR shops produced a delightful little 4-wheeled railcar, on a Baguley chassis with Ford T motor. No doubt this played a role in military "scouting" at the time. It was fitted with a "passenger" compartment and used for inspecting the line. When GSR took over, it was drafted to Ennis (West Clare) and made available for use on all the GSR/CIE 3ft. gauge lines. (It thus returned to Tralee on occasion). It looked well in GSR red livery with their crest on the side panels. In 1938 it was re-engined with a more modern Ford 8 unit. In 1953 it made a return to Tralee in connection with assessing a suggestion for operating the line with railcars (like the West Clare). This was after cattle trains had ceased. Beyond Blennerville they only just pulled up in time before hitting a section where rails were missing. A local "Scrappie" had anticipated complete closure! Nothing further came of the proposal. The little car was surplus to requirement when the West Clare closed (no more public 3ft. gauge to inspect!) and sadly it was scrapped in 1961-2. What a pity it did not survive.

Table 1 gives full details of the T&DLR locomotives.

127. Arguably the most successful loco on the T&D, No. 8, seen here at Tralee in 1938 is freshly out of Inchicore shops and resplendent in black paint with red front beams, following her final major overhaul. She bore the brunt of working on the latter-day cattle specials and ran on the very last train to operate on the Tralee & Dingle section in July 1953.

(W.A. Camwell)

128. No. 8T at the back of the shed, sandwiched between 6T and 5T. October 1949.

(Ivo Peters, copyright Julian Peters)

INSPECTION RAILCAR

129. As built at Tralee 1922, awaiting body shell. *(Per Padraig Kennelly)*

130. In Ennis shed, 1938, still with original Ford T radiator, as GSR No. 6. Note crest at rear and number 6 on door panel. *(W. A. Camwell)*

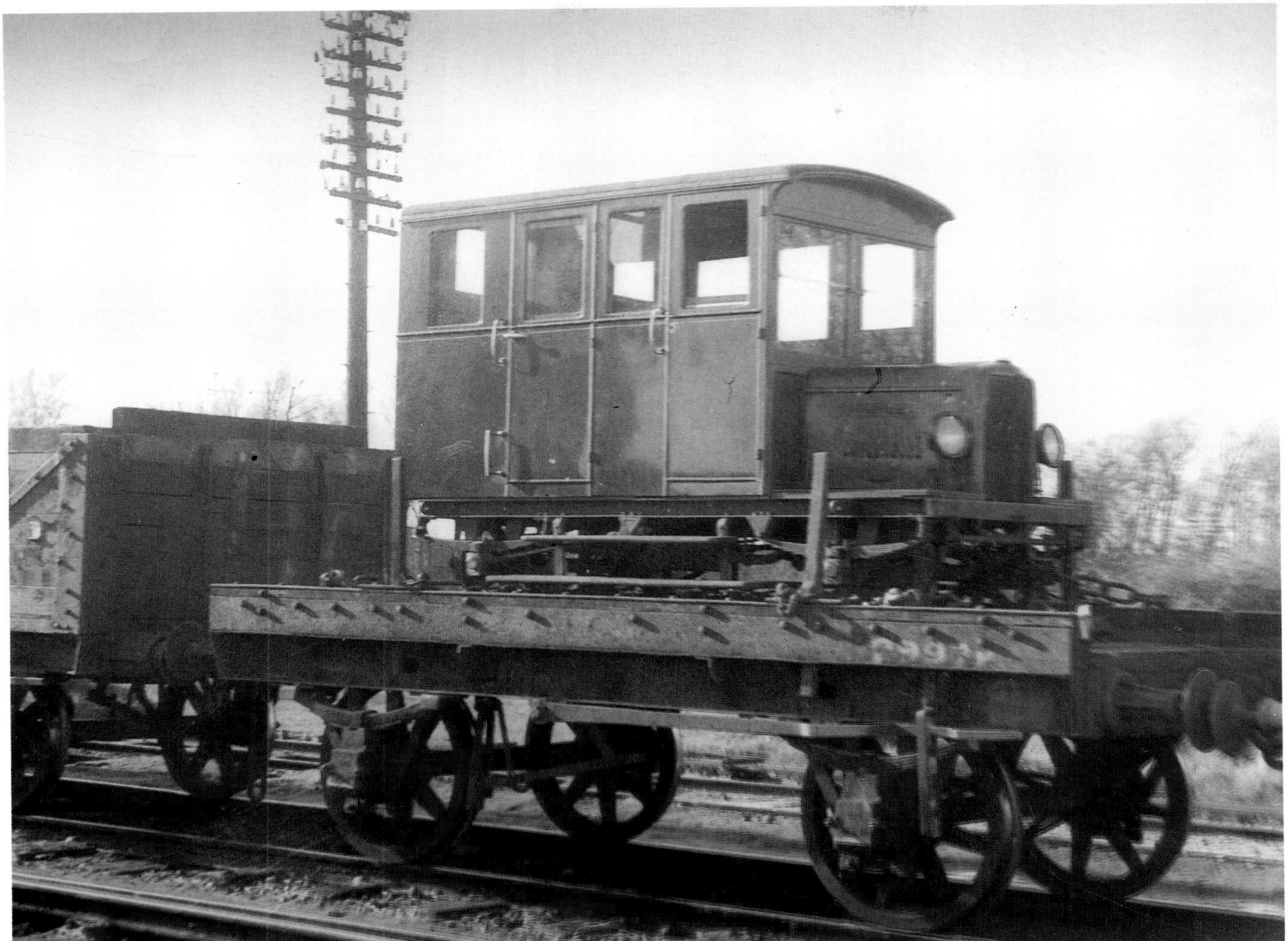

131. Returning from one of her jaunts to other NG lines, she is here taking it easy and passing Athlone in 1959. *(R. N. Clements)*

132. Derelict at Ennis in 1961, just prior to cutting up. What a shame no-one then thought to save her! *(H. C. Casserley)*

Tralee & Dingle Railway

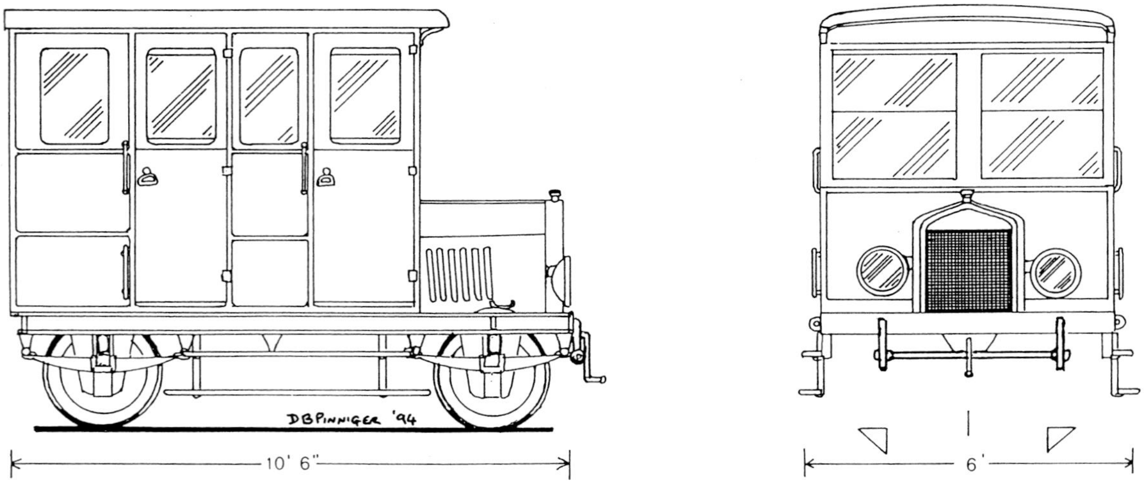

Inspection Railcar
As built, with Ford T engine
Built in T&DR workshops on Baguley chassis, 1922
Drawn by David Pinniger

SCALE **1:43.5** FEET
12 0 1 2 3 4 5 6 7 8 9 10

LOCOMOTIVE PERFORMANCE

Many enthusiasts are interested in locomotive performance. It is perhaps unfair to look at that by two worn-out locos at the very end of their working lives, but this record of a loaded cattle special returning from Dingle in 1953 is the only example I know on the T&DLR. It was recorded by Ian Duncan.

Log of Return Trip, 28th March 1953
(Locos 1T & 8T, crew of 7 + 3 visitors, 1 wagon, 9 loaded cattle vans, 1 brake van)

	Miles	Times	Av. Speed
Dingle	0	0	0
Lispole	4.7	25-47	10.9
Garrynadur	1.6	14-03	6.9
Ballinasare	1.8	7-20	14.7
Annascaul	2.5	11-25	13.1
Annascaul	0	0	0
Camp Junctn	10.8	72-47	8.9
Camp Junc	0	0	0
Curraheen	4.4	15-29	17.1
Blennerville	3.1	12-05	15.2
Tralee	2.3	11-45	11.7

Time Dingle-Annascaul:	58-35, 10.6 miles, Av. speed 10.8mph.
Annascaul-Camp J.:	72-47, 10.8 miles, Av. speed 8.9mph.
Camp J.-Tralee:	39.19, 9.8 miles, Av. speed 15.0mph.
Dingle-Tralee:	170-41 mins., 31.2 miles, Av. speed 10.9mph.

Advertised departure: Dingle 11-3-45 am;
Arrival Tralee: 3-26-53 pm.
Overall Time: 231min.-08sec.;
Running Time: 170min. 41sec.
HORSEPOWER DEVELOPED CLIMBING GLENAGALT BANK:–
2 locos, each 38t, maintain 6.9mph up 1 in 29 with trailing load of 74t.
At 10mph, loco resistance ca 10lb./t. Double this for T&DR.
At 7mph wagon resistance ca 4.2lb./t. Double this for T&DR.
Rolling resistance = (38 + 38)20 + (74) 8.4 = 1520 + 6220 = 2142lbs.
Gradient resistance = (76 + 74) 2240/29 = 150 x 2240/29 = 11590lbs.
Indicated HP (total) for balancing speed = (2142 + 11590).6.9/375
= 13732. 6.9/375 = 252, i.e. **125.1 HP per loco.**

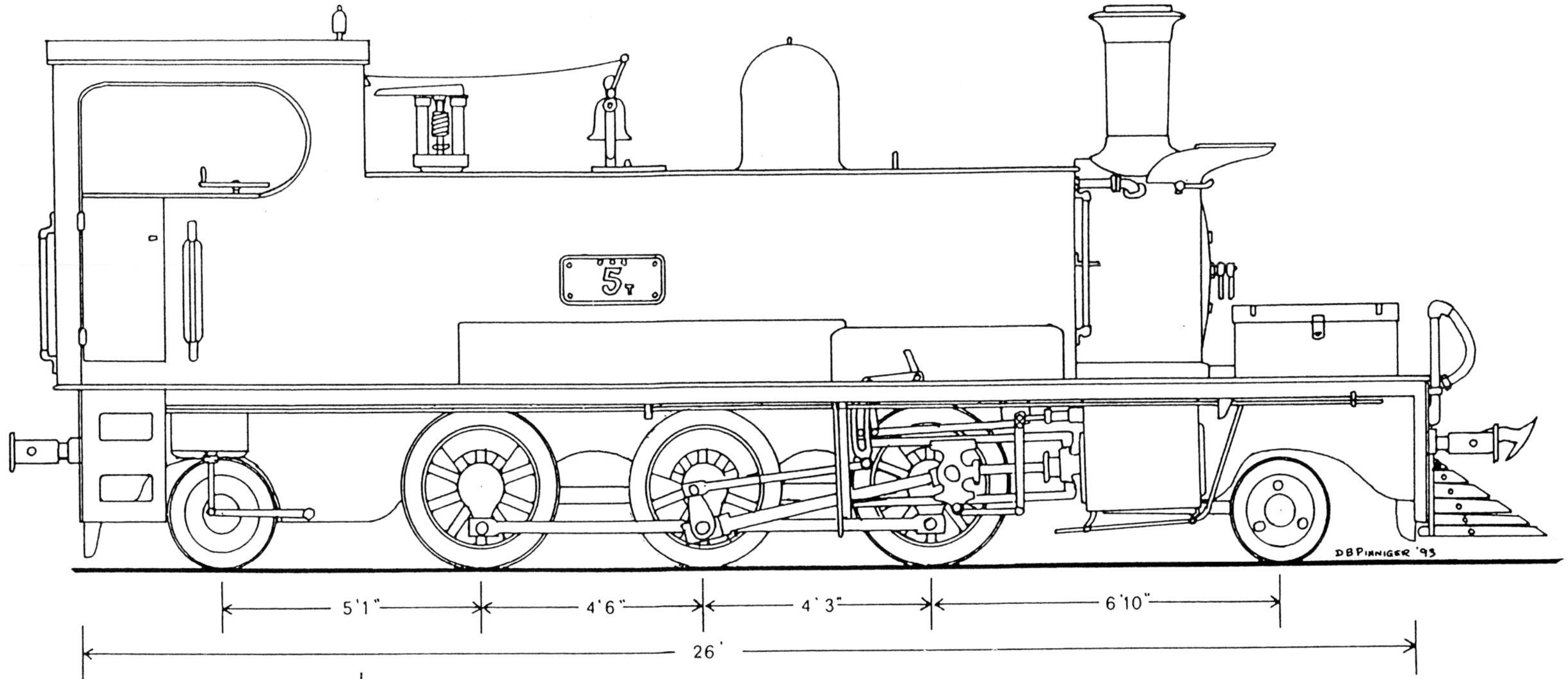

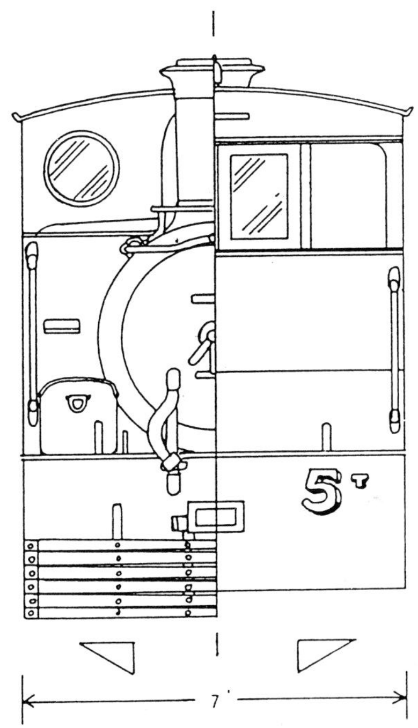

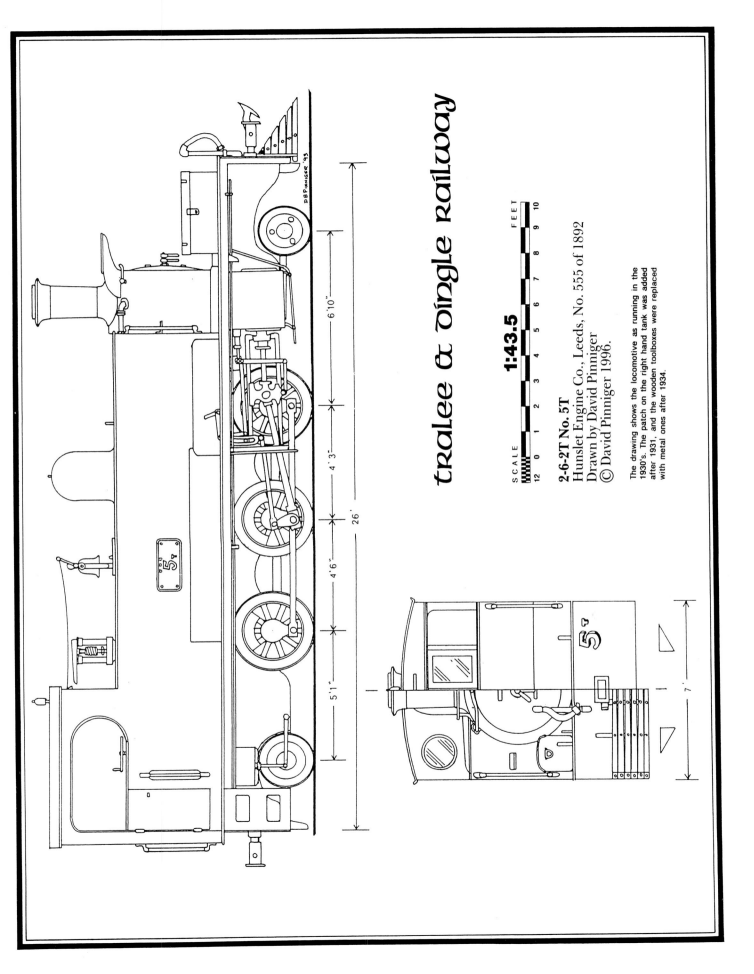

tralee & dingle railway

SCALE **1:43.5** FEET

12 0 1 2 3 4 5 6 7 8 9 10

2-6-2T No. 5T
Hunslet Engine Co., Leeds, No. 555 of 1892
Drawn by David Pinniger

The drawing shows the locomotive as running in the 1930's. The patch on the right hand tank was added after 1931, and the wooden toolboxes were replaced with metal ones after 1934.

TABLE 1
LOCOMOTIVES OF THE T&DLR

Loco No.	Maker & No.	Date	Wheel Arr.	Reboilered	Last Major	Scrapped	Remarks
1 (1T)	HE 477	1889	2-6-0	1902 1920	1934	1955	Rebuilt 1895 (Curraduff)
2 (2T)	HE 478	1889	2-6-0	1903	1933	1955	Withdrawn Nov. '52
3 (3T)	HE 479	1889	2-6-0	1902	1954	1959	Drafted to C&L 1941
4	HE 514	1890	0-4-2	—	—	1907	Front cab removed 1892. Castlegregory Branch loco. Withdrawn in 1902
5 (5T)	HE 555	1892	2-6-2	1906	1990	Extant	Drafted to C&L 1950. To USA 1959. Back to Tralee '86
6 (6T)	HE 677	1898	2-6-0	1911 1954?*	1957	1959 1952.	Drafted to West Clare To C&L 1957
7	K, S 800	1902	2-6-0	—	1920	1927	Branch Loco from 1920
8 (4T)	K, S 836	1903	2-6-0	—	1938	1959	Renumbered 4 in 1907 Drafted to C&L 1941
8 (8T)	HE 1051	1910	2-6-0	1938	1938	1956†	Dismantled 1953, sent to West Clare (see notes* †)
"9T"	Green 200	1893	0-4-4	1936	1936	1952	Paper transfer. Went instead to S&S 1938

* Did anyone see 8T *working* on the West Clare? Informed opinion has it that No. 6T received No. 8's boiler in 1954 but there are no records to confirm this.
† This is believed to be when the "remains" (less boiler) were cut up.

In 1995, Eire Post issued a set of stamps featuring narrow gauge railways. The First Day Cover, reproduced here, showed the T&D, but the stamps themselves, unfortunately, did not. *(collection D. H. Smith)*

Chapter 6
CARRIAGES AND WAGONS

Records of the rolling stock owned and used by the Tralee & Dingle were confused, contradictory and fragmentary. That we have a listing at all is due largely to the painstaking research undertaken by John Powell in the 1950s within the official records and from surviving stock. The difficulty of his task should not be underestimated. It is indeed a testimonial to his thoroughness that little new material has come to light since then, and the only amendments to his records have been the updating in terms of survivors and their locations.

A Survey of T&D C&W stock undertaken in 1950 by the ex-T&DLR Wagonmaster, Dick Heaslip, for CIE has also been of great value. Much additional information has been provided by Henry Orbach, Desmond Coakham and John Gardiner.

THE CARRIAGES

The contractor, Worthington, handed over an original stock of 8 third-class bogie coaches supplied by the Bristol Carriage and Wagon Company and the embryo C&W department must have adapted some at least to First Class use, since this facility was available at the opening of the line. At best this probably consisted of partitioning and placing of cushions on the longitudinally-slatted seats, since the coaches later reverted to full-third class use. These were 27ft. bogie coaches, 5 full-thirds and 3 brake-thirds, one of which became a brake-composite. The brake-end coaches appear to have had a pair of observation windows fitted at that end to enhance the Guard's look-out: these are shown in some of Goodlake's early (1898) photos.

Additional stock was ordered in 1891, including a composite, another full-third and a brake-third. All these designs were austere and spartan, and were painted a brownish plum colour, lined out in yellow and black above and below the windows. Doors were marked 1st or 3rd and the letters T&DR were painted on the body sides. The T&DLR crest was not used on the rolling stock.

Maintenance problems in the C&W Department do not seem to have been quite so severe as those in the Locomotive shops, though in 1902-4 extra staff were needed to tackle arrears of turning and retyring wheels. The lack of Guard's automatic vacuum valves (criticised in the Curraduff Report) was not made good until 1902.

In 1896 the T&D built its own 27ft. full-third class coach (No. 11), quite an achievement given the difficulties of the time. In later years it was mounted on a Bristol chassis and this was probably purchased originally.

The origins of coach No. 12 are obscure, but it is possible that it, too, was built at Tralee on a Bristol underframe. Records show that it was converted to a Breakdown van in 1919 for emergency work during the "Troubles", and it appears to have been scrapped around 1940.

In 1898 an additional 27ft. coach was obtained from the Bristol C&W Company, but this vehicle appears to have been rebuilt in Tralee shops in the 1920s, with panelled sides. Thereafter it was a brake-third but records are not clear whether it was so originally.

Two more brake-thirds, thirty-footers this time, were ordered from the Bristol C&W Co. in 1903 and paid for by instalments.

In 1904, the T&D shops built the longest and most elegant coach on the railway, a 32ft. composite (No. 16), and details of this and a bogie goods van (No. 42) were given, with photos, in the Locomotive Magazine, May 1905. The coach was made of American white oak with outside baywood panels and moulding. Divided into 3 compartments: 1st and 3rd Saloons, with a 1st class smoking compartment in the centre, approached by a door from the 1st class saloon only. Interiors of the saloons were 12ft. long, the smoker 6ft. 8in. First class seats were veneered in oak facing with walnut mouldings; seats were longitudinal in the saloons, but transverse in the smoker. All were upholstered in moquette. Fittings included mirrors over the seats and at compartment ends, linoleum on the floors and curtains (dark crimson) on brass rods. Ventilation was via "Eros" extractors on the roof and lighting by carbide. Altogether a prestige vehicle.

The funds obtained by Tom O'Donnell MP in 1907 enabled two additional 30ft. composites and two 30ft. brake thirds (plus wagons) to be obtained, this time from the Midland Carriage & Wagon Co. On arrival the handbrakes were found to be missing from the Guard's compartments, and these had to be hastily fitted in Tralee!

Under the Great Southern Railway from 1925, all coaches were finished in the regulation red, which suited them very well. With the GSR crest in the centre of the body panels, and the "1", "3" or "Guard" on the doors, these coaches looked extremely handsome.

All coaches survived until 1939, except No. 15 which was gutted in the "Troubles" of 1922 and never rebuilt.

Oil lighting was used as standard (except in No. 16) until 1917-18 whereafter battery lighting was installed as standard. Coach dynamos having proved useless in service, batteries were charged in rakes standing alongside the C&W sheds at Tralee, such rakes being a familiar sight in photos of Tralee station in the 1920-40 period.

After withdrawal of the passenger service in 1939, all but six of the coaches were sent to the West Clare which, until then, had never had bogie coaching stock. During the 1940s the remaining brake vehicles at Tralee were gradually and crudely converted to brakevans for use on the cattle trains. They were then painted in the grey goods livery and had "flying snails" (CIE's logo) applied in some instances.

In some of these conversions there was no partition provided between the Guard and the cattle; in others the Guard would find the brake-handle in the cattle compartment, surrounded by cows! Railway enthusiasts who travelled in these brakevans on the monthly cattle trains of the early 1950s were sometimes given the "comfort" of a platform bench seat brought down from Tralee Main station, for the round trip.

Two of these brakevans that had been hastily repaired for the LRTL/IRRS "Last Passenger Train" of 1953, were sent to Limerick on closure of the T&D Section and refurbished before onward transmission to the West Clare. One of those (5T) and another ex-Dingle composite (18T) then went to the Cavan & Leitrim section. No. 18T went with loco 5T and the C&L's own 4-4-0T, Lady Edith to Steamtown, USA, in 1959.

From there the van accompanied Lady Edith to New Jersey where they still run together.

On closure of the West Clare in 1961 there was no further use within CIE for 3ft. gauge bogie stock and most of the vehicles were scrapped: the bodies being sold as hen-houses, sheds etc.

In 1986 two of these were discovered by Great Southern Railway Preservation Society members. One of them is clearly the former No. 10T (44C). The other is another of the Bristols that went to the Clare in 1940 but has not yet been further identified. Whether these can ever be restored remains an intriguing question.

The sole horsebox (also numbered 1T in its own solitary class) was supplied by the Bristol C&W Co., allegedly in 1897, though earlier Company Minutes mention a horsebox, and 1890 is more likely, unless, as John Powell has suggested, it was built from the mysterious and unaccounted-for 4-wheel brakevan of the Curraduff disaster train (see p.82). Though in reasonable condition it received little use after 1939, and was not used in the cattle trains. It gradually decayed at Tralee. Special workings for Horse Fairs, of which there were several in the 1940s, used cattle wagons.

Such details as are known of the coaching stock are summarised in Table 2.

WAGONS

Documentation of the wagon stock of the T&DR has always been difficult but luckily there were two exhaustive studies of it conducted in the 1950s which have helped to clear up most of the puzzles. On 18.9.50 Dick Heaslip, the Wagonmaster at Tralee, checked all the existing wagons, classified them and reported on the condition of the bodies, frames, wheels (tyres) and breakgear. It made sobering reading: most of the stock was in very poor condition. He had a number of vehicles or their gear sent to Limerick for repair and it is suspected that much of it never returned to Tralee. By 1953 when John Powell and Henry Orbach spent many hours in the narrow and broad gauge yards at Tralee, which were graveyards of derelict and mouldering wagons, measuring and identifying vehicles, only about 20 cattle trucks were in running order. That some had been refurbished in the late 1940s was shown by the number decorated with CIE's "Flying Snail" motif as they were out-shopped from the Limerick paint shops.

All T&DLR wagons were painted grey (though the shades varied from dark to light) throughout the life of the line. Ownership lettering "TDLR", "GS" or the aforementioned 'Flying Snail' and the running numbers were always in white.

The first batch dated from construction of the line and it is reckoned that Nos. 1-37 were in stock by the Railway's opening day. As an early expedient to assist with conveying large numbers of cattle, horses and pigs, a number of the dropside open wagons for ballast and coal conveyance were fitted with "slot-in" rails to increase the height of the sides. This use was discontinued around 1904-5 when extra wagons were purchased from the Hurst Nelson and Pickering companies. The Government Grants of 1907 also enabled purchase of more goods and cattle wagons from the Midland Carriage & Wagon Co.

Regarding bogie stock, there were two vans in 1892, one from Bristol (39) and the other from the Tubular Wagon Co. (40), and an early photo shows them being loaded with fish. In 1904 the C&W Department of the T&DLR built a bogie van (No. 42). This achievement and the building of coach No. 16 were written up by the prestigious trade journal *The Locomotive Magazine* for May 1905. The shops had previously built two bogie bolster wagons and in 1922, the mysterious bogie livestock van 79T of which the only known photographs are one taken by Cyril Fry of it derelict at Tralee in 1949 (and which shows only the bogies in close-up!) and one of it in a train behind loco 3T at Annascaul, taken by W. A. Camwell in 1938. Here the detail is hidden by the loco crew! Very frustrating! It does not feature in Mr Heaslip's report, having been scrapped in 1949.

Although the locomotive No. 6K did not transfer from the closed Cork & Muskerry section in 1935-6, a few wagons did, one covered van and two open wagons of Oldbury Carriage & Wagon Co. manufacture. These took the stock numbers 80-82.

Such details as are known of the wagon stock are summarised in Table 3.

TABLE 2
COACHES OF THE T&DLR

No.	Date & Builder	Remarks
FULL THIRD CLASS (some initially converted to compo)		
1 (T)	1890 Bristol 27ft.	Transferred WC 1940, became 46C. Converted to railcar trailer (bus body) 1952.
3 (T)	1890 Bristol 27ft.	Transferred to WC, 1940 as 39C.
6 (T)	1890 Bristol 27ft.	Transferred as 47C, converted to trailer 1952.
7 (T)	1890 Bristol 27ft.	To WC, 1940 as 45C.
8 (T)	1890 Bristol 27ft.	To WC, 1940 as 48C, converted to trailer, 1952.
10 (T)	1891 Bristol 27ft.	To WC, 1940 as 44C. Body sold 1961, survives today w GSRPS.
11 (T)	1896 T&DLR 27ft.	To WC, 1940 as 49C.
COMPOSITES 1/3		
4 (T)	1891 Bristol 27ft.	Originally Full-third, converted to compo TDR shops 1904. To WC, 1940 as 43C.
16 (T)	1904 TDLR 32ft.	To WC, 1940 (41C) and converted to brakevan.
17 (T)	1907 Midland 30ft.	To WC, 1940 (40C).
18 (T)	1907 Midland 30ft.	To WC, 1940 (42C); to C&L 1954 as 21L; to USA 1959 – rebuilt.Extant.
BRAKE-THIRDS		
2 (T)	1890 Bristol 27ft.	Converted for cattle traffic 1940 To WC, 1954 as 51C.
5 (T)	1890 Bristol 27ft.	Converted for cattle traffic 1940 To C&L 1954 as 22L; to WC 1959.
9 (T)	1891 Bristol 27ft.	Cattle 1940; To WC 1954 (52C).
14 (T)	1903 Bristol 30ft.	To WC 1940 as 50C.
15 (T)	1903 Bristol 30ft.	Destroyed in Troubles, 1922
19 (T)	1907 Midland 30ft.	Cattle traffic 1940. Scrapped 1954.
20 (T)	1907 Midland 30ft.	Cattle traffic 1940. Scrapped 1954.
BRAKE-1/3 COMPO		
13 (T)	1898 Bristol 27ft.	Cattle traffic 1940. Scrapped 1954.
OTHER		
12	Origins not known	Converted to breakdown van 1919. Scrapped 1940?
1 (T)	1890? Bristol	Horsebox. Derelict 1950. Scrapped 1954.

TABLE 3
T&DLR WAGONS

No.	Maker & Date	Scrapped/ 1954	Body sold	Remarks
COVERED GOODS 5 TONS				
3T	Bristol 1890	—	✓	Ventilated
5T	Bristol 1890	✓	—	
6T	Bristol 1890	✓	—	
7T	Bristol 1890	✓	—	
8T	Bristol 1890	—	✓	
9T	Bristol 1890	—	✓	Ventilated
11T	Bristol 1890	✓	—	
12T	Bristol 1890	—	✓	
13T	Bristol 1890	✓	—	
16T	Bristol 1890	✓	—	
26T	Bristol 1894	—	✓	
28T	Bristol 1894	—	✓	Ventilated
37T	Bristol 1894	✓	—	derelict 1950
41T	Bristol 1894	—	✓	Ventilated
43T	Bristol 1897	—	✓	
64T	Midland 1907	✓	—	derelict 1950
65T	Midland 1907	?	—	Limerick 1950
66T	Midland 1907	✓	—	derelict 1950
80T	Oldbury ?	?	?	ex C&M 61K
BOGIE COVERED GOODS VANS 10 TONS				
39T	Bristol 1892	—	✓	derelict 1950
40T	Tubular 1892	✓	—	derelict 1950
42T	T&DLR 1904	—	—	Store, Tralee
79T	T&DLR 1922	1949	—	Ventilated
COVERED CATTLE & GOODS, 5 TONS				
1T	Bristol 1890	✓	—	Ventilated
2T	Bristol 1890	✓	—	Vent. Limerick '50
4T	Bristol 1890	✓	—	Ventilated
10T	Bristol 1890	✓	—	Ventilated
14T	Bristol 1890	✓	—	Ventilated
15T	Bristol 1890	✓	—	
18T	Bristol 1890	—	✓	
19T	Bristol 1890	✓	—	
20T	Bristol 1890	✓	—	
23T	Bristol 1894	✓	—	
78T	T&DLR 1922	—	✓	
BUTTER WAGON 5 TONS				
17T	Bristol 1890	—	✓	drop louvres
RAIL BOGIES (BOLSTERS) 10 TONS				
38T	T&DLR 1911	✓	—	derelict 1950
77T	T&DLR 1911	✓	—	derelict 1950
BALLAST TRUCKS (DROPSIDE) 5 TONS				
25T	Bristol 1890	—	—	To C&L as 226L
27T	Bristol 1890	—	—	To C&L as 227L
30T	Bristol 1890	—	—	To C&L as 228L
32T	Bristol 1890	1944	—	
35T	Bristol 1890	✓	—	

No.	Maker & Date	Scrapped	Body sold 1954	Remarks
COAL TRUCKS (3-plank) 5 TONS				
21T	Bristol 1894	✓	—	derelict 1950
34T	Bristol 1894	✓	—	
36T	Bristol 1894	✓	—	
44T	Bristol 1894	✓	—	
45T	Bristol 1894	✓	—	
COAL TRUCKS (5-plank) 6 TONS				
81T	Oldbury ?	✓	—	ex C&M 34K
82T	Oldbury ?	✓	—	ex C&M 46K
OPEN CATTLE 5 TONS				
22T	Bristol 1897	✓	—	orig. covered
31T	Bristol 1897	✓	—	
33T	Bristol 1897	✓	—	
46T	Bristol 1897	✓	—	orig. covered
47T	Hurst Nelson 1905	—	✓	
48T	Hurst Nelson 1905	✓	—	
49T	Hurst Nelson 1905	✓	—	
50T	Hurst Nelson 1905	—	✓	
51T	Hurst Nelson 1905	✓	—	
52T	Hurst Nelson 1905	✓	—	
53T	Pickering 1904	✓	—	
54T	Pickering 1904	1935	—	
55T	Pickering 1904	✓	—	
56T	Pickering 1904	✓	—	
57T	Pickering 1904	1936	—	
58T	Pickering 1904	✓	—	
59T	Pickering 1904	✓	—	
60T	Pickering 1904	✓	—	
61T	Pickering 1904	✓	—	
62T	Pickering 1904	✓	—	
63T	? 1907	✓	—	orig. covered
69T	Midland 1907	✓	—	orig. covered
70T	Midland 1907	✓	—	orig. covered
74T	Midland 1907	✓	—	orig. covered
75T	Midland 1907	✓	—	orig. covered
COVERED CATTLE WAGONS 5 TONS				
24T	Bristol 1897	✓	—	
29T	Bristol 1897	✓	—	Powell says open
67T	Midland 1907	✓	—	
68T	Midland 1907	✓	—	
71T	Midland 1907	✓	—	
72T	Midland 1907	1947	—	
73T	Midland 1907	✓	—	
76T	Midland 1907	✓	—	

There follows a photographic review, along with drawings, of the T&DLR coaches and wagons. *The text resumes on page 123.*

133. Original all-third class coach, as running in 1907, No. 8. Painted brownish-red, lined out in yellow and black above and below the windows.
(H. Fayle/IRRS)

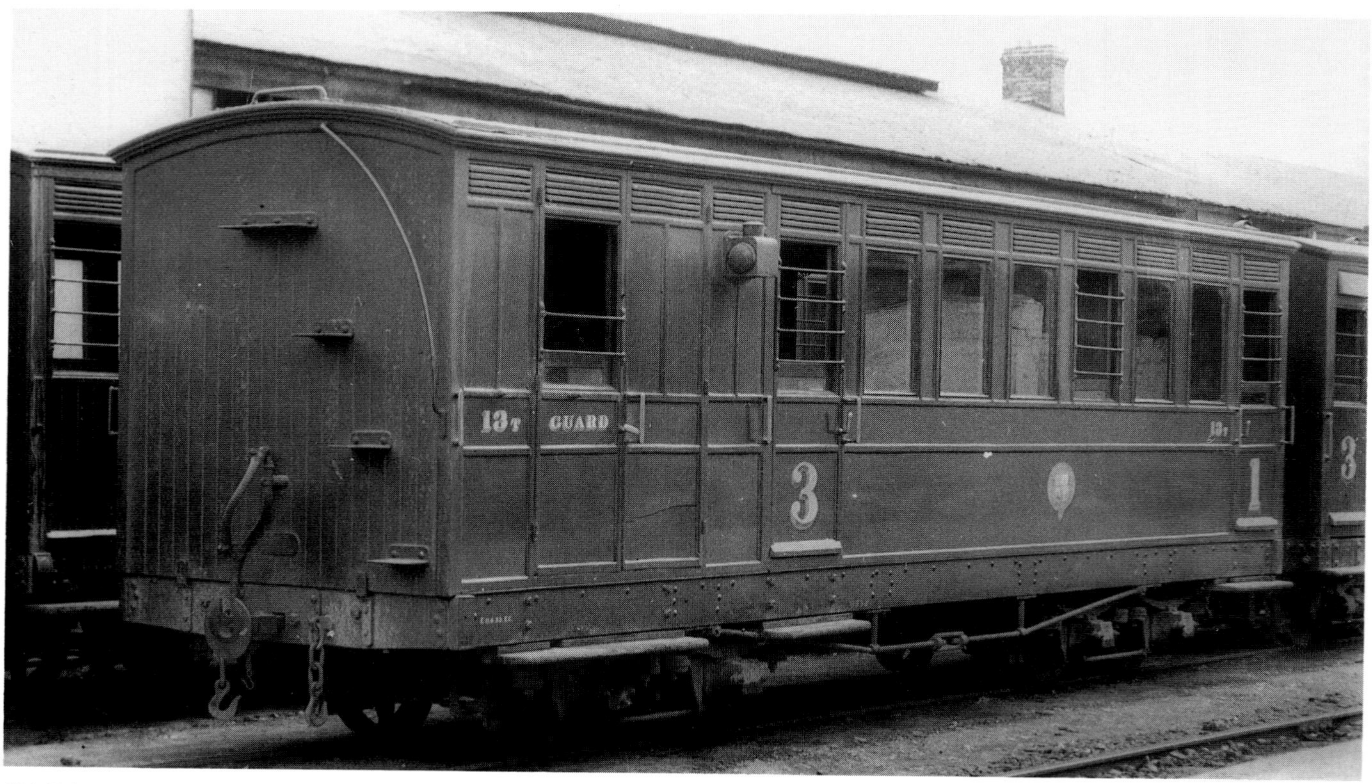

134. Bristol brake-composite No. 13T seen here at Tralee in the lovely GSR dark red livery. Converted to brakevan in 1940 for cattle traffic.
(H. C. Casserley)

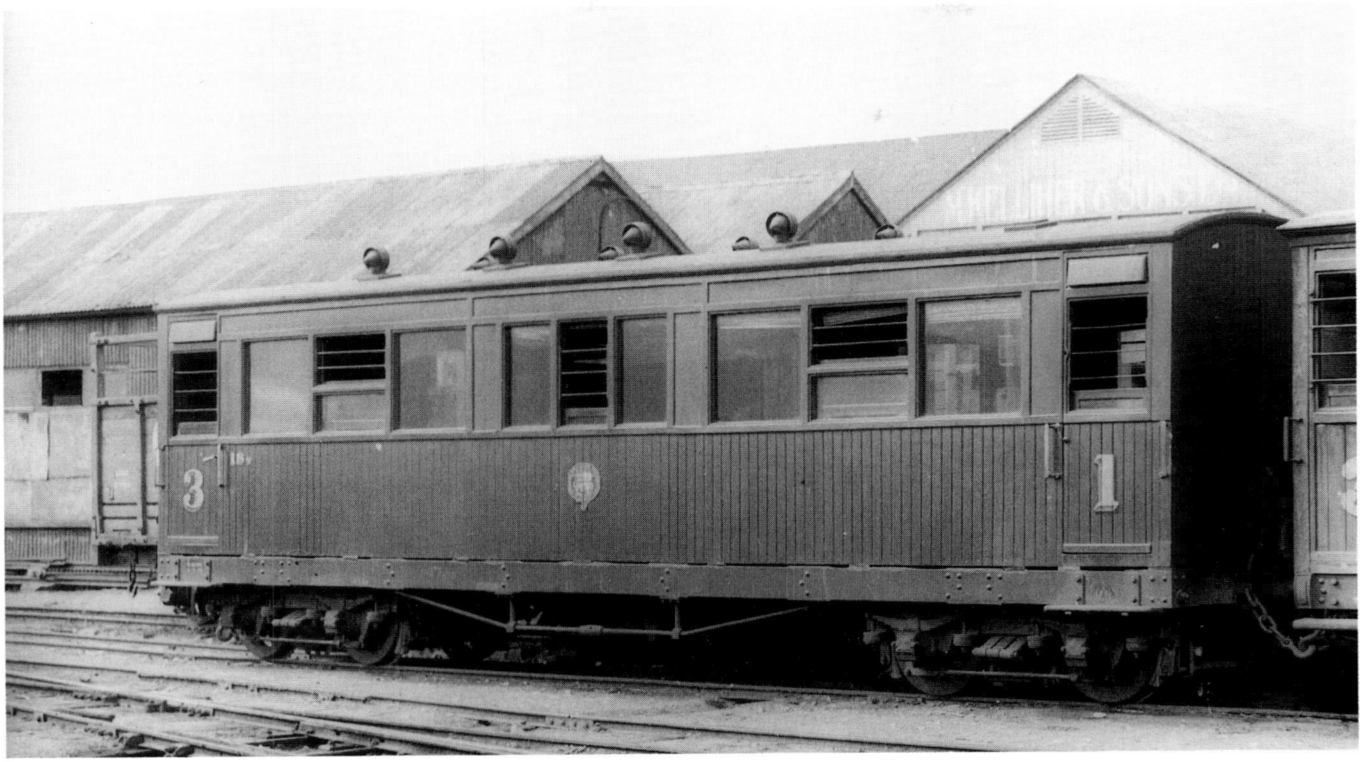

135. Midland C&W Co. No. 18T, a 30ft composite, seen at Tralee in 1934. Transferred to the West Clare in 1940 (became all-third, 42c). Survives (much altered!) in USA. *(H. C. Casserley)*

136. All-third No. 4T as transferred to the West Clare (43c), had been converted to composite in 1904 but reverted to full-third on West Clare. *(C. L. Fry)*

137. No. 6T as transferred to the West Clare (47c), shown here in 1949 in ³/₄ view. *(R. N. Clements)*

138. Interior of coach No. 6T (derelict on West Clare 1951) detached from underframe. Note "garden seats" and bars removed from droplights. *(R. N. Clements)*

139. **The Tralee & Dingle's own handiwork, the 32ft composite, No. 16T built by the C&W department in 1904. Seen here at Tralee, charging batteries in the last week of passenger services. Next to her is brakevan 14T.** *(G. J. Aston)*

140. **And this is how No. 16T ended up on the West Clare – as brakevan 41c.** *(D. G. Coakham)*

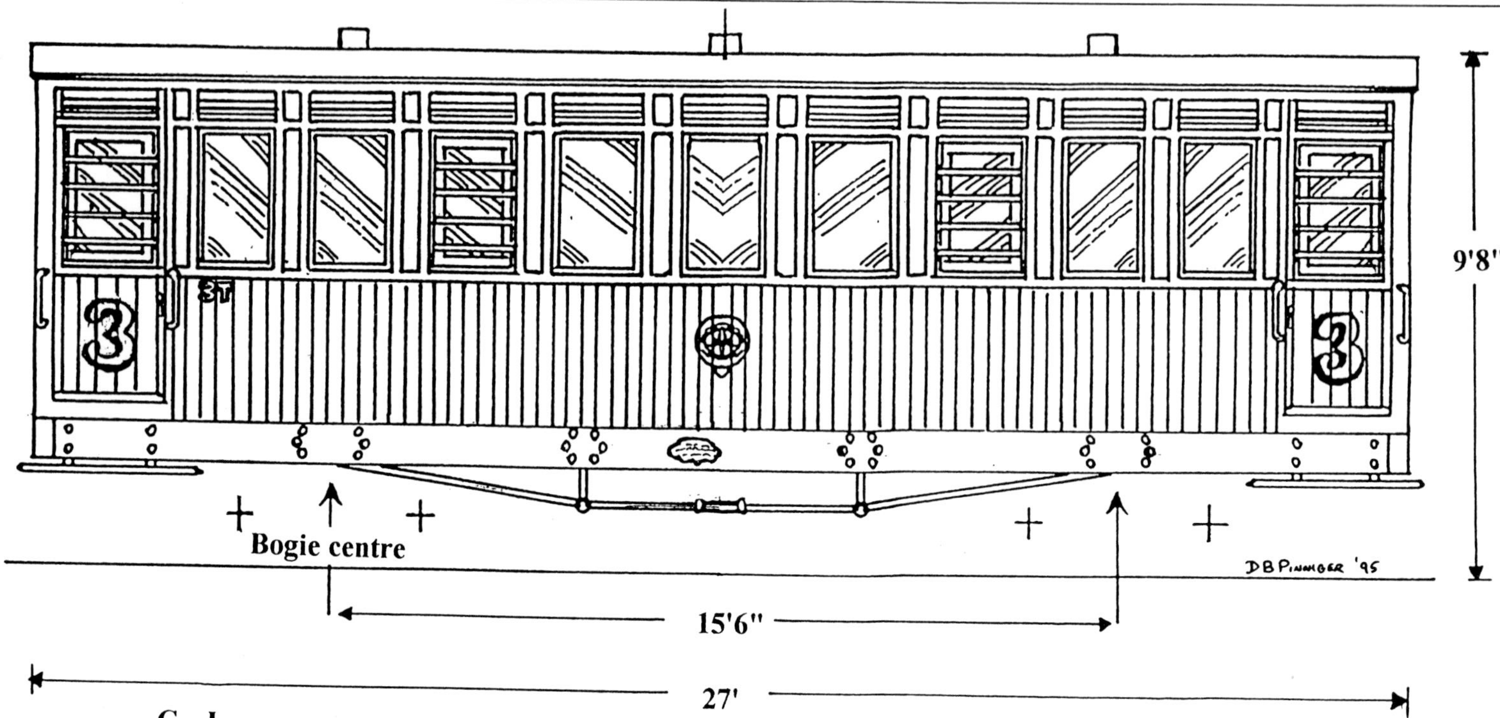

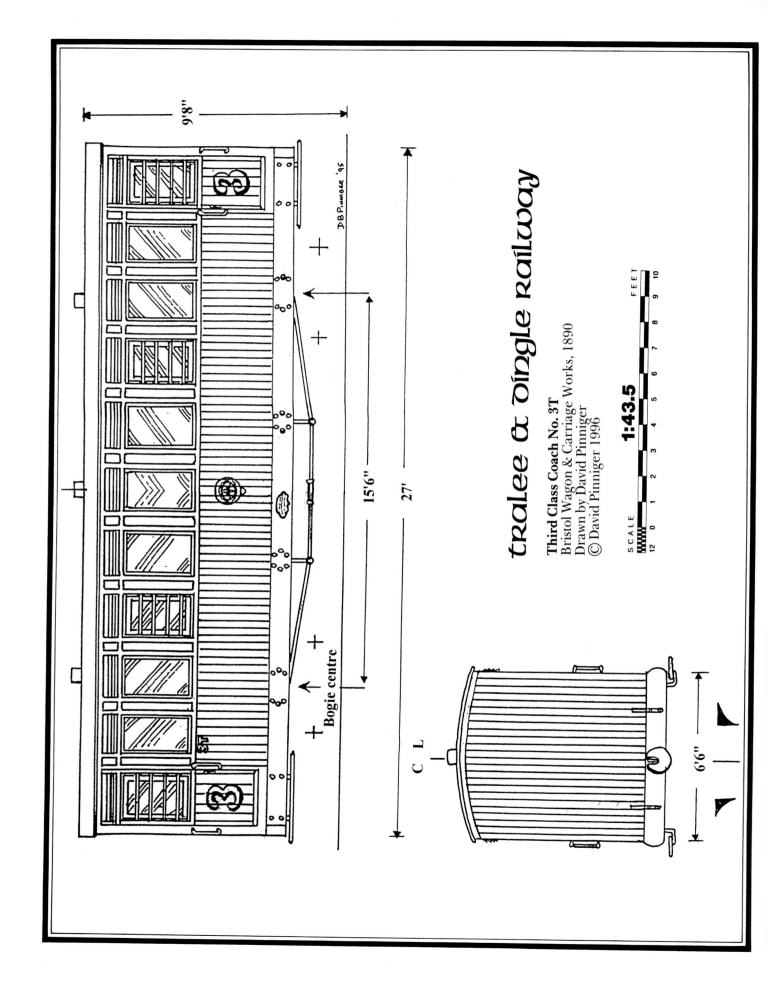

Tralee & Dingle Railway

Third Class Coach No. 3T
Bristol Wagon & Carriage Works, 1890
Drawn by David Pinniger
© David Pinniger 1996

SCALE **1:43.5** FEET
12 0 1 2 3 4 5 6 7 8 9 10

141. The rediscovered Bristol coach No. 10T, as surviving. *(D. Parkes)*

142. Interior of 10T, as surviving. *(D. Parkes)*

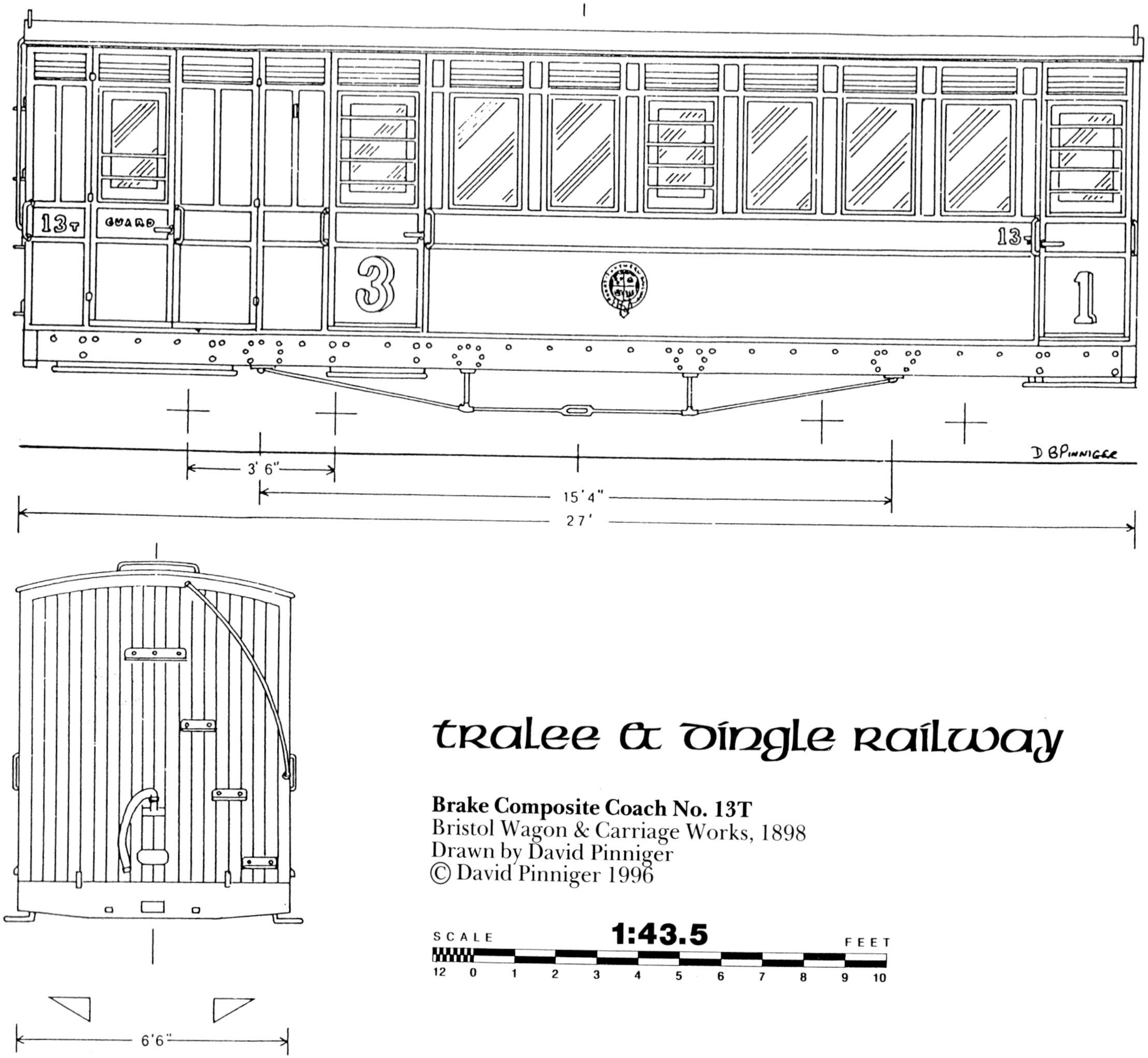

Tralee & Dingle Railway

Brake Composite Coach No. 13T
Bristol Wagon & Carriage Works, 1898
Drawn by David Pinniger

1:43.5

SCALE 12 0 1 2 3 4 5 6 7 8 9 10 FEET

143 & 144. Two views of brakevan 5T at Annascaul in 1952, still showing some signs of her palmier days! *(H. S. Orbach)*

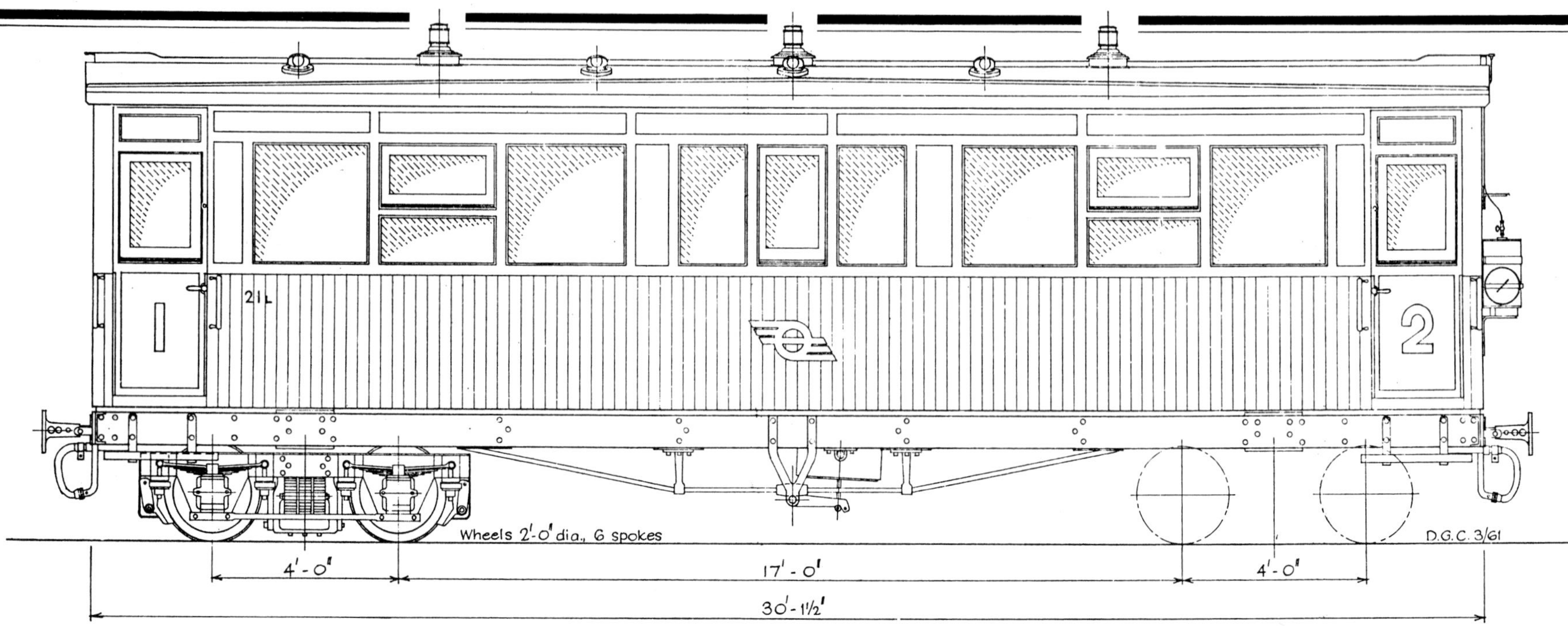

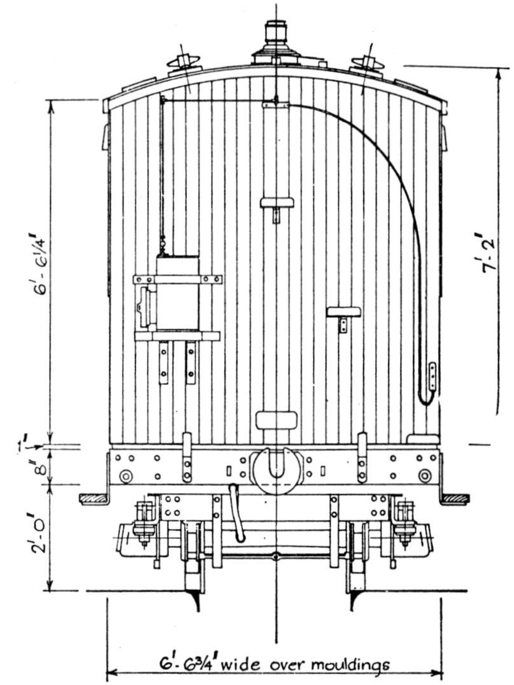

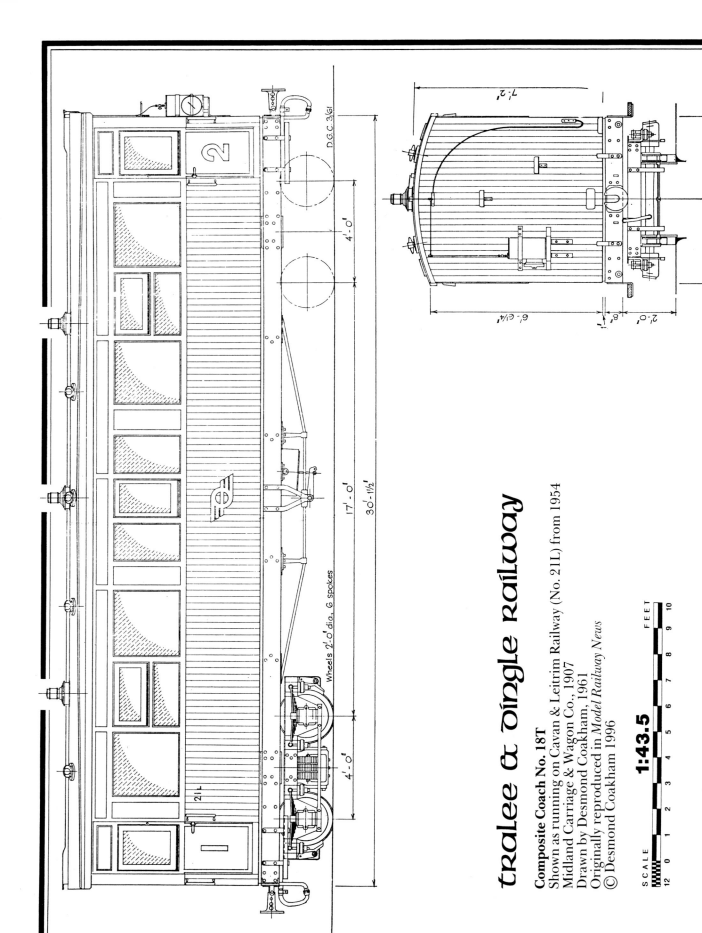

Tralee & Dingle Railway

Composite Coach No. 18T
Shown as running on Cavan & Leitrim Railway (No. 21L) from 1954
Midland Carriage & Wagon Co., 1907
Drawn by Desmond Coakham, 1961
Originally reproduced in *Model Railway News*

SCALE **1:43.5** FEET
12 0 1 2 3 4 5 6 7 8 9 10

145. (Above) The T&D Horsebox, No. 1T in its own solitary series, seen here derelict at Tralee in 1953. *(D.G. Coakham)*

146 & 147 (Below) When "lady" passengers were to travel on the cattle specials, a modicum of comfort was provided with a station seat from the Main Line yard, seen here being installed in brake van 5T, in both longshot and close up. Glimpse of horsebox 1T in photo 147. *(Author's Collection)*

148. No. 3T in June 1931 with train marshalled and ready to cross over and reverse into passenger platform. Bogie van 40T – the "tubular" – next to loco. *(C. R. Gordon-Stuart)*

149. HOW FRUSTRATING: A close-up of the bogie of mystery van 39T. Cyril Fry is known to have photographed the entire van (and measured it, too!) but a search has so far failed to find the negative or even a print. *(C. L. Fry)*

150. PW STORE: **The T&DLR's own home-built bogie wagon No. 42T survived closure of the line, the body being used in Tralee main yard as a store for many years.** *(A. J. Powell)*

151.END VIEW of bogie van 42T, tarpaulined over. *(A. J. Powell)*

152. From the first series of vans, No. 3T at Dingle in 1953; planks removed for cattle ventilation. *(D. G. Coakham)*

153. No. 12T derelict at Tralee, next to it (R) is covered cattle van 76T. *(H. S. Orbach)*

Tralee & Dingle Railway

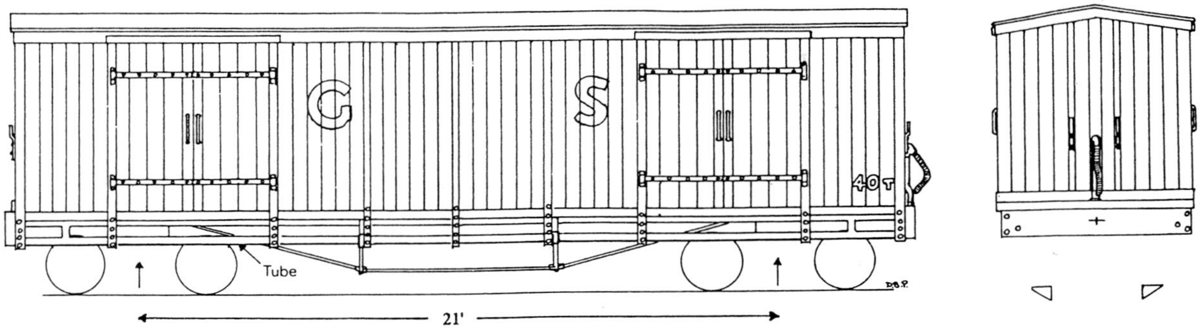

Bogie Van No. 40T
Tubular Frame Wagon Co., 1892
Drawn by David Pinniger

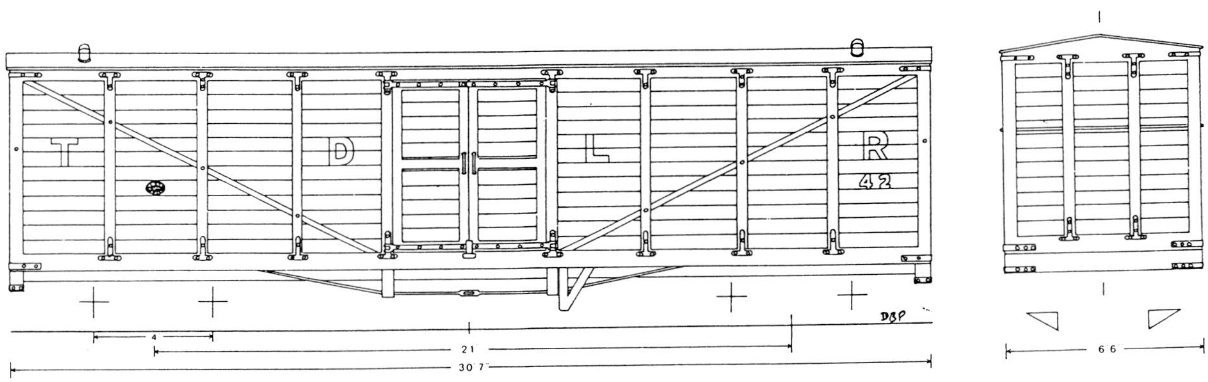

Bogie Van No. 42T
Built in T&DR Workshops, 1904
Based on a photograph in *The Locomotive Magazine* May 1905
(Diagonal supports were later modified)
Drawn by David Pinniger

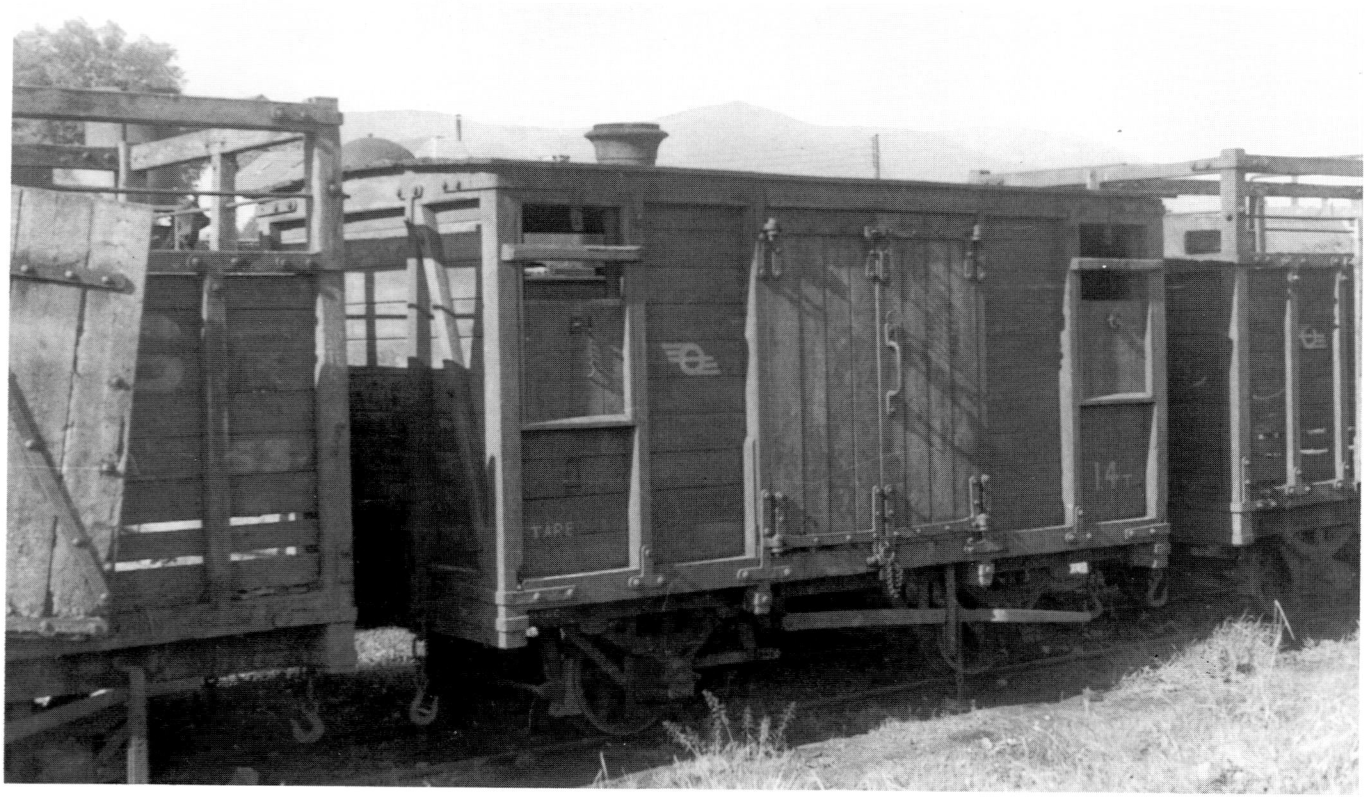

154. Centre is No. 14T with drop ventilators; at left the first of the 1904 Pickering open cattle wagons, with another at R. (Loco 8T in background).
(H. S. Orbach)

155. End view of 14T less draw gear, in Tralee yard awaiting sale or destruction, 1954.
(A. J. Powell)

Tralee & Dingle Railway

4w Vans and Cattle Wagons

Drawn by David Pinniger

SCALE **1:76.2** FEET

12 0 1 2 3 4 5 6 7 8 9 10

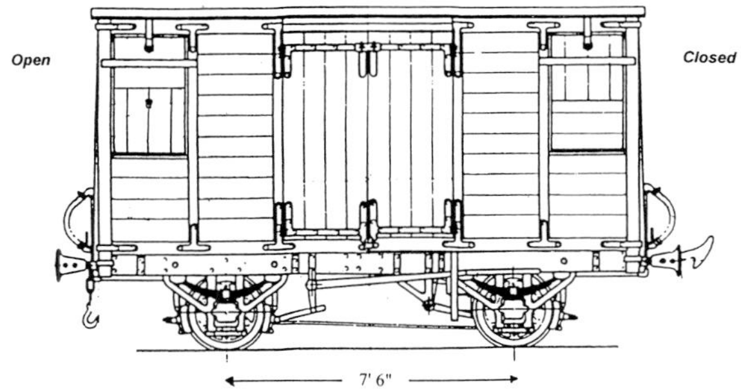

"Standard" van 14T
as modified in 1940 with side drop vents for carriage of livestock
[Drawing derived from Powell 1958]

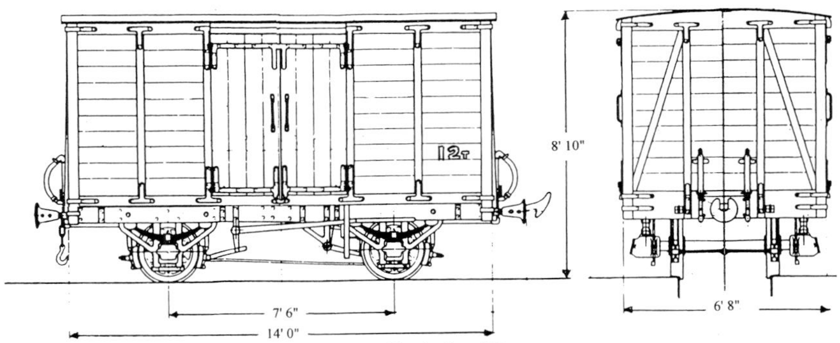

"Standard" van 12T
as built by the Bristol Carriage and Wagon Co in 1890
[Drawing derived from Powell 1958]

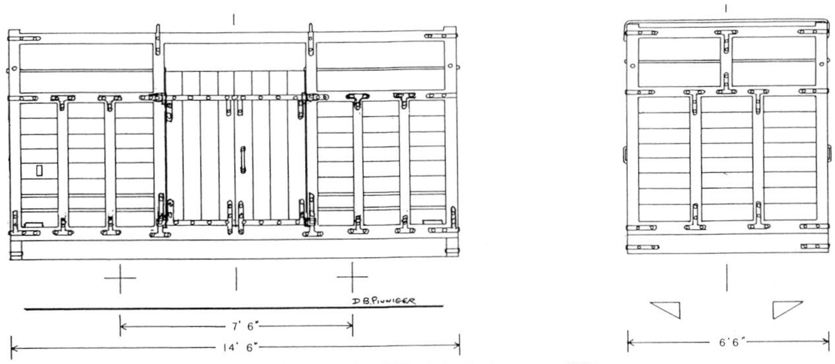

Cattle wagon No 56 built by Pickering in 1904

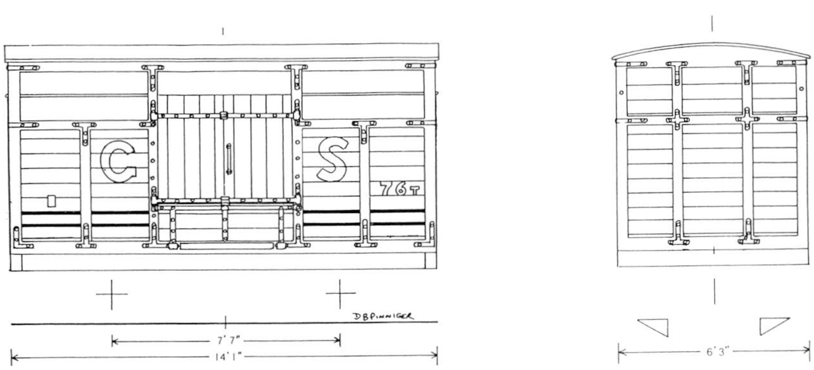

Midland Carriage & Wagon Works cattle wagon, originally built in 1907, as running in 1934.

156. Open cattle wagon 29T (end of it visible in photo 152) from Bristol C&W Company of a batch of five supplied in 1897. Seen here still in running order at Dingle, 1953. *(D. G. Coakham)*

157. An end view of 29T taken a few years earlier at Tralee in 1948. *(Ian Duncan)*

158. Another of the first series of vans, with planks removed for ventilation (compare with photo 152), No. 41T at Dingle, 1953. *(H. S. Orbach)*

159. John Powell's records (usually meticulous) say this is No. 60T derelict at Tralee 1954. That would make it a Pickering open cattle truck . . . however maker's drawings show only single uprights on either side of the door . . . *(A. J. Powell)*

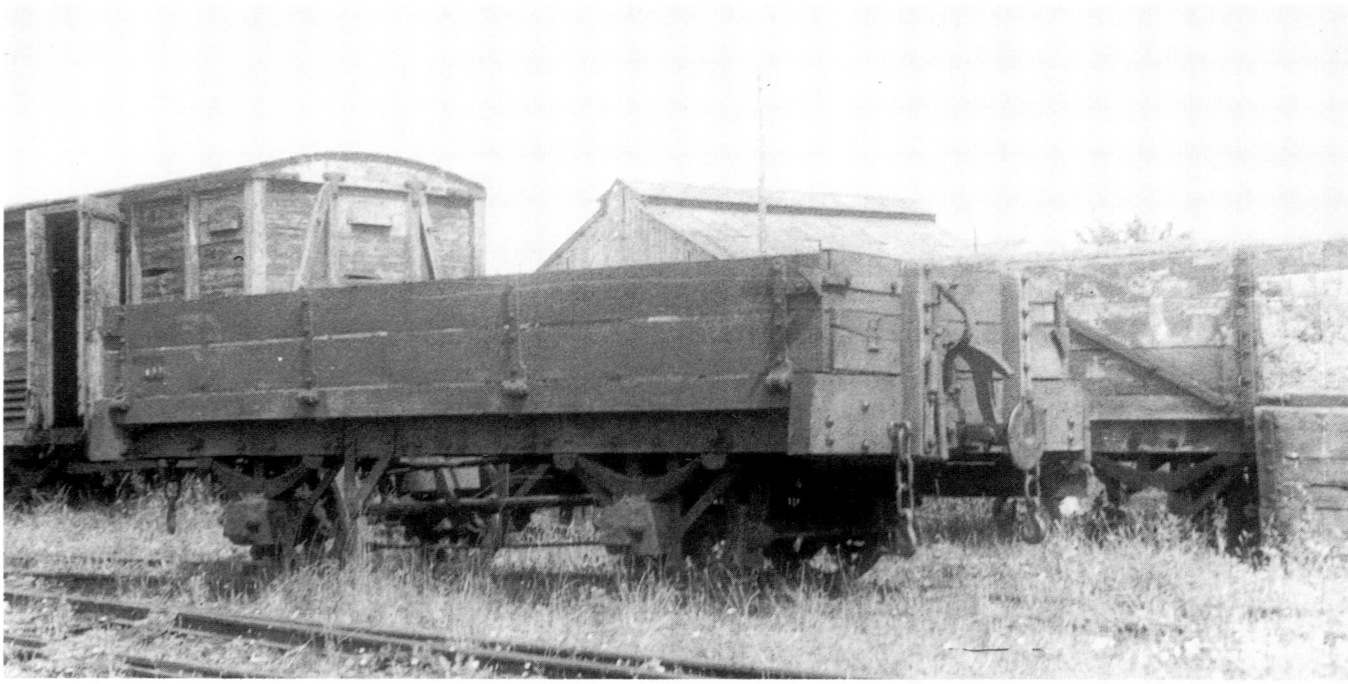

160. Dropside ballast truck, 25T, note faded CIE "snail" emblem. Behind it at left, is the former butter van, 17T, taken at Tralee, 1953.
(H. S. Orbach)

161. Seldom seen in action (except photo 49), this is the bogie bolster built in the T&DLR's own shops in 1911, No. 77T, here seen derelict in the "no hope" siding at Tralee.
(H. S. Orbach)

Chapter 7
LORE AND LEGEND OF THE DINGLE TRAIN

So far the Dingle railway has appeared in two guises: a financial liability and an adventure for the railway enthusiast. In their custom of bestowing floral association on a railway of character, railfans could have called it 'The Fuchsia Line'.

In fact it was often called the 'Home Rule Railway'. Indeed it had three phases of political evolution: unionist and ascendancy (1891-1900) with Lt. Col. Rowan as chairman and Orangeman Richard A. Parkes as manager; 'Home Rule', under the chairmanship of Tom O'Donnell M.P. (1900-18), O'Donnell being a member of the Irish Nationalist Party and a colourful character who electrified the House of Commons by making his maiden speech in Irish[1]; and Sinn Fein (Republican) after 1918 with Austin Stack (nominally) and Tadhg Ó Cinnéide, in effect, acting as chairman. During the latter period, avers John Joe Sheehy, the IRA protagonist who worked on the T&D both before and after the 1921 Treaty, 'Practically everyone, from the chairman to the newest loader had active connection with the Republican movement'. Under Tom O'Donnell's Chairmanship many improvements were made to the Railway: his was the driving force behind many excursions and publicity (the "Rare West Kerry" booklet for example), he badgered Government for capital grants to make the safer trackbed diversions and landed the major coup of £23,000 for such purposes.

To the present writers, however, it has always been the railway of surprise and amazing coincidence. Typical of these was that 'Traein an Daingin' should be mentioned in the Radio Éireann broadcast[2] on Fr Tadhg Ó Murchú. Fr Tadhg was known to have made scores of visits west of Dingle but only one such rail trip: his very first in 1935 and he could recollect nothing of it at all, which was surprising. However, in the course of the programme, one contributor, Molly O'Connor of Dunquin, was telling that her father often would relate how, returning from Tralee Horse Fair in 1935, on the Dingle train, he was approached by a small priest who asked him about life in Dunquin, Ballyferriter and the Blaskets. They conversed all the way to Dingle. Molly O'Connor only travelled on the train once herself but said her father would often tell how he had introduced Fr Tadhg to the Kerry Gaeltacht on board the Dingle train. No wonder Fr Tadhg's recollection of the rail trip was so hazy, since he had talked all the way! By such coincidences do the pieces of the jigsaw puzzle fit together.

This jigsaw consists not of the economic, mechanical or political history of the line, for this is already known. Rather, it is the involvement of the railway in the lives of the inhabitants of the region it served, as distinct from the heavy financial burden carried by the ratepayers. Tom Francis, son of the late stationmaster of Lower Camp, has pointed out the social and educational benefits made possible by the railway, particularly in giving access to youngsters for education beyond that of primary schools.[3]

Perhaps more than most rural communities, the people of Corcaguiny have, to an observer, an in-built acceptance of the foibles of man or machine that gives complacent certainty to their philosophy. If the train doesn't run today, then surely, she'll come tomorrow or the day after.

Padraig Kennelly has told [4] of the English visitor on the Dingle train in the 1930s whose exasperation at being delayed by a cow on the line was only exceeded by the disgust he expressed when they caught up with the cow once again! This yarn rings true and seems to depict quite accurately the conflict of two different sets of values.

So, too, with Desmond Fitzgerald, a Cabinet minister of the Free State Government, 1922-7, though few animals encountering the train were as lucky as Padraig's cow. Of his 1913 trip on the railway, Fitzgerald wrote:

> 'The fact that we should have to wait [in Tralee] for hours before the little train was due to start for Dingle was not an inconvenience, rather an assurance that here one escaped from the outer world of large towns and modern efficiency and haste . . . Even the wearisome delay of the train after its time to start pleased me'.[5]

This train hit and killed a donkey on the line. Fitzgerald was travelling out to the Gaeltacht of course.

Until passenger services ceased, the Railway was an important link in what has aptly become known as "The Scholars' Path"[6], westward to Ballyferriter and the Blasket Islands. The storytellers and poets of the Blaskets, where the Gaelic language was still in constant use, drew celebrated scholars and linguists from all over the globe. The names of those pilgrims adds a lustre to the story of the Dingle train which carried them. Not only the islanders themselves, of whom Tomas O'Criomthain himself must surely be the first – despite his dislike of the train which he termed "Scuan", likening it to a fussy hen with gaggle of chicks[7], but also men and women of the calibre of Robin Flower[8], Carl "The Viking" Marstrander[6], Kuno Meyer[6], George Thompson (Maurice O'Sullivan's pupil then mentor and who with Moya Llewellyn Davies[9] translated "Twenty Years A-Growing" into English)[10], George Chambers (who called it: "A very primitive railway!"[11]), Maurice O'Droigheain[12], James Cousins and his wife Gretta[13], the Gaelic League secretary Fionan MacColuim[13], Marie-Louise Sjoestedt[14], Richard Best and Osborn Bergin[6], the quartet of youthful philosophers and literary campers: Bede Griffiths, Martyn Skinner, Hugh

Waterman and Geoffrey Hayward[15] and Jeremiah Curtin[16]. Their names run off the pen like a poem!

Most of them left impressions of the Dingle Railway in their writings, even if only a few sentences. Thus Jeremiah Curtin, who had the doubtful pleasure of crossing the original Curraduff viaduct four times, wrote of his 1882 visit, that the views from the train were magnificent, but the progress slow. Four nuns from Tralee shared his compartment (Nuns were allowed first class as a privilege by the Company) and he wondered that they knew nothing of the country through which they passed. (He overlooked that "enclosed" Sisters would not have relished conversation at all, let alone with a strange male!).

In a letter to the writers, Seán Ó Lúing the celebrated biographer and historian, described travel in the opposite direction, a journey which he had previously recorded in verse.[17]

> I am sure you know the kind of sidecar [cart] used most in the country here. After sitting in this for eight miles (i.e. Ballyferriter to Dingle) with a cushion of hay if you were lucky, and in any kind of weather, you thought the Dingle Train, with its wooden benches and all, was the acme of comfort.

Fr Senan Moynihan, mentor and patron of many Irish writers, referred aptly to these benches as 'the garden seats'.

> Again it is Christmastime and you are on your way home on holidays from Saint Brendan's in Killarney and at Tralee the guard invites you into a crowded and cosy special half-compartment where you find a debonair and big-hearted Franciscan who is travelling to Annascaul to spend Christmas with his people there. The friar must be big-lapped too, for rather than see you standing he takes you on his lap; and there in comfort you listen to him 'drawing out' Tom Crean, lately back from immortal deeds of heroism at the Pole.

Of course, the first class had cushions and divided compartments. We may be sure that Padraig Kennelly's traveller went first class! Latter day railfan travellers from England were often touched by the courtesy of the T&D staff which extended to offering them the first class compartment even though they held third class tickets.

Peig Sayers making her only rail trip had less trouble finding a seat than Fr Moynihan. Returning from a pilgrimage to Wether's Well near Tralee, she wrote:[18]

> . . . everyone was at his best to get to the station. When we reached it, you'd think nobody ever died, there were so many people there. Every carriage was full. 'Come into this carriage', said Kate. 'We surely must find room somewhere'. When we went in a wren couldn't find room on any of the seats, but there was a place where an overcoat was stretched the length of the seat. 'What about the overcoat, Kate,' said I, 'Isn't there room for three under it?' 'I don't know in life, my treasure', said she, 'I suppose it's somebody put it there to keep room'. 'If so, musha', said I, 'It will keep only his own place, whoever it belongs to'. I caught the coat and I folded it and I planked it down on the seat with so much room under it that if it was the devil himself he'd have room. Then Kate and I sat on what was left of the seat. We were squashed enough but it was better than to be standing.

Songs and singing were very much a part of the journey. Fr Moynihan mentioned the man who was merry:

> '. . . and all he wanted to do was to sing, but never a note could he utter until he had clasped someone's hand in his. Then away he would go soaring! It was always so'. Peig Sayers too: 'There was no more talk about the overcoat, but that didn't leave us without company, because Michael and more of the people of the island were at one end of the carriage, his hat on his knee, singing. 'Dark Woman's Slope', he was at, and he taking an echo out of the carriage'.

Similarly, on one of the rail trips west, undertaken by the dramatist J. M. Synge, he recorded

> 'An interruption was made by a stop at a small station and the entrance of a ragged ballad-singer, who sang a long ballad about the sorrows of mothers who see all their children going away from them to America'.[19]

On a previous trip he had mentioned at Tralee:

> 'A drunken young man got in just before we started, and sang songs for a few coppers, telling us that he had spent all his money, and had nothing left to pay for his ticket'.

Peig Sayers' son, Micheal Guihean, was one of the few emigrées who went out and returned over T&DLR metals. It is to him that we owe the transcripts of his mother's stories.[20]

Payment for the ride was not always of overriding importance in the eyes of the staff, whatever may have been the view of management.

Among courtesy passengers were occasional distressed sailors whose ships had come to grief around the rocky coast, or in the case of survivors of the Norwegian barque *Carmanian,* torpedoed by a German submarine in WW-1. Rescue of those survivors was heroically organised by the then curate of Ballyferriter, Fr Tom Jones, Irish handball champion, musician and native of Rock Street, Tralee.[21]

In Pádraig O'Snodaigh's pamphlet[22] there are recollections of people from Ballyferriter and nearby parishes who marched from Dingle to Tralee in 1916 to link up with the arrival of the German arms ship the *Aud.* The march was unsuccessful in its mission and the marchers had perforce to return by train without paying, having no money for fares. Pádraig Martin recorded how Eamonn O'Connor of Tralee spoke to the train crew 'Take these men as far as they want to go. I am giving you that order'. 'We got in, paid no money or anything. It brought us safe and sound to the town of Dingle'. 'We came home on the train. I experienced one touch which did not please me. A man who spoke in English. 'Ye have done great good', he said 'to the

Dingle Railway, whatever else good ye may have done'. It was the ticket man who said that'.

To prevent free travel during the Civil War period when a number of stations were broken into and tickets stolen, the T&DLR immediately overprinted their issued tickets with a diagonal red line to identify them as official and not those stolen in the raids. Among collectors these are known as 'civil war tickets'. There are, of course, a number of roadside crosses alongside the route of the T&D at Tonevane, Derrymore, etc., commemorating IRA volunteers killed at those spots in either the War of Independence or the civil war.

In late 1922 came the dramatic episode of the "Flour Train" (see Chapter 7).

For many at the lineside, passage of the train marked the time of day. Sean Ó Lúing mentioned the local phrases 'she is going over' (i.e. east to Tralee) or 'she is going back' (to Dingle). This 'time by the train' theme runs all through Tim O'Donnell's delightful 'Lament for the Dingle Train'[23] wherein passage of the train proclaimed teatime in Tralee, milking at Camp, work over at Annascaul and for the blacksmith at Lispole.

Cmdt Pat O'Donnell, historian of faction fighting, lived alongside the line at the Basin 1925-41 and recorded

> 'When we were on a picnic at Spa or nearer Tralee, we used to watch for the whistle and smoke of the train across the way by Derrymore and know it was five o'clock'.

Earlier accounts of 'The Train' in verse are given by Mícheal Ruiséal in his 'Song in Praise of Dingle'[24] wherein he mentions its arrival in clouds of smoke, whistling shrilly and 'coming with the tea to Dingle to be put cheaply on sale'. Tea was a luxury in West Kerry at the time of writing (early 1900s: Ruiséal died in 1928). A longer evocation of the commercial and passenger traffic of the railway, obviously written soon after the line closed, was given by Micheál Ó Se.[25] The most recent being that by Micheal O'Dubhslaine.[26]

To those who for many years did not travel out of Corcaguiny, the train would remain 'The Train', as Fr Colman Foley, O.C.S.O. has recalled so delightfully in his picture of Dingle station and harbour extension,[27] in the 1900-26 period.

> 'To me it was the mother of all trains. Look at all the notions it gave birth to . . . Every other train is only a modification of the Dingle train, a variation of the root idea'.

His father, Patrick Foley, in his justly-renowned History of Corcaguiny, makes only brief mentions of the railway.[28]

Fr Colman's essay mentions the funeral wakes.

> 'And sometimes the bodies of our people who died away came back to us on the train and that evening there would be a big gathering at the station to await the corpse'.

One such he poignantly remembered was that of 'Miss Bridie Neligan, a young lady organist of our church who died of TB in a sanatorium. Her boyfriend Mr Ross Lenergan marched with her family behind her coffin, from the station – a very sad occasion'.

Fortunately for the present writers, Fr Colman's interest was such that he undertook to aid their researches by contacting old friends who had cause to remember their railway. Surprise and coincidence became rife again! To give an example, there was the matter of the film company visiting Dingle. Between 1910 and 1914, the Kalem Film Co. of the USA visited Ireland, chiefly Killarney, making silent films such as 'Colleen Bawn', 'Ireland the Oppressed', 'Kerry Dances', 'Robert Emmet' and others. They travelled most of Kerry too, and though it is recorded that on one occasion 'they forgot their cameras', they must surely have filmed the Dingle railway at some time in that period? However, all enquiries came to nothing. One of the people mentioned in Fr Colman's reminiscences was Miss May Bailey, daughter of the Dingle stationmaster, and now Sr M. Malachy Bailey of Carlow. Imagine the writers' delight when, completely without foreknowledge of their quest she wrote among her recollections to Fr Colman:

> The fish season was always very busy at the station as great quantities of fish were sent to the markets in Dublin and to Billingsgate, London. There was a famous Dingle fish-woman called Biddy Johnson who used to sell delicious fish from her cart near the school and occasionally she would send some fish to Tralee. One time (around 1912) a gentleman from one of the film companies was anxious to make a 'short' of emigrants going out to America, and the Railway said they would send a mock train out a mile or two from Dingle and then return when the film men had departed. On the same day, Biddy asked my Dad if there was a train going early to Tralee. He said 'No' because the local train had just gone. Biddy was anxious to send her fish, however, and when she heard the whistle later of the film train, she ran up and tried to get into a carriage with the 'emigrés'. Dad tried to pull her back and explain that the train was only going a short distance but Biddy wasn't having any, and the film (which we saw later) showed them locked in a 'death grip'. Thank heavens it was a silent film as Biddy's language wasn't very choice on that occasion.

Fish traffic was, of course, a major *raison d'etre* for the line, but with road improvements it dwindled as did everything else, in the 1930s. Even so, when travelling the route with one of the authors in 1977, Bill Kinnerk and Paddy Martin of Tralee reminisced about the huge consignments of fish from Dingle that were transhipped at the Basin to barges working down the Tralee canal and across Tralee Bay to export ships at Fenit.[29]

The Basin was noted in season, of course, as the disembarkation point for passengers heading for Tralee, as was Blennerville if cattle or the Ballyard tidal floods blocked the line. Miss Ciss Duffy and Cmdt O'Donnell both mention seeing passengers leaving the stranded coaches to walk into Tralee while the train waited, perhaps up to its ashpan in water. Fr Dermot Healy,

162. AFTER CLOSURE: Two generations of ex-T&D men, Driver Paddy Martin (right) of Tralee could take his career right back to independent days. Bill Kinnerk (left), Tralee Councillor and ex-Kerry and All-Ireland football international, was a loader at Tralee in GSR days. They are standing in the entrance arch to Castlegregory Junction (Lower Camp) only a few weeks before the site was bulldozed to make way for road widening, 1977. Immediately behind them was the branch track and bay platform. The two men are examining a copy of David Rowlands' 1977 book The Tralee and Dingle Railway. *(Cork Examiner).*

former editor of the *African Missionary* and who, like Cmdt O'Donnell lived alongside the line near the Basin, said that his most vivid remembrance of the railway was of 'The Floating Train' in the tide water – indeed he carried this mental picture during many years in Nigeria. Fr Healy's father was a fireman, later driver, on the railway in GSR days – but more of his adventures later. Next door to them on the Castlecountess estate lived another GSR driver, Johnny Sullivan, who also drove on the Dingle, and of whom it was said he held the record for the number of crossing gates demolished!

Historian, former president of the Kerry Archaeological and Historical Society, Fr J. McKenna travelled often on the train. He wrote:

> I remember on one occasion coming home for Christmas when it ran through the gates at a crossing on the outskirts of Tralee. The window behind my head was smashed on impact. There was a long hold-up. No-one was injured and presently the train was on its way. On another occasion, when returning to St. Brendan's (Killarney) after the Easter holidays, about four miles out of Dingle the engine derailed. Again, there was a long delay while we strolled the nearby fields. It ended with the announcement that the train could not proceed and we all walked back to Dingle for an extra day's holiday. Many have recorded the bustle of messenger boys at Tralee arriving with parcels etc. They were claimed and piled at the end of the carriage between the doors. I was on board a couple of times when stranded by floods. I will never understand why the train left Tralee on these occasions – to travel 3/4 mile and come to a full stop for perhaps 2-3 hours while we all waited in the cold and wet was ridiculous! Didn't they know in Tralee about the tide? We could have been having a cup of tea in Tralee during the

wait, instead of marooned at Blennerville in the wind blasts! I can remember coming home on Sunday afternoons on the train with the victorious Dingle football teams. The cheering, singing and good fellowship – no bars on the train. Often in the long summer evenings we would cycle a few miles out of Dingle to meet the train and race it from the Racecourse to the station – with great risk and some success. I have happy memories of being frozen with cold in winter, there being no heating at all.

Tom Francis and Cmdt O'Donnell both recall Tom O'Leary (formerly a guard on the Camp disaster train) as gateman and factotum at the Basin. His son Paddy, county council clerk, later stayed with the O'Donnells and used to take them on the train. Cmdt O'Donnell remembers one such excursion when they had to walk beside the train along by Curraheen and Derrymore.

Miss Cis Duffy lived at Blennerville as a child and went to school in Tralee by train. The fare (3rd class) was 1½d. Her father had been paymaster on the T&DLR during its construction.

Construction of the line and a typical works train which gave them a welcome ride into Dingle, were described by Joseph O'Connor in *Hostage to Fortune*.

Sr Malachy's father, Tom Bailey, succeeded O'Connor Senior at Dingle, having also been with the T&DLR right from the start. He had worked as guard on construction trains. Tom's brother, John, was later guard on the railway also. Another of Tom's daughters, Miss Agnes Bailey, wrote this memoir:

> One of my very earliest recollections is of the crowds and sidecars that congregated outside the station to see the train coming in at about 7pm. The Dublin morning papers *Independent* and *Freeman's Journal* arrived on this train, and the newspaperman, John O'Connor, was the centre of a chattering, jostling crowd for a good quarter of an hour, while he undid and distributed papers from his exclusive pitch on the grassy ditch about 50 yards from the station. I'm not quite sure how this ceremony was carried out on wet winter evenings – no doubt an alternative site was found possibly in one of the waiting rooms . . . When the Volunteer movement was active just before and in the early years of the First World War, some businessmen from the town (Pat Neligan, Main Street, Paddy Devane, Greer Street etc.) congregated in the station office with my father and had very interesting and animated political discussions. This was where I got my early initiation into the Irish situation as I listened enthralled to quotations from the current and previous MPs right back to Gladstone. To me at least it was a blessing if the train was a bit late. On a summer's evening the clunk-clunk could be heard as the train rounded the shoulder of Greenmount. From that point too, the passengers had a magnificent view of the harbour with Reen towering above it and reflected on the water in calm weather. But not all trains brought such rapturous thoughts. One of the saddest spectacles I remember was when emigrant ships were due to leave from Queenstown [now Cobh] and batches of young boys and girls, mostly from west of Dingle, left by train, about 4pm. An immense crowd of relatives and friends accompanied them to the station; the scene was reminiscent of funerals and the grief has left a never-to-be-forgotten memory in my mind. There were however happy times such as the exodus when Kerry was playing in the All-Ireland final at Croke Park in Dublin. Cars were few and far between, and a special train left in the small hours of the morning in order to connect with the main train in Tralee. I'm afraid I don't remember the names of many employees. Bob Knightly and Vincent O'Brien were clerks in the office as was Bertie O'Donnell who later went to America. Bob Knightly became stationmaster at Annascaul and later at Castlemaine. I remember two porters, Paddy Sullivan and Tadhg Kennedy.

To these staff Sr Malachy and Miss Duffy have added Jamesie Moriarty (night watchman), Mikie Bowler (later chemist in Main Street), Paddy Griffin (head porter), guards Jim Ashe (of whom more later) and Jack O'Connor.

Mrs Dunton, daughter of Inspector Murphy of Dingle, who also lived there in this 1900-20 period recalled in addition, driver Quinn and Murphy his regular fireman; Johnny Donoghue (PW Inspector), George Hoffman stationmaster at Annascaul, and Peter Casey at Lispole. She mentioned too, Crean's pub at Camp which was Aunty's to the railwaymen.[30] Aunty was a great character down the road from Fitzgerald's bar, just opposite the branch turntable.

CIE Locomotive Inspector (retd) Jack Manning, of Cork, who began as a cleaner at Tralee and learned fireman's duties on the T&D, remembered stationmaster Bailey of Dingle as a strict disciplinarian but who in good humour would sometimes travel with his staff on one of the engines to pubs on the pier extension for a social drink. Mr Manning has interesting recollections of his spells on the Dingle. He drove several times with Tom Cournane, notably when Cournane and he reopened the line, which had been closed for some months during the 1944 fuel shortages, with a racehorse special of 6-8 vans (18 horses) to Dingle. Driver Cournane, he said, was perhaps the most characteristic of the old T&DLR men in those early GSR days. Kindly, friendly and great company – but say a word against 'The Dingle' and you were his enemy immediately. The Dingle men went to their own pub in Tralee and the Southern men to theirs and rarely did the twain meet. Cournane, however, was kindly to young cleaners and firemen, provided they acknowledged by their conduct and conversation that the T&DLR had done a great favour to the Southern in condescending to amalgamate with it! Similar views were expressed into CIE days and even into the 1950s by the other ex-T&DLR drivers (and proud of it!) Jack Cotter, Paddy Martin and Billy Hanlon. In part, the present authors suggest this stems from the fact that the general manager of the T&DLR, who succeeded R. A. Parkes, John P. Tooher became Tralee district superintendent of the GSR upon amalgamation. Thus in office at any rate, the T&DLR manager did take over the Southern in the district!

Richard Parkes had been manager since the line's opening. A Protestant and leading Orangeman he must have found his job increasingly difficult with the changing atmosphere and sympathies. For a while, 1910-11, there was a father-and-son partnership as his son Albert, trained by Hunslets of Leeds (who supplied the locomotives), became locomotive engineer. Albert Parkes' daughter has supplied an interesting memoir.[31] Other members of the family had been manager's assistant and telegrapher. The family emigrated to Canada in 1912.

Tom Francis has also given us a memoir of some of the staff at Tralee. Among drivers not already mentioned were Jerry Donovan, 'Big Mick' Moriarty and 'Small Mick' (Jack) Moriarty, Eddie Murphy, Paddy Ryan, Ned Dunne and Jim Hanlon (father of Billy). Indeed, Jim was the driver of the 1904 train referred to by both the Whitehouse-Powell history and by Fr Moynihan, which knocked down four men at once at Aughacasla on the branch. Manager's secretary was Kerry footballer Tom Ryle, of Rock Street; secretary of the Company was Tom O'Connell with Matt Sweeney as his clerk. Tom Sampson was the auditor – he died tragically, in a fire at Tralee. Dan Finn was the storekeeper and until 1925 Jim Bailey from Tonevane was stationmaster, with his son Stephen as clerk. Tom O'Gorman was loco superintendent in those days with Dick Heaslip carriage builder; fitter James Veale, Eugene Landers, carpenter; Paddy O'Shea, painter; while Paddy Foley of Blennerville was a linesman and brother of Guard Foley, whose wife looked after Blennerville; Mr Foley was guard on the train which derailed at Lispole in 1907. Other guards were Jim Courtney from Castlegregory, who succeeded Jack Alec Fitzgerald, and Mick Duhig.

Paddy Martin and James Ashe, both old T&DLR men were reminded of the GSR's baptism of fire to the Dingle, on the very first day, 1 January, 1925 of GSR operating the line. This occurred at Glenmore crossing, an accident blackspot already familiar to the writers for a wagon derailment in 1951. Martin was driving and Ashe was guard of a train which bisected a Model T Ford on this crossing, leaving the driver of the car still holding his steering wheel.

The whole of one side of his car was found up on the front of locomotive No. 6, one hundred yards away. When Ashe ran up to the demolished car he expected to find a corpse, but the dazed driver was uninjured and wondering where the rest of his car was!

Guard Ashe became famous for his calling out at each station stop: "Anyone there for here?" and at the lonelier wayside halts this was often followed by "Devil a one here, Driver, Away wi' ye".

Needless to say, Martin and Ashe both regarded all post-1925 affairs on the line as anti-climax to the glorious days of independence. Driver Martin recalled firing excursions on Sundays in pre-GSR days. Young men and teenagers were on the roofs, for every coach was crammed full. Near Derrymore the fun turned to tragedy when a telegraph post struck young Tim O'Donnell of Tralee. He was killed outright. The occasion was a Sunday excursion to Lispole, marking the 4th anniversary of the death of patriot Thomas Ashe.

'The strangest special I ever drove' for driver Martin was from Tralee to Upper Camp halt (Camp platform). It conveyed in solitary state, P. J. Floyd, general manager of the GSR in Dublin. The priest at St. Mary's, Camp, had applied to the GSR to release a plot of land at Camp halt as a playground for the school, beside the railway. Floyd travelled to see the plot required and the children put on a sports and gymnastic display for him at the lineside. Martin saw Floyd give £1 (then a large sum) to a young girl for winning one event. Anyway, they got their playground.

Mention of Camp brings another of the coincidences that typify research into T&D lore. Most people who used the line remember Pat O'Connor (Pat Cooper O'Connor), long-serving honorary helper at Camp church and who worked on the railway as a labourer on the branch, signalman, porter at Camp, halt-keeper there, and later at Tralee. He died in 1977 aged 92. While Bill Kinnerk, Paddy Martin and Walter McGrath were revisiting old scenes at Camp they stood outside his cottage, debating whether to call. They decided not, knowing he was ill. Afterwards they learned that he had died at his cousin's that very afternoon. Standing by his cottage door, they visualised the scene there 70 years previously. There would have been rails on both sides of his cottage, because it was within the western apex of the Curraduff diversion, made in 1907. Pat's brother and John Knightly of Killelton both worked on the construction of this diversion, as did Michael P. Griffin. Of this work on the diversion, Mr Griffin recalled most interestingly, that they received 2/6d (12½p) per day (nothing if the weather was bad) and that all payment was in sovereigns, half-sovereigns, crowns or half-crowns. The metal girders and superstructure for the bridge came from Scotland and were landed at Dingle Pier, thence by train to Camp. The new tracklaying began from the junction and he, Knightly and O'Connor all worked horses and tipper wagons of spoil and ballast, along with some twenty five others.

Bob Fitzgerald, nowadays general secretary of the Irish Rugby Football Union, but in the 1930s living on the family farm at Meenascorthy, Deelis, on the branch, had many warm recollections of Pat O'Connor who was then porter at Camp. Jack O'Leary, son of guard Tom O'Leary – the hero of the Curraduff disaster whose presence of mind despatched a warning to the following train – was stationmaster at the junction from 1920, following Tom Francis Senior. The young Bob Fitzgerald who travelled daily to primary school in

Tralee from Deelis in 1926-33 caused consternation once by getting his head firmly stuck between the bars of the carriage window. It delayed the train for 20 minutes and Bob wrenched free 'just as a search for a screwdriver was about to be successful'. He and his sisters survived a derailment at Derrymore in 1939 when a pony was hit and killed. On this stretch between Camp and Blennerville, Bob remembers seeing All-Ireland Gaelic footballer Charlie Sullivan keeping fit for matches by pacing trains on his bicycle. Bob wrote:

> I remember the little old man who during the 1930s would, in season, travel every morning from Castlegregory to Tralee with a 56lb. Butter box full of cockles, covered with a nice white cloth. The fishy smell filled the entire carriage as we faced each other on the seat of wooden laths. The boys going to the Christian Brothers' school in Tralee were always copying one anothers' Latin exercises. Apparently punishments were most severe in that subject!

Pat "Aeroplane" O'Shea taught at Derrymore School in the years 1910-15 and travelled by train from Castlegregory each day. He occupied the time by teaching himself Gaelic, and thanks *The Dingle Train* for his grasp of Irish.[32]

Fr Moynihan mentioned the landing on Banna strand of the ill-fated Roger Casement during the First World War. This brings to mind an incident of the Second World War. Mrs O'Neill, daughter of stationmaster Jack O'Leary, remembered that during the period of infrequent goods-only trains in 1942, fireman Charlie Flaherty was walking the rails near Derrymore, when he saw a tall stranger waiting on the disused platform there. He saluted him, and the stranger in clipped accent asked 'Vot dime vor Dralee der negst drain kommst?' or words to that effect. Charlie replied: 'The last one was three years ago and heaven knows when the next will be'. Shortly after, the German stranger was arrested for questioning, having parachuted in near Brandon.

Two of the eight Deane sisters of Camp are today widows of T&DLR stationmasters, namely Mrs O'Leary and Mrs O'Donnell. Another sister, Mrs Quilter, recalled that the signalbox at the junction was a favourite playing-area for the local children and courting couples in the days when Tom Francis Snr. was stationmaster there.

He was locally esteemed as a most lovable man who always kept a cheerful fire in the waiting room in winter, so much so that it became a social centre for the community at the time.

Before temporarily leaving the branch to Castlegregory, it is worth recording the tongue-in-cheek solution supplied by former driver Paddy Martin to another mystery. Since taking over in 1925 the GSR had continuously tried to close the branch, despite heavy excursion traffic and, later, the beet trains which ran late into the night. Their probable reason was the state of the track which, according to their permanent way records in our possession, had received little maintenance. When the junction was relaid in the mid-1930s, only a few yards of the branch were renewed. If trains of any sort were to continue running, very expensive track renewal would be necessary. (The line to Dingle was much better maintained). The wonder was that the GSR had not summarily closed the branch once roads began to improve. However, there lived at Castlegregory, an eminent woman county councillor, Kate Breen. It was rare in those days for a woman to hold such office. She was a personal friend of Dev. Whenever the GSR mooted closure, it is said that Kate would descend on the GSR general manager's office in Dublin and demand retention of the service. She would apparently succeed. At any rate, it was shortly after she died that the GSR closed the branch to all traffic!

Three decades earlier, another county councillor from Castlegregory was father of Rt Rev Mgr O'Donnell of Barking Road, London. The late Mgr O'Donnell remembered vividly his travels over the branch to school in Tralee from 1903 onwards. By virtue of his county deputyship Councillor O'Donnell was sometime among the directorate of the line. Annually for some years a 'Directors special train' ran slowly over the entire system, of which Mgr O'Donnell wryly commented: 'They were inspecting the line, moryiah, but more interested in the refreshments provided'.

There was published a 70-page Board of Trade report on the enquiry into the Curraduff disaster which makes interesting reading. Richard Adams QC, renowned wit of the Irish Bar, and later a famous judge, was the legal assessor. Shorthand evidence on the scene of the accident was given by Police Sergeant Noble RIC. He was later to compose a dramatic and lengthy poem on the disaster.[33]

Only one of the present writers was born to the Tralee & Dingle: Tom Francis. Not just born to it, but related to many of the Company staff and surrounded by its daily events, legends and gossip. He was in the best possible position to evaluate its true place in the communities it served. He did so in articles published in the *Cork Evening Echo,* 15 October, 1981, which ran as follows:

"It would seem that the Tralee and Dingle Light Railway was the subject of more discussion, controversy and adverse criticism than any other light railway in these islands.

On reading early complaints about its shortcomings one would be prompted to ask why was the line ever built; what purpose was it intended to serve; did it justify its existence, and did the ratepayers get value for the financial burden it entailed?

One must try to envisage the isolation of the Dingle Peninsula up to 1891. It is a matter of regret to me that I did not record some of the many stories both gay and grim recounted by an uncle of mine who carted for some years between Dingle and Tralee before the train came. He spoke of carters' anxiety to be clear of certain lonely localities before nightfall as there was constant danger of losing part of their loads – perhaps a sack of flour or a box of tea!

Many had experiences of being joined by "ghostly passengers" who on departure would appropriate some valuable part of the load.

The hardships of coach travel between Tralee and Dingle were ably outlined by the late Joe O'Connor in his book, "Hostage To Fortune". Joe's father, who was first stationmaster at Dingle, initiated my father into the T&DLR and he became stationmaster at Castlegregory Junction (Camp).

With the advent of the railway a much more facile mode of travel was provided for the people. It helped to widen commercial and social contacts, and it provided a means of travel to Tralee secondary schools for pupils as far west as Annascaul and Castlegregory who could not have gone beyond their local primary schools had the railway not been there.

Over the years many hundreds of people from the Peninsula attained positions of worthy note in church, state and professions. In most cases such progress would not have been possible without the railway.

Business in the towns was enhanced, and one cannot forget the market activity at Tralee N.G. Station when the "touts" would be canvassing for various shops and competing in prices offered to the incoming housewives for their eggs, butter and other products. And at train departure time in the evening the excitement at the station was intense with harassed shop messengers delivering goods to the purchasers before the train left. It was a happy atmosphere, full of good humour and neighbourly friendship.

Such was the competition for business from the West, that it was said one of the reasons for establishing a station at the Basin near the old Tralee canal was to facilitate shoppers wishing to patronise the lower end of the town rather than the Castle Street/Ashe Street area.

Castlegregory Junction was my home for 17 years and I recall it as a social focal point where people gathered to wish God-speed to departing emigrants or to welcome home the returned exile.

In summer activity was at its peak when crowds gathered to meet excursionists from Tralee on Sunday afternoons, and occasionally on Wednesdays. The railway management erected a refreshment room adjacent to the Junction to cater for the crowds. For many years this was managed by the late Mrs Mary Kennedy of Boherbuee.

In those days Camp had an annual sports meeting and pony races in Deane's Field – "Gort a' Duna". This function, as well as the Castlegregory Pattern Day (August 5) were two big events which brought the people in their hundreds by train to enjoy the sport and the beauty of the locality.

Of the commercial activity at the Junction I recall the weekly butter market conducted by a man representing a Cork firm. Camp fair days were other events of much activity, but most impressive of all were the constant daily queues of carts at the station, collecting merchandise sent from Tralee.

The "Troubles", 1920-23, caused much disruption, Curraheen and Derrymore bridges being demolished, and when times became normal again the pattern of life was just not the same any more. Cars were appearing on the roads – and then came the bus which was a more convenient form of travel.

The operating staff have often been unjustly branded, many because of alleged insobriety. Anybody not knowing the truth would get the impression from some things which have been written that train staff would only leave the pub at the Junction when a flood was threatened on the line in at Blennerville. That is a confounded untruth and a reflection on the conduct of many good men who rendered faithful service, often under trying conditions. For 17 years I had close association with the railway at the Junction and I cannot recall one staff member who could be accused of being a drunkard.[34]

I travelled by T&D to school in Tralee for five years and in that period never once was I late by reason of train failure. We would sometimes be delayed by floods at Blennerville but that was not the fault of the T&D or its staff!

Postal services improved from the earlier situation in which the mail was carried in easy stages between Tralee and Dingle. It took some time before the Post Office would agree to pay the transport rate demanded by the Tralee and Dingle Light Railway Company. The improvement was a matter of wonder to the people when it became possible to have a letter from Dublin delivered in Dingle within 15 or 18 hours of time of posting. There was a mail out of Dingle in 1903 postmarked 7am. I have a postcard to prove it.

The line was kept busy with transport of cargoes of cured fish for the American market. The facilities for serving fairs and markets were of inestimable value; and the management was over-generous in the amount of goods a passenger was allowed to carry without extra charge.

Dingle had a flourishing trade through its port. There were more local industries in those days.

The railway brought The West into regular daily contact with places beyond the Barony of Corkaguiny. Its popularity with the people in its early stages might be gauged from the strong pressure used to have the Castlegregory branch line extended to Brandon. Early working losses, however, made this impossible.

It was only with the coming of the railway that the beauty of the culture of the barony was opened to hosts of scholars who found beyond the terminus of the line treasures which had been a source of study and inspiration to only a few before the railway era. It opened up the Gaeltacht including the Blaskets.

The more tragic phases of the line's history have been covered in many detailed reports and analyses, but there are many aspects of the history of the line as yet unrecorded. These await the researchers.

There is material for many stories which should be put on record now before all contacts have disappeared. There are the yarns and legends of accidents or mishaps to men and beasts; the burning of thatched houses by sparks from the hard-pressed engines; the runaway milesmens' bogey going through the level crossing gates; the early morning specials to All-Ireland finals; the rescued French sailors who sang The Marseillaise on Dingle platform in appreciation of the valour of their rescuers; the facilities given to a group of Norwegian sailors rescued in 1916 at Ballinabuck by famous handballer Fr. Tom Jones and the men from Ballyferriter, for which a gold cup was presented to Fr. Jones by the King of Norway!

These, and many other events in which the Tralee and Dingle was a focal centre remain to be written about in more detail.

On a number of occasions recently it was my privilege to be entertained by Mr Bob Knightly, now the "grand old man" of the few survivors of the Dingle railway staff. This veteran, still hale and hearty, resides with his daughter in Co. Wexford. He was stationmaster in Annascaul from the time of the first Great War until the ending of the passenger services on the "Dingle" in 1939. What a host of memories of the line he possesses – not least his tales of the famous old pattern fairs of Ballinclare, Annascaul, every May and October.

Yes, it can be said indeed that the railway played an important part in the development of West Kerry, and the hopes of that far-seeing Committee who founded it in the 1880s have been justified in an immeasurable and socially satisfactory manner.

The new "Steaming Monster", the old lady in Annascaul called it, when she ran down the village street telling people to run "for here comes the devil himself belching fire and smoke!" But what a significant part this monster played in the development of rural life in the Barony.

What a pity the line was closed, when it could have been continued as a scenic line as has been done with many narrow-gauge lines in Wales and elsewhere. One last word of appeal to lovers of the Old Line – let's take steps to perpetuate its memory with a T&D Railway Museum in Tralee."

The train has been gone for forty years but lives on in the memories of those who worked or travelled on it. At this time, the concluding lines of Tim O'Donnell's poem seem particularly appropriate.

Now often in my dreams I see
Tralee, the sea, the sky
And a small train struggle bravely on
Across the mountains high,
A memory of the days that were
A ghost from out the years
Climbing the heights of Gleann na nGealt
Like an old man full of tears.[23]

1. J. A. Gaughan, *A Political Odyssey: Thomas O'Donnell* (Dublin, 1983).
2. Radio Eireann broadcast 7th October 1975.
3. T. Francis, *Cork Evening Echo* 28 December 1977.
4. P. Kennelly, *Kerry's Eye*, 18 December 1975.
5. D. Fitzgerald, *The Memoirs of Desmond Fitzgerald* (London 1968) 6-12.
6. S. O'Luing, *The Scholars Path, Cork Holly Bough,* 1982 p.16.
7. W. McGrath, *Cork Evening Echo,* 2 August 1982, p.5.
8. S. O'Luing, Studies, 1981, 121-133.
9. T. Enright, *Cork Evening Echo,* 17 August 1983.
10. W. McGrath, *Cork Evening Echo,* 20 December 1983.
11. G. Chambers, *Letters from the Great Blasket* (date?).
12. S. Moynihan, *Bonaventura,* 1937-8.
13. W. McGrath, *Cork Holly Bough,* 1985, p.23.
14. S. O'Luing, *Cork Holly Bough,* 1983, p.32; J. Kerry Arch. & Hist. Soc., No. 20, 1990.
15. W. McGrath, *Cork Holly Bough,* 1980, p.23-4.
16. W. McGrath, *Cork Evening Echo,* 8-10 August, 1983, pp. 9.
17. S. O'Luing: *Traein an Daingin in Feasta* 2 (1971) 16.
18. P. Sayers, *An Old Woman's Reflections* (Oxford 1972) 77-9.
19. J. M. Synge, *In West Kerry* (1907), included in *In Wicklow and West Kerry* (Dublin 1912) 60-61; 126-30.
20. T. Biuso, *The Poet's Road,* Irish-American Magazine, December 1988; *Cork Evening Echo,* 27 July, 1984 p.9.
21. T. Francis, *Cork Holly Bough,* 1982, p.23.
22. P. O'Snodaigh: *Paróiste an Fheirtéirigh agus 1916* (Dublin 1966).
23. T. O'Donnell, *Lament for the Dingle Train* in *Sigerson Clifford's Book of Irish Recitations* (Dublin 1960) 37-9.
24. M. Ruiséal, *Duanhaire Duibhneach* (Ed. J. O"Dowd N.T.) (Dublin 1933) 43.
25. M. Ó Sé, *Traein an Daingin,* in *Danta le Mícheal Ó Sé* (Dublin 1968).
26. M. O'Donoghue, *Cork Holly Bough,* 1982.
27. Fr. Colman Foley, *Cork Evening Echo,* 24 May 1977.
28. M. Foley, *A History of the County Kerry in Baronies: Corkaguiny* (Dublin 1907) 6,167.
29. W. McGrath, *Irish Weekly Examiner,* 2 June 1977.
M. O'Ruairc, *Cork Evening Echo,* 11 July 1983.
30. K. Dunton, *Irish Weekly Examiner,* 30 June 1977.
31 P. Piddington, *Cork Evening Echo,* 28 December 1977.
32. W. McGrath, ROS, Vol. 10, No. 1, 1980, p.3.
33. Known to have appeared in *The Kerry Reporter,* date unknown.
34. Allegations of drunkenness and hard drinking have always dogged the Dingle Railway. There are records of disciplinary action against staff, but these are common to all minor railways and not just in Ireland. The North Wales Narrow Gauge Railway (later the Welsh Highland) for example can provide several examples of accidents caused through drunken staff.

What hit particularly hard were the accounts of visiting railfans in later years who – in trying to convey the adventurous atmosphere of the Tralee & Dingle invoked the "Stage Irishman" a little too often. Yes, the crews often partook of a drink or two at Aunty's, Fitzgerald's and elsewhere . . . but it was often at the invitation first of those enthusiasts to whom they had given footplate rides or stopped to allow them to take a posed photograph en route. Liquor was seldom carried on the trains, the brew favoured was as often as not cold (or hot) tea . . . or even that curious brew mentioned by Pat Whitehouse: aerated lemonade and goat's milk.

The late Willie Garrett, Foreman at Tralee, was often hurt by the allegations that his crews drank heavily on duty. As a matter of fact if the Dingle had its drinkers (and no-one denies that it did) then it also had its teetotallers: men like Pat "Cooper" Connor, Sacristan of Camp Church, who had worked on the Curraduff diversion in 1908, become porter at Lower Camp and finished his railway service with the Freight Depot in Tralee.

THE FLOUR ROBBERY

163. Castlegregory Junction: Scene of the night-time unloading of the commandeered train. Here in 1952 a returning cattle special is taking water before the last stage of the journey to Tralee. At right with CIE cattle lorry and trailer outside, is "Fitzgerald's Bar" and in the centre distance is Crean's pub (Aunty's). *(C. L. Fry)*

THE CIRCUS COLLISION

164. Scene of the accident: No. 5T on the daily goods (ex-Dingle) is drawing up to the dangerous Lougher crossing in 1940. *(Author's Collection)*

Chapter 8
THREE COLOURFUL INCIDENTS

The people of Kerry and the Blaskets have a natural talent for poetry and story-telling, and The Dingle Train has featured in many of these. They also possess phenomenal memories for past incidents. In our experiences of tracking down the records and bases of dozens of these stories, none of them have ever been invented. The Dingle Train did not need invention: the reality was quite incredible enough!

Indeed there is only one attested example of The Dingle Train in fiction: Michael O'Sullivan's "An Fear Aduaidh" (Dublin, 1978).

What stories then shall we pick? Engine No. 2T losing its chimney one Fair Day? The "Floating Train" marooned in the Blennerville floods? The train blown off the line at Skylough on Christmas Eve, 1912? The prize cockerel that escaped from the train at Lispole? How the first pedigree donkey came to Corkaguiny? How the train of paraffin barrels caught fire from a "hot box"? How the priest at Camp had his garden set ablaze? Why the General Manager had to purchase a pony and trap to carry the railway mails?

Well, we will settle for three. They come from different periods of the line's history and present different facets of its operation. During the "Troubles"; in the early years of WW-2 after passenger services had been withdrawn; and in the very last years when running the cattle specials once a month was such a headache to Willie Garrett.

THE GREAT FLOUR ROBBERY OF 1922

We are recounting the salient facts of this exciting Civil War incident not to resurrect any bitterness of that dread period, or to ascribe guilt or notoriety, but simply to record the memories of a few of the surviving actors in the drama, taken when they were still with us in 1980.

Two octogenarians, Paddy Martin of Tralee (a native of Dingle) and Joe Spillane of Fermoyle, beyond Castlegregory, and a nonogenarian, Pat O'Shea of Farrantane, Castlegregory, all kindly answered questions on the subject, while Tom Francis, a much younger man, has given boyhood memories of what was to him almost a "ghost train" which arrived mysteriously in Camp Junction, ten miles west of Tralee, one pitch black night.

The period was late 1922. Kerry was tragically sundered, in politics and in arms. The Free State troops had occupied Tralee, and the Republicans were entrenching themselves westward throughout the Dingle Peninsula. Railway and road bridges were blown up at Curraheen and Derrymore, west of Tralee, and all railway traffic on the narrow-gauge T&DLR was disrupted, in fact no trains had run on the line, or on its branch from Lower Camp to Castlegregory, for several months. The threat of food shortage and of actual hunger was very real.

It was under those circumstances that the Republican Command of that area (E. Coy., Camp, 4th Batt., Kerry Brigade) learned that a food ship had left Cork for Dingle harbour and Ballykissane Pier, near Killorglin. It was laden with flour ("St. Louis" brand) and other supplies. Much of the flour was invoiced to Killarney Mental Hospital, and the nearest unloading point to that was Ballykissane, far up at the eastern end of Dingle Bay, and in shallow water.

The vessel, as expected, hove to off Dingle and cast anchor, awaiting high tide.

An elaborate plan, involving the use of a train of several wagons and a multitude of horses-and-carts was devised to gain possession of that valuable consignment of flour, and distribute it among dozens of households around Camp, Gleann na nGealt, Curraduff, Deelis, Meenascorthy and Castlegregory – mainly to homes known to be "friendly to the cause."

Paddy Martin, then living in retirement in Tralee after a long and honourable railway career, took up the tale: "I was then a fireman, and later a driver, of the Dingle Railway. No trains had run for months and one night I was sitting in my home in John Street, Dingle, when two armed volunteers entered, and ordered me to get up to the station immediately and get steam up in an engine, as a food train was to be run to Camp. I demurred at first but a gun was quickly produced!

"I was then told that a party of officers had earlier hi-jacked a ship in Dingle harbour, and had brought it to the pier, where a large number of carts were lined up. Tons upon tons of flour and some other goods were unloaded from the ship on to the carts and driven up to the railway station."

When Paddy Martin got to the station he found one engine already in steam. It had come all the way from Castlegregory (under driver Tom Bailey and fireman Jerry O'Donovan – and also under "armed guard"). Driver Jack Cotter, and Paddy (as fireman), then set about getting a fire going in the Dingle engine's firebox, while all the time wagon after wagon was being loaded up with the bags of flour from the horse carts.

"Eventually we set off double-headed for Camp. There was supposed to be an armed lorry following us on the road (which ran near the track for long stretches). There were also armed men on the train.

"My only memory of the strange journey is that at Annascaul, stationmaster Bob Knightly was waiting for us. On re-starting he travelled with us for a short distance and pointed out some "friendly" houses where we threw out a few sacks of flour to waiting hands."

It must have been a strange journey indeed as the train, after leaving Dingle, wended its way past Ballintaggart and Ballinasteenig, then over the high

Lispole Viaduct, up Bawnogue Heights, down into Annascaul and then up the long climb through Emalough and Glenmore to the summit of Gleann na nGealt. Ghostly indeed the train must have seemed as it hugged the side of the famous "Glen of the Mad."

It was at Lower Camp (Castlegregory Junction) that the greatest scenes of activity were enacted late that night. Tom Francis was only a child, but he remembers the mysterious hustle and bustle, and the nightlong comings and goings of carts and traps. Tom's father had been stationmaster at the Junction but had died two years earlier.

Joe Spillane, now one of the best-known residents of the Fermoyle area, on the road to Cloghane and not far from the Connor Pass, was a young volunteer billeted in Camp during the early days of the Civil War. "I travelled on the famous 'flour train' in both directions," he told me. "I went west to Dingle with the Castlegregory engine as one of the unit in action, and returned to the Junction after the sacks of flour had been loaded. It was a mysterious journey."

Joe's wife, Mrs Bridget Spillane (who incidentally was well known to many of the stars and production crew of the film "Ryan's Daughter" ten years ago) put in here: "I often heard that the whole countryside was saturated with St. Louis flour for weeks after the incident."

And Mrs Spillane had a few other memories of it for Tom Francis. "There was more than flour. There was tea in timber chests – and I can tell you there were many cans of sweets going the rounds too."

Pat O'Shea of Castlegregory, then a sprightly 91, had the last word. He would not comment on whether the whole affair had been an important military exercise or not. He presumed some of the flour in the Camp area, and around Killelton and Derrymore, had probably been put to good use. Before long, however, the Free State troops arrived in Castlegregory and the hidden stocks of flour were soon unearthed. "Alas, for the clever plans of mice and men in times of Civil War."

THE CIRCUS COLLISION OF 1940

It could only have happened on the "Dingle"! We have all heard about the steamroller that crashed into the Muskerry Railway train on the Carrigrohane Straight Road, Cork, but who would have thought it possible that a circus on its leisurely way to Dingle would come to grief in an encounter with a locomotive on the mountainy, roadside Tralee and Dingle Light Railway? Yet that is what happened at Lougher near Annascaul, Co. Kerry, exactly 50 years ago.

I would never have heard of it but for a conversation in Cork with Father Dermot Healy, S.M.A., then editor of a Cork religious magazine. Learning that he was from Tralee I asked him if he had any anecdotes of the Dingle train, and he replied that his late father had been a fireman and later a driver on it in "Great Southern" days (after the Amalgamation of 1925) and that the most exciting incident of his father's career was when his train crashed into a circus one day, and he had to make many journeys to the High Court in Dublin as a result. Fr. Healy could remember the incident but had no ideas as to date.

Here was a fascinating subject to research – something that had escaped the attentions of all Tralee and Dingle Railway chroniclers hitherto. On a visit to Tralee I interviewed former T&D driver Paddy Martin, guard Jim Ashe and former GSR guard Bill Kinnerk (all since deceased). All of them remembered the incident as having taken place during the Second World War (that narrowed it down greatly) but they couldn't date it. However, I got three more "detectives" on the job – Paddy Mercer of Tralee; Seamus Crowley of the Kerry A. and H. Society and Tom Wall of the Irish Railway Record Society, Dublin, and between us we pieced the story together. Tom Wall found the vital "date" reference in the pages of the invaluable *Fayles Bulletin,* a journal of railway lore preserved at the Drumcondra headquarters of the I.R.R.S. Fayle, a noted rail enthusiast, had not recorded the incident itself, but had given the High Court ruling eighteen months later.

Several horse-drawn vehicles of Fosset's Circus were making their way westward for a performance in Dingle on April 26, 1940. One of the heavy floats was being driven by a middle-aged employee of the circus, Albert Marloe, described as an acrobat and entertainer. It is thought that he was dozing at the reins (possibly after a late night's work and early morning dismantling of the "big top") and was taking little note of the roadside track of narrow-gauge railway. This was the time of "goods only" GSR trains on the Dingle line. At a number of points around Glenmore, Lougher, Emalough and Annascaul the railway criss-crossed the public road, and at the Lougher crossing the engine of the daily goods crashed right into the front of Marloe's circus float.

At this passage of time we may perhaps regard the collision as humorously typical of the vagaries of the old remote railways of rural Ireland, but it was tragic for Marloe. Both his legs were very seriously injured, and there are reports that one might have been amputated. Certainly he was walking with the aid of a crutch for years later. The first local resident on the scene was James Terry O'Herlihy. He is reputed to have had many memories of the incident, but died in 1977. He, too, had to make a number of court appearances in the subsequent litigation.

The two horses pulling Mr Marloe's float or caravan were killed instantly by the force of the crash with the locomotive. We do not know now what animals, if any were in the float, or in the other vehicles of the cavalcade, but the legend has come down that there were memorable scenes of excitement.

Fr. Dermot Healy's father, John Healy, as a 'passed' fireman was learning the road under instruction from Tom Cournane. Cournane was letting Healy drive the train and was firing for him when the accident occurred. This complicated things for the GSR which did not want to admit that a fireman was driving at the

THE LONG WEEKEND

165. STALLED: Due to wet grass and dew, No. 8T and 2T have stalled on the climb up from Lispole viaduct and have just set back. About the centre of the train you can see the Guard watching the fireman of 2T uncoupling to divide the train. The footplate passenger has walked over the viaduct to secure this view. *(C. L. Fry)*

166. GOING BACK FOR THE REST: Annascaul, and at left 2T is at the head of the first (divided) portion of the train. 8T (right) is pushing the dead 1T out beyond the loop, prior to returning to Lispole for the remaining portion. The goods depot is at right, and the rails to Tralee actually climb up that road in the centre distance at 1 in 30 grade. *(C. L. Fry)*

167. 8T heading for Garrynadur, leaves the roadside for the T&DLR's own right of way, with the rest of the train collected from Lispole. *(C. L. Fry)*

time, although he was entitled to. Anyway, Cournane and Healy had to pay several visits to Dublin during the legal proceedings. The *Cork Examiner* for 27 April 1940 reported: 'Killed by train. Two horses fatally injured in Kerry. A middle-aged man named Edward Marloe, an entertainer of Fossett's Circus received a compound fracture of the leg when two horses drawing a circus caravan which he was driving to Dingle ran on to the railway line near Annascaul. Both animals were killed by a train! The eventual legal outcome recorded was: '12 Nov. 1941. A circus acrobat was awarded £650 and costs by consent in a claim against the GSR in the High Court, Dublin, for injuries received when a train collided with a horse-drawn vehicle owned by him, at Annascaul, Co. Kerry, last year'.

THE LONG WEEKEND: 1952

It was spring 1952, with only three locos available and a large number of cattle awaiting trans-shipment from Dingle. Trouble began on the Thursday evening when 1T was found to be steaming badly for no clearly discernable reason. On the Friday morning early, a single train comprising loco 8T, a coal truck, eight wagons and a brakevan left for Dingle, getting there about noon. Meantime a double-header (1T and 2T) left Tralee with twenty-two wagons and two brakes, depositing six wagons and a brake at Castlegregory Junction. It proceeded up Glenagalt and over the switchback section between Glenmore and Emalough to be met at Annascaul by 8T which had run back, light engine, from Dingle after coaling. The pilot (1T) dropped off the double-header, as she was still steaming indifferently, and ran back to the Junction, while the other two slogged up to Garrynadur and on to Dingle with the main train. From the Junction, 1T set out with the remaining vehicles, but developed trouble and failed near Glenmore at about 3.30pm. Meantime 8T had returned yet again from Dingle to Annascaul, where she was waiting to pilot the portion stuck with 1T. About 5.30, 1T's fireman arrived with his tale of woe, having got a lift in a lorry, and 8T then ran back to Glenmore, where she hauled the stranded train to Annascaul. Here she pulled 1T into the loop to await a repair gang from Tralee who, in the event, did not materialise. (Eventually 1T's fire was dropped and her crew caught the evening bus back to Tralee.) By this time 8T was short of sand, and acquired most of No. 1's supply before starting out for Dingle. Unfortunately a soft drizzle had set in, which made the going difficult, and she stalled near Baunogue top (Puckisland) just short of the helter-skelter descent.

Setting back did not help. Well off the regular road, Bill's fireman had to walk to Lispole in order to phone through to Dingle. No. 2T's crew were snug in the PW hut at Dingle, brewing tea after marshalling the first train for next day's workings into the cattle sidings. Having coaled and watered her, they were not pleased to be routed out by the Agent at Dingle, to revive No. 2 and go out to Garrynadur again. Luckily they had plenty of sand; they needed it since the rain had become torrential. The crew and enthusiasts on 8T were very glad to see them arrive, it being a lonely spot, far from the crossing keeper's cottage at Ballinaclare gate. They finally reached Dingle at 9.30pm, after a near miss with sheep near Ballinasteenig.

Next day there was the usual loading chaos. Then 8T and 2T set out from Dingle at 12.45 with 17 vans and a brake fully-loaded, having then marshalled 10 vans and brake into the cattle bay and decided to leave one brakevan at Dingle. It was a soft day, and despite running at the viaduct the whole train stalled on the climb upwards. Setting back was no good and they divided the train. Two locos and 10 vans got up to Baunogue and coasted down to Annascaul where they ran into the loop occupied by the dead 1T. While 2T's fireman went to phone for more sand, 8T uncoupled and pushed 1T out beyond the loop on the East side.

After watering, she ran back to Lispole for the remaining six vans and brake. No. 2T now ran out of the loop up to 1T while 8T uncoupled from her flotilla and ran up to head the outgoing train in the loop. Then 2T pulled 1T back on to the passing line, uncoupled, and went back to Dingle for the remaining 10 vans and brake. Returning with these, she ran up to No. 1, and coupled up. She then pushed and pulled the train out of the loop and backed on to the remaining six vans and brake left by 8T. Meantime 8T had performed the incredible and hair-raising feat of humping 14 vans up to Glenmore without a brakevan, and anyone who has seen the switchback course of the line, will appreciate how nerve-wracking this must have been! How the cattle fared was not recorded! She stuck for a while near Glenmore but ultimately made it to Glenagalt and literally slid down to the junction, where the footplate passenger declared he had had enough, and would walk until a bus came along! After a breather, the crew and 8T returned to Annascaul to pilot out the convoy headed by 2T, with 1T dead between them – sixteen wagons and two brakes. Stalling on the 1 in 29 out of Annascaul, they were met by the pick-up truck with sand. Finally they made it to the Junction, after which the other enthusiasts, who had been party to these manoeuvres, had to set out with their car-driver for Tralee. So, we do not know how the trains were got back to Tralee, except that it was 11pm before the men finished. All in a weekend's work to the men of the Tralee & Dingle! Over this one weekend, loco 8T clocked up some 160 miles on a 63 mile round trip.

Chapter 9

LOCOMOTIVE NO. 5T's LAST RUN ON THE DINGLE RAILWAY

This account is culled from a long letter to David Rowlands by the late Cyril Fry, doyen of Irish railway enthusiasts and a builder of superb model locomotives. He provided much help and many photographs for David Rowlands' 1977 book "The Tralee & Dingle Railway". Mr Fry rode on 5T's footplate for this last run and took a few photographs of the occasion. How he would have delighted in her return to Tralee!

Incidentally Mr Fry secured the bell from No. 2T prior to scrapping at Inchicore, through the good offices of Willie Garratt. He put it to good use as the doorbell of his house in Dublin. The bell from No. 1T was also secured by Mr Garratt and sent via Walter McGrath to a Mission in Nigeria to act as its church bell.

It is interesting that David Rowlands first wrote this account for the Narrow Gauge Times Magazine, Winter 1976-7 where it was titled "Bearings & Buckets". At the time No. 5T was still at Steamtown, Vermont, USA and although Edgar Mead her owner had hinted she was for sale, there seemed a real and dreadful prospect of her being "converted to non-European outline and sold to an amusement park". Mr Mead himself wrote a short account of her adventures in 1987 for the magazine Narrow Gauge and Short Line Gazette, entitled "The Saga of Tralee & Dingle No. 5". She had originally been intended for the "Pleasure Island" park in Wakefield, Mass.; but the park failed and Edgar Mead was able to acquire the Dingle engine for his Steamtown Exhibition at Bellows Falls.

None of us at the time, not even in our wildest dreams, dared hope that she might return to her home in Tralee AND STEAM AGAIN over part of the original right-of-way!

The locomotive which has so dramatically and excitingly returned to Tralee from the USA, where it had been preserved, last ran in service on the Tralee & Dingle in 1949.

Passenger services on the line were withdrawn in 1939, after which a single goods train worked down to Dingle and back each day. It is not clear when that daily train, leaving Tralee at 7.30am and returning from Dingle at noon, finally ceased – if it was regularly resumed after the coal shortages of 1944 – leaving only the once-monthly special traffic for Dingle Fair. But there is no question that the five locos remaining at Tralee were in poor condition. This was particularly true of No. 6T (one of the "standard" Hunslet 2-6-0Ts) and the only 2-6-2T – No. 5T, both of which had been used extensively for the daily workings of the '40s. Since 1939, when passenger services ceased, luxuries like boiler wash-outs had been few and far between and who, on seeing the bulk of 5T, stuck at the back of Tralee shed in 1949 "Not Moveable", or rusting quietly away in the rain in Inchicore yard in 1950, would have guessed that she would survive all her sisters?

Built in 1892, Hunslet's No. 555, she was the first inside-framed 2-6-2 NG loco in the British Isles and – surprisingly – an oil-burner! However, despite its success the Holden apparatus was removed and coal-firing supervened. As supplied, she had triple rear windows and was the last to arrive with motion skirts fitted. She was re-boilered only once, in 1906, and was extremely popular with the T&D crews, being worked hard all through the '20s and '30s. As well as coal and oil, she was also tried – ignominiously – with turf during the 1944 fuel crisis, but in the event not only ran out of steam, but out of fire as well and was abandoned near Emalough for about a week until coal arrived again in Tralee. Such drivers' reports as survive from the '40s suggest she was deteriorating fast – a sorry tale of lost power, ominous "knocks", heating bearings and leaking tanks – already patched twice in the '30s.

The spring of 1949 produced a goodly number of cattle for shipment to the Midlands and awaiting transport from Dingle Fair. Two double-headed specials were the "norm" for this event, but it was realised that unless there was an extra "relief" working (to return the same day) a lot of juggling with locos and stock – already decrepit enough – was going to be necessary. For some while past, No. 5T had been "stopped", wearing a "Not Moveable" sign after continuous bearing trouble. However, it was decided to steam her for the relief: 6 vans plus brake, with the main portions to follow later.

Driver Martin and Fireman Fitzgerald, old T&D men, who knew the line well, got their train away sharply at 08.50 hrs on the Friday morning. Accompanying them by road went the loco Foreman's car, leaving an Inspector to get the two main specials away. At Basin crossing, the Foreman's car awaited them and they anxiously felt the cranks and axles – warm as toast!

On, slowly, across the springy trackbed – wet from the Spring tides hitting the Ballyard flats, to another inspection stop alongside the road at Blennerville; Hot enough to fry an egg on! Further discussion, Irish-style, and a decision to carry on to the junction at Lower Camp (Castlegregory Junction). Here, bucketfuls of water were liberally applied from the standpipe until the desired coolness was achieved. However, the Foreman was dubious and it was decided to wait for the first double-header, to give further time for the bearings to cool, and Tralee was phoned from the junction (bar!) to get her under way. This duly arrived behind 2-6-0T's Nos. 6T and 8T in the form of some 20 vans and a brake. No. 6T (herself in no very good shape) took over the relief and changed crews with '5T' to keep the roster correct. They reached Dingle without difficulty, after a lineside stop on falling gradient close to the

"South Pole" (!) at Annascaul. Meantime No. 5T clanked to the head of No. 8T's train, the Inspector climbed aboard after receiving a call that '6T' had reached Annascaul (only the pub in actuality, not the end of Section!) and was proceeding. Nos. 5T and 8T headed away on the stiff climb to Camp and Glenagalt, while the second double-header (behind '1T' and '2T') left Tralee.

In the cutting just beyond the disused passenger platform at Glenagalt summit, the usual brake stop was made and the Inspector vetted the wagon brakes before the switchback section to Emalough and steep drop to Annascaul. On the principle that if something smells bad you don't stick your nose in it, they forbore to feel the offending cranks and axles, but contented themselves with throwing a couple of buckets of cold mountain water over the parts and a generous libation of oil. Then away! Tortuous squealing of flanges on Glenmore curves, a narrow escape with a sleepy CIE lorry driver on the crossing at Emalough and down,

168. NOT MOVEABLE: This was the situation for 5T during the late 1940s at the back of Tralee shed with various troubles, including "shot" bearings. This was taken in 1948. *(Ian Duncan)*

169. Her last run! No. 5T actually on her last run on the Tralee & Dingle in June 1949. Here she has arrived at Lower Camp Junction with the Relief portion from Tralee. The main train is in the background. *(C. L. Fry)*

helter-skelter, to Annascaul. With the Inspector aboard, only a longing glance at the "South Pole" – so near – as the train swept downward; but not to worry, the Foreman's car had been there first and all were catered for. A minor fracas ensued on entering the yard at Annascaul, as the porter sent for the weekend had left his bike leaning against the standpipe at the Tralee end, after helping water '6T' earlier. It had fallen over and was foul of the track. Nosing over the points like a hound on the scent, No. 5T's catcher tossed the bike contemptuously aside, as its crazy flotilla of empty stock bumped into the yard. Just another problem to be solved! The oil on 5T's bearings was smoking nicely, but a few well-aimed buckets of water cured that. After all, it was good sound metal – no "white" to cause trouble by melting. Like all Hunslets, No. 5 was steaming well, the valves were blowing off gently and the fire was good, despite the loose state of the sootbox door. That fireclay in the smokebox seemed to have done the trick! It was pleasant in the midday sun, there was porter for everyone and, sure, there was no need to feel the bearings – until they'd cooled anyway! Water into the left hand tank at the standpipe; ease up to let '8T' do likewise, then slowly up the yard, driven by our raconteur this time, over the crossing to the water-tower, and fill the right-hand tank too. Here it was noticed there was a rusty bulge at the patch – spotted at Lower Camp indeed, but now it was weeping water – what a pity it wasn't over the troublesome axle! Anyway, the road was getting blocked. (This watering procedure differed with various crews: some filled the left tanks at the standpipe and reversed the entire train back, and entered the loop to fill the right-hand tanks; especially if there was a passing train in the opposite direction). Drivers of carts were getting impatient to cross. The porter ran up with another bucket found in the derelict buildings. It was filled and left on the footplate. So, away, into the cutting and up the steep climb to Baunogue top, after a farewell to the Foreman and mate who were returning to Tralee. At least the rail was nice and dry. On to Ballinaclare Gate and a wave for the crossing keeper's wife and children. Four trains in a day are quite an event here: usually it's two Friday and two (returning) Saturday: and only once a month at that!

Never short of steam in that long boiler, No. 5T was blowing off as she topped the summit. With synchronised movement, driver and footplate passenger sloshed buckets of water at the motion either side: most of it missing the target, while the fireman opened the firedoor, and they coasted down through Garrynadur to Lispole viaduct, which was approached on a nasty curve. An incredible shuddering shake convulsed the entire train, to the tune of frantic whistle signals for Guard's braking, and see-sawing of the centre couplings, as the train stopped for the viaduct – just! No. 5T was uncoupled and trotted alone across the spidery structure, carrying on round the bend to the overgrown Lispole platform close by the farm. At one time, past goods trains had been scheduled for long stops here and there had been a short siding. At any rate, this stop was to fill buckets at the nearby stream. Again, cold water fizzled fussily on hot metal. While oil was being coaxed where needed, No. 8T appeared with her train and gingerly coupled up behind. Ho, then for Dingle! – but not before a bit of excitement at Garfinney crossing where a cyclist stood mesmerised, bicycle across the track, despite the fact he could see (and hear!) the train on the "long straight" for about a mile! Then the final creep down the hill into Dingle, where '6T' was simmering at the head of her short train, already loaded with cows. She wheezed throatily away, as the in-coming train arrived, and duly passed the third portion with '1T' and '2T' at Annascaul.

On Fair Day following, '5T' piloted the first portion out, with '8T' again, and made it back to Tralee, despite a soft day and a suicidal gamecock at Lispole; but it was a sick engine that limped into the yard and, uncoupling, eased thankfully into the shed without being turned. There she remained – wrong way round – until the crane came to the Broad Gauge station to take her to Inchicore. This was the 20-ton steam crane from Limerick, the one at Tralee not being hefty enough. No. 5T was propelled "dead" to the exchange siding by No. 2T when steamed for the October Fair, 1949, and stood there several weeks until the crane came to load her. Later in 1950 the same was done for '6T'; neither returned again to Tralee. Mr Garrett, the Locomotive Foreman at Tralee, said he wasn't sending-in any more engines for repair: they would just be drafted away to other sections. The Dingle would have to make do with what running repairs could be provided on the spot. He was left with only Nos. 1T, 2T and 8T to run the monthly cattle trains.

After a long period out to grass at Inchicore works, No. 5T was taken in by the fitters and overhauled. She got a new smokebox (with wheel-type key), "pop" safety valves and new side tanks. She had lost only the big lamp bracket of her Dingle fittings when she was transported by rail to Ballinamore on the Cavan & Leitrim section, late in 1950. They subsequently removed the bell and cowcatcher. Her toolboxes remained at Tralee where they were used as extra sandboxes, primarly on No. 2T whose "own" sandboxes were noted for constipation!

No. 5T was worked hard on the Cavan & Leitrim, both on passenger and coal trains until that line closed in 1959, when she worked a number of demolition trains. Edgar Mead had secured her for Preservation in the USA during one of his visits to the Cavan & Leitrim, along with one of the C&L's own pretty little 4-4-0 locomotives. They were shipped out to Massachusetts, in October, 1959, along with some carriage stock that included an ex-T&D coach. The C&L loco, "Lady Edith" was restored to steaming condition and leased out; but No. 5T remained outdoors for 20 years: a static exhibit. Her subsequent rescue is detailed in the next chapter.

170. AWAITING OVERHAUL: Her T&D service over (at any rate for more than 40 years!) No. 5T is seen at Inchicore, awaiting attention in October 1949. Her toolboxes have remained at Tralee, but she is otherwise complete. *(R. N. Clements)*

171. THE TRAVELS OF No. 5: Seen here at Ballinamore, Cavan & Leitrim Section, in 1956. Note they have given her a pair of diminutive toolboxes. She has lost her cowcatcher but still has the bell, and a painted numeral on the tank side replaces the GSR numberplate. *(T. J. Edgington)*

Chapter 10
STEAMING BACK TO BLENNERVILLE

In 1985 decisions were made in the USA to reclocate the huge Steamtown railway preservation centre from Bellows Falls, Vermont, to Scranton, Pennsylvania. Space was more limited at the new site and priority was given to American prototypes. Tralee & Dingle No. 5T thus became surplus to requirements. There was a stirring of interest in the UK and Ireland and a Mr Dallimore of Hornchurch in Essex – writing to the railway press – began to co-ordinate an attempt to raise funds. Unfortunately he died suddenly and the scheme lapsed. However, journalist Peter Levy had seen the appeal and he set to, forming a fund-raising group: The Tralee & Dingle Engine Committee who, along with well-wishers in the USA, contacted Edgar Mead, the owner of 5T. Mr Mead had already got token acceptance of the loco at the New Jersey Museum of Transport, but he was moved by the thought that she should return to Ireland, and not only did he donate the locomotive, but also cleared things with the New Jersey Museum.

There was some competition to claim the locomotive from the Leeds (England) Industrial Museum (No. 5T was built by Hunslet of Leeds, of course) and from the Ulster Transport Museum, who already had a number of Irish Narrow Gauge locomotives in their collection. Luckily Edgar Mead decided in favour of return to Tralee.

There then remained the little matter of shipping costs . . . $15,000 to be precise! A major donation came from Con Kelly of Boston, whose father had worked as a steam raiser on the T&DLR and who had lived for many years in the station house at Blennerville.

So finally the negotiations were completed and No. 5T began the journey from the New Jersey Museum to Port Highway and thence aboard the "Atlantic Compass", a container ship, in early July, 1986 . . . twenty-seven years almost since she had left the Cavan & Leitrim for the trip to America. The ship docked at Liverpool on 23rd July and 5T was craned on to a low-loader for movement to Fleetwood, from where Pandoro Ro-Ro transported her to Dublin. She arrived in Dublin on 4th August and Tralee on 7th, being unloaded on the 8th. An early visitor to see her was the Deputy Premier, Dick Spring.

After examination at Tralee by the Great Southern Railway Preservation Society (GSRPS) members who formed the Tralee-Dingle Locomotive Committee, revealing that she was in good enough order to warrant restoration to working condition, she was placed on public exhibition. Long queues of people were happy to pay 80p per visit to see her, a good augury for the restoration project.

The Dingle Engine Committee moved her to the GSRPS workshops at Mallow and established links with Tralee UDC and the Irish Training and Employment Agency (FAS) training schemes which were involved in the superb restoration of the old windmill at Blennerville – always a landmark in photos of the T&DLS at Blennerville – which had been built in the 1790s but had been derelict from the 1880s.[1]

They envisaged a project to run a mile of 3ft gauge line on the old T&DLR trackbed from Basin to Blennerville and for it to be far enough advanced to have 5T in steam for the T&DLR Centenary in 1991. The scheme was also linked with the future restoration of the nearby Tralee Ship Canal.[2]

During 1989 No. 5T was moved back to Blennerville where a loco shed had been erected for her and where FAS could begin initial restoration work. Much help and expertise came from the North York Moors Railway (NYMR) in England who repaired boiler and firebox, provided training and overall supervision of the two-year restoration. In the event things took a little longer and 5T missed the Centenary, being first steamed in June 1992. Shannon Free Airport Development and Tralee UDC also provided funds or carried out contributory works.[3]

In January 1990 the Tralee-Dingle Steam Railway Company was incorporated, under the Chairmanship of Ned O'Shea a Tralee businessman, and including the original committee as well as representatives of the local authority, businesses and the Tourist industry. The Secretary, John Griffin, provided much of the drive and enthusiasm for the project that saw it through to the official opening in 1994.[4]

The Committee's immediate priority was to re-acquire the former trackbed from private owners. Tralee UDC accomplished this and leased it back to the Company at a nominal rent.

Irish Rail provided free technical advice on the tracklaying and cheap sleepers from the disused North Kerry line. FAS trainees working on the trackbed were supervised by Irish Rail staff and the work included not only a bridge of 15-metre span over the Lee at Ballyard marshes, but an existing road/rail bridge decking also had to be replaced. Due to the continued flooding, the new line is laid about a metre higher than the old. New platforms have been built at the Tralee (Ballyard) terminus and at Blennerville Mill.

During 1989 another GSRPS group discovered two derelict ex-Tralee & Dingle coaches in Co. Kilkenny, in use as garden sheds. The interior seating ("The garden seats" – Fr Senan Moynihan had called them once, with unconscious prediction!) was still intact. Whether they can in due time be restored or made available is yet to be decided.

Coaches were obviously needed, however, and in 1990 an Irish Rail executive visiting Spain happened to see a rake of disused metre-gauge coaches. After due

172. ON EXHIBIT AT STEAMTOWN, USA. Seen here at Bellows Falls, Vermont in 1968. *(C. M. Whitehouse)*

173. ARRIVAL AT TRALEE: On low-loader, 7th August 1986. *(P. Levy)*

174. ON DISPLAY/FUND-RAISING: Seen here during August 1986, in Tralee with display boards setting out the story of her life and rescue.
(D. Parkes)

175. Awaiting restoration in the skeleton of the new shed at Blennerville in 1989. *(D. Parkes)*

TRALEE & DINGLE RAILWAY (IRELAND)

The Chairman & Directors of
Tralee - Dingle Steam Railway Company
have the pleasure of inviting

Mr. David Rowlands

to the Official Opening of The Tralee - Blennerville Steam Railway
by Mr. Dick Spring, T.D.
Tanaiste & Minister for Foreign Affairs
at Ballyard Station, Tralee, on Saturday July 10th 1993 at 12.30pm
and afterwards at Blennerville Windmill Visitor Centre.

R.S.V.P. Tel: 066-28888, before July 8th **Beidh an-failte romhat**

negotiation, these four, metal-bodied coaches were purchased and shipped to Tralee. Four bogies were re-gauged to 3ft by Storey of Morpeth, while the bodies and interiors of two coaches were restored at Blennerville by FAS trainees guided by NYMR and Irish Rail staff. These two are currently in use.

And so it all came together. In January 1994 over a thousand invitees and guests were present in Tralee for the first special trips to Blennerville prior to the formal opening on 1st April.

Services currently run from April to October, daily, with trains leaving Tralee (Ballyard) on the hour and returning from Blennerville on the half-hour. Full details can be obtained from the Tralee-Dingle Steam Railway Co., Town Hall, Prince's Quay, Tralee, Co. Kerry, Eire. Telephone: 066 28888, fax 066 27444.

1. D. Parkes, A Railway Migrant Returns, *Steam at Mallow,* Journal of the GSRPS, No. 2, 1986-7 p.19.
2. D. Hickey, *Cork Examiner,* 6 January, 1990.
3. D. Gaffney, Chairman's Letter, *Southern Steam,* Newsletter of the GSRPS, January, 1990.
4. J. Griffin, "Tralee & Dingle back on the rails", *Railway World,* May, 1994, pp. 41-3.

176. Her replica number/works plate as originally fitted.

177. Work progressing at the site of the new station at Blennerville in 1992. The original track ran alongside the road at left. *(J. St. Ledger)*

178 & 179. Two 1995 scenes of the current operation. No. 5T with re-gauged metre-gauge coaches alongside the road, and on railway right of way, both near Blennerville. *(J. St. Ledger)*

POSTSCRIPT
The Tralee and Dingle Today – by Dave Cooper

Visitors to the Dingle Peninsula today hoping to find a wealth of relics of the line will not be completely disappointed as there is still a wealth of knowledge and history in the memories of the local people who are only too willing to impart tales and experiences, despite the fact that the line closed to traffic over 40 years ago.

Hard evidence of the line's existence is somewhat harder to find in some places and in others the shape of a bank or wall can almost play tricks on the enthusiast looking for that item of interest, indeed the writer was fooled at Camp when he discovered the remains of the turntable pit, the land around the pit having been landscaped as a picnic area, the wall surrounding the pit – the top of which was once at ground level – now stands some two feet higher than ground level. Do look hard, there is more than first meets the eye, as in most of Ireland, change is slow and even 40 years cannot entirely hide all the line's features.

To try to follow the old trackbed from Tralee now presents a problem as the old station site appears to have entirely disappeared beneath a new shopping area and any route that had existed through the town is long gone. There still stands the crossing keeper's cottage where the line crossed the Blennerville Road but within the town proper, all is now lost to progress.

As one crosses the Blennerville Road today it is impossible to miss the new Water Sports arena, and next to this splendid facility, a railway station. The town of Tralee sports, once again, a section of the Tralee and Dingle Railway, rebuilt on the old trackbed towards Blennerville and hauled by the restored No. 5 visitors can now travel the first few miles of the old line in the comfort of modern coaches imported from the Continent and restored and painted to match the line's old livery. Facilities at the ends of the line are not extensive but the pleasure of riding behind No. 5 should not be missed.

On from Blennerville the line can be traced for a mile or so across the fields but is soon lost under the developments and extensions to front gardens that edge the road towards Camp.

The Camp junction station site does offer some relics of the line in the shape of the water tank and base, now in use as a Public Works Department office, and the remains of the turntable pit as previously mentioned. The water tower now sports a commemorative plaque, explaining for the benefit of the less knowledgeable visitor that it is a relic of the T&D. "Fitzgerald's Bar", captured in many a view of the station in working days, still stands, now called the Junction Bar. Little altered structurally, it has been tastefully updated inside and makes the most of its railway heritage with a fine display of photographs of the line.

If one chooses to follow the line to the resort of Castlegregory, the visitor may well enjoy the drive and the exploration, however, Castlegregory station buildings were demolished in 1994 to make way for a new house on the site.

Following the line on towards Dingle from Camp is possible without difficulty, care should be taken however, as this is now a busy road with few places to stop. The first major feature is Curraduff Bridge. The scene of the fatal 1893 accident, the bridge is still in sound order and can be viewed from the road with ease.

Following the line on brings one into open country and the famed Glenagalt Bank. It is not that difficult to imagine the loco powering up this fearsome incline. The figure of 1 in 30 means very little somehow until you see the ascent in reality. Reaching the top of the series of climbs, the trackbed passes under the remains of the aptly named structure at Glenagalt Bridge, summit of the line.

On reaching the pleasant town of Annascaul, it is still possible to see both the water tanks and the bridge over the River Owenascaul even if the bridge is now swathed in a coat of ivy.

Lispole comes as something of a surprise along the road towards Dingle and this surprise is compounded to wonder when one realises the gradient that led onto Lispole viaduct. The route of the line can still be clearly seen and should be appreciated for the feature it surely is, when viewed along with the slowly decaying remains of the once handsome viaduct. Standing truncated in a field as it does, the viaduct looks somewhat forlorn today but was surely a splendid sight when occupied by a hard working loco and train.

After leaving Lispole, the line swung down onto the almost flat plain just prior to entering Dingle. This area of the landscape today can yield almost no evidence that the line ever existed. That is until when approaching Dingle itself, one is confronted by the sight of Dingle station house, cleverly hiding its past under a modern usage as a funeral director's premises but the building still retains enough features to make it impossible to miss. Indeed the train shed that once protected passengers from the elements also appears to have survived as part of the adjacent motor vehicle business, a strange irony.

In addition, Dingle station water tank still survives, somewhat battered and almost hidden by trees just adjacent to the road, yet this was the feature that gave the writer the clue to the station's location.

Unfortunately, no evidence of any features relating to the harbour line now exist, Dingle has seen extensive development within the last 10 years and all traces are now gone.

THE LINE TODAY

180. This was the view at Dingle harbour in June 1974, looking towards Dingle, with the trackbed on the right in use as a footpath. *(A.J. Powell)*

181. Dingle station in July 1995, in use as a funeral director's premises, with garages behind. *(Dave Cooper)*

182. Lispole viaduct, pictured during a visit by the Kerry & District Archaeological Society in 1978. The view is substantially unchanged today. *(Author's Collection)*

THE LINE TODAY

183. The disused trackbed at Ballinsare, pictured on 14 June 1974. *(A.J. Powell)*

184. The water tank at the site of Annascaul station, July 1995. *(Dave Cooper)*

185. The overbridge at the top of Glenagalt bank, looking towards Dingle, a view taken during the hot summer of 1995. *(Dave Cooper)*

CURRADUFF BRIDGES

186. Curraduff Bridge, photographed in 1978, and still surviving in good order today. *(Author's Collection)*

187. The "new" bridge on the Curraduff diversion, pictured in August 1979. Co-author Walter McGrath poses on the decking. *(Author's Collection)*

Appendix One
WAY AND WORKS

Colonel Marindin's Report to the Board of Trade on the Curraduff disaster included some factual statements on the original constructional proposals and on the practice and operation of the system. Some aspects are worth quoting, as follows:

Extracts from Proposals

The undertaking consists of a tramway (chiefly on the public road) from the stations of the Great Southern and Western and the Limerick and Kerry Railways at Tralee to the pier at Dingle, with a branch of the town of Castle Gregory. It is divided into four tramways, Nos. 1, 2, 3 and 4.

	On Roads			Through Fields, &c.			Total		
	M	F	C	M	F	C	M	F	C
Tramway No. 1	26	1	8	1	1	3¾	30	6	1¾
Tramway No. 2	0	1	7½	0	1	7	0	3	4½
Tramway No. 3	4	2	7	1	6	1	6	1	1
Tramway No. 4	0	0	6	0	2	9¾	0	3	5¾
Total	31	1	8½	6	4	1½	37	6	3

Tramway No. 1 commences at the Tralee station of the Limerick and Kerry Railway, passes through the town of Tralee, crosses the River Lee close to and at the east side of the bridge over it near Blennerville, passes through the village of Blennerville, and close to the villages of Anniscaul and Camp, and terminates a quarter of a mile from the town of Dingle in a field beside the public road leading from Dingle to Tralee in the townland of Farran and parish of Dingle.

Tramway No. 2 commences at the termination of Tramway No. 1, and is a continuation of its, passes close to the entrance gate to the revenue station, and along and near the edge of the strand, and terminates at the north end of Dingle Pier.

Tramway No. 3 commences by a junction with Tramway No. 1 in the townland of Knockglassmore, and parish of Kilgobban, at 9 miles 3 furlongs 2 chains on Tramway No. 1, and running principally upon the public road it terminates at the south end of the town of Castle Gregory.

Tramway No. 4 commences beside the Great Southern and Western Railway six chains to the east of the passenger station at Tralee, and terminates by a junction with Tramway No. 1, at 1 furlong 3 chains on that tramway.

The gauge proposed is three feet.
Tramway No. 1:–
The steepest gradient is 1 in 30.
The ruling gradient is 1 in 30.
The sharpest curve has a radius of 2½ chains.
Tramway No. 2:–
The steepest gradient is 1 in 41.
The ruling gradient is 1 in 41.
The sharpest curve has a radius of 9½ chains.
Tramway No. 3:–
The steepest gradient is 1 in 32.
The ruling gradient is 1 in 32.
The sharpest curve has a radius of 4½ chains.
Tramway No. 4:–
The steepest gradient is 1 in 66.
The ruling gradient is 1 in 66.
The sharpest curve has a radius of 2½ chains.

On Tramway No. 1 the gradients are favourable from the commencement to 9 miles 4 furlongs 5 chains, but at this point begins a long ascent to summit at 13 miles 1 furlong 1 chain, the gradients being as follows:–

	M	F	C
Rising 1 in 38 for	0	4	0
Level	0	0	7
Rising 1 in 30	0	2	3
Level	0	0	3
Rising 1 in 30	1	0	1
Rising 1 in 31	1	5	2
Total length	3	4	6

On this incline the line is fairly straight with the following four exceptions:–On the 1 in 38 (in the middle of it), there is a curve of seven chains radius for a length of five chains, on the first level portion there is a curve of three chains radius for its whole length, on the second 1 in 30 (2½ furlongs from the top of it), there are two curves reversing of four chains and five chains radius respectively, for a length of six chains, and on the 1 in 31, three furlongs from the bottom of it, there is a curve of five chains radius for a length of one furlong.

At the summit there is a level portion for a length of five chains, and then a gradient of 1 in 30 falling towards Dingle for a length of one mile; on this incline the line is tolerably straight with one exception, there being a curve of nine chains radius near the top of it for a length of 4½ chains; on the remaining portion of this Tramway (No. 1) there are three other inclines falling towards Dingle, viz., at 17½ miles of 1 in 34 for a length of a mile; at 19 miles of 1 in 30, 1 in 31, 1 in 32 and 1 in 11 for a total length of 1 mile 7 furlongs 8 chains, the 1 in 30 (10 chains long) being at the top of this incline, and at 25¼ miles of 1 in 30 for a length of 1 mile 1 furlong; on the last of these inclines (1 in 30) there is a short curve of nine chains radius; on the other two inclines there is no bad curve.

Generally where the tramway runs along and upon the public road, it is intended to form it upon a raised path (like a footpath) along the side of it, but where it passes through streets or villages, it is intended that the upper surface of the rails shall be on the level of the surface of the road.

Where the tramway shall be upon the public road or streets, and the upper surface of the rails on the level of the surface thereof, it is proposed that the spaces between rails and sleepers shall be filled with ordinary macadam well grouted and rolled, the flange of the wheels forming their own groove.

The rails proposed to be used are intended to be steel, Vignoles pattern, weighing 40lbs to the yard, fished at the joints with steel fish-plates, to be secured to sleepers by dog-spikes and fang-bolts at joints and intermediate places.

The sleepers are proposed to be of timber, 9 inches by 4 inches and 6 feet long, laid 2 feet 10 inches apart, except at joints, where they are intended to be 1 foot 6 inches apart on a bed of ballast, the lower 6 inches of which is intended to be pitched.

Where the tramway shall be upon a raised path at the side of the road, it is proposed that a channel course shall be formed at the road side of the tramway connecting with built gully-traps and drain pipes laid underneath the tramway connecting with roadside ditches.

It is proposed to have passing places at intervals of about one every three miles, the additional line required for these and for sidings will be laid generally upon land to be acquired for the purpose.

It is proposed to have eight stations, viz.:–

	M	F	C
Tralee–			
Blennerville, at	2	2	0
Junction of Tramway No. 3	9	3	0
Camp, at	10	4	0
Annascaul, at	19	4	5
Lispole, at	26	0	0
Dingle–			
Castle Gregory–			

Locomotives proposed to have two pair of wheels (coupled). Wheel base, six feet; weight not to exceed eight tons on a pair of wheels. Passenger carriages to be constructed on bogie frames, and to have inside longitudinal seats; weight about five tons. Cattle trucks to be capable of carrying eight to ten cattle; goods waggons to weight about two tons.

It is proposed to make use of 33 public road bridges and culverts (varying in span from 4 feet to 31 feet), either wholly or partially (some of them having to be widened from 3 feet to 9 feet). All of these bridges with the exception of one (at 3 miles 3 furlongs 8 chains on Tramway No. 1) appear sufficiently strong – for the tramway traffic.

I recommend the following modifications to be carried out in construction of these tramways:–

That where the tramway is upon the road, and the uppermost surface of the rails on the level of the surface of the road, the rail to be used shall be a grooved rail, and that the surface of the road shall be finished with such paving or metalling as the county surveyor may require.

That where a grooved rail is used it shall be laid upon longitudinal timber sleepers, or upon a bed of cement concrete 12 inches deep, below the surface of the road, and that the rails shall be kept in gauge with three wrought iron tie-bars in each rail, in straight lines as well as in curves.

That where the Vignoles rail is used the sleepers shall be not more than 2 feet 6 inches apart (centres), and that they shall be boxed up to their upper surface in the spaces between, and also for a width of at least 12 inches outside their ends.

That where the tramway shall be on a raised path on the side of the road there shall be such kerbing, pitched slope, or walling, as the county surveyor may require, between the tramway and the roadway. Where curbing is used its height shall not exceed 8 inches above the surface of the road. That the clear width between the fence at the field side of the tramway and the rail next to it, and between the outer edge of the curbing and the rail next to it, shall be such as the county surveyor may require, and that the drainage of the roads shall be provided for by such drains, under and parallel to the tramway as the county surveyor may require.

That the Vignoles rail shall weigh not less than 45lbs. to the yard, and the grooved rail not less than 56lbs. to the yard.

I recommend that all works upon or in connection with any public road be carried out to the satisfaction of the county surveyor.

I recommend that special and ample brake power shall be provided and always ready for use on the heavy inclines.

With reference to the general engineering merits of the undertaking, I am of opinion that, having regard to the object of uniting Dingle and Castle Gregory with Tralee by means of a road tramway, that object could not be better attained than by the route the proposed tramway take.

The country is mountainous, and although there are long heavy inclines I am of opinion that with powerful engines and an assistant engine for heavy loads on those inclines, the proposed tramway may be efficiently worked.

(Signed) BENJAMIN F. FLEMING,
35, Dawson Street, Dublin,
9th July, 1884.

Factual observations on construction and operation

Description of the Line

The line is single, except at stations, and the gauge is 3ft.

The main line from Tralee to Dingle, on which the accident happened, is 31 miles 52 chains in length, of which 27 miles 61 chains are laid along the side of the public road, and may be considered as a tramway, the remaining 3 miles 71 chains being a light railway through fields and mountain land.

The permanent-way, which is laid in accordance with the specification, mostly consists of:–

1. Flat-bottomed steel rails, weighing 45lbs. per yard, fished at the joints, and secured to the

sleepers by six 3/8-inch fang-bolts, and 16 dog-spikes, to each 30ft. rail.

2. Transverse sleepers of larch, Scotch fir, or oak, laid 1ft. 8in. apart at the joints, and 2ft. 10in. apart elsewhere, the smallest of the sleepers being 5ft. 11in. in length and 8in. x 4in. in section.
3. Ballast of broken stone.

The steepest authorised gradient has an inclination of 1 in 30, and the sharpest authorised curve has a radius of 3 chains.

Mode of Working

The line is ordered by the Board of Trade to be worked, and the Company has given an undertaking to work it, dated 2nd March 1891, in accordance with the following rule:–

"The line between (1) Tralee and Camp Junction, (2) Camp Junction and Annascaul, (3) Annascaul and Dingle, (4) Camp Junction and Castle Gregory, shall be worked by only one engine in steam, or by two or more coupled together, at one and the same time, such engine or engines to carry a distinct staff for each of such sections."

Limits of Speed

The speed of trains throughout this light railway is limited by the Order in Council to 25 miles an hour at any point, and by Board of Trade Order, dated 13th May 1891, issued after the inspection of the line, and following the special recommendations of Major-General Hutchinson, C.B., the officer who made the inspection, the speed was restricted at certain places, to the following extent, viz.:–To 12 miles an hour where the railway is laid along the side of a road, to six miles an hour through any town or village, to two miles an hour at certain street and road crossings, and to five miles an hour.

(1) At the oblique crossings of all roads when approached on the level or on a falling gradient;

(2) On the sharp curves on each side of the viaduct at 10 miles 58 chains on the journeys from Dingle to Tralee.

A further limit was imposed by the Company, enjoining a speed of six miles an hour all the way down the incline from Glen-na-galt to and beyond Curraduff Viaduct as will be seen from the following extracts from the instructions issued to the servants of the Company, applying, among other matters, to the use of brakes and speed of trains:–

"Instructions to Engine Drivers and Guards. – Before starting at the beginning of each journey the train must be examined to see that the brake fittings are in good working order and tested, also that the engine and all vehicles are properly coupled and in working order, and that the tender hand-brake is in proper working condition, and carriage and waggon axles oiled and trimmed."

* * *

"Before starting the guard must see that the proper vacuum is registered by the indicator in his van for the effectual use of the brake.

"All up trains must come to a dead stop at the top of Glen-na-galt incline, and, if more than three vehicles are on, to pin (*sic*) down the waggon brakes, and the speed to Scrallaghbeg Cottage not to exceed six miles an hour. After passing this point the brakes may be lifted. The engine hand-brake must also be used on this incline."

* * *

"Speed of Trains, &c. – The speed of trains on approaching the junction should not exceed five miles an hour, and should be reduced to two miles an hour when passing over the facing-points. Drivers must be prepared to pull up at once if at any station or gate the signals are against them.

"The speed between Tralee terminus and Great Southern and Western Company's terminus not to exceed two miles an hour. The speed over the crossings on the line to be reduced to 10 miles an hour, and over the crossings near Tralee to five miles an hour. The speed on the county roads, where the line is tramway not to exceed 12 miles an hour, and where the line is fenced off not to exceed 25 miles per hour, slowing off to 10 miles an hour for the sharp curves or down the steep gradients of 1 in 30.

"The drivers must always be prepared to pull up if necessary when on the road in passing restive horses, cattle, &c.

"In crossing the road at Blennerville from the curve to the station the speed must on no account exceed two miles an hour.

"In crossing the road at 17¾ miles not to exceed two miles an hour.

"At the oblique crossings of all road s the speed must not exceed five miles an hour.

"On sharp curves on each side of the viaduct at 10 miles 58 chains not to exceed five miles an hour.

"In crossing Lispole Bridge 10 miles an hour."

From GSR/CIE permanent way records:–

The last 2-3 miles into Dingle (excluding the pier branch) were relaid in 1936 with 68½ and 72lb. rail from the Cork, Blackrock and Passage line, with second-hand sleepers, soleplates and spikes and new fangbolts.

In 1933 Castlegregory Junction was relaid with 74lb. N. Cumberland rail (ex-GSR), second-hand sleepers and new spikes and fangbolts.

Appendix Two
RULES AND REGULATIONS

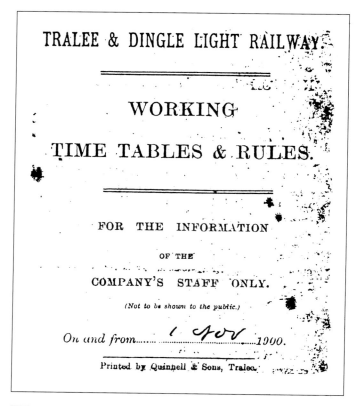

TRALEE & DINGLE LIGHT RAILWAY.

WORKING TIME TABLES & RULES.

FOR THE INFORMATION

OF THE

COMPANY'S STAFF ONLY.

(Not to be shown to the public.)

On and from 1 Nov 1900.

Printed by Quinnell & Sons, Tralee.

NOTICE TO ALL SERVANTS OF THE COMPANY.

It is expected that all Servants of the Company, and more particularly those who are employed in the working of the trains, will constantly exercise the utmost vigilance while performing their duties, so as to avoid accidents and to secure the safety of life and property.

Facing Points—The greatest care must be taken by Stationmasters and all concerned to see that Facing Points are always secure for approaching Trains, and made for the proper road.

Departure Times—The times shown for Trains at Intermediate Stations are those at which Trains should be ready to leave the Stations.

Extra Carriages—Stationmasters to be careful to provide extra carriages for increased number of passengers, when necessary, and to notify Manager.

3

Delays—Stationmasters are to send special reports and explanations of delays at Stations beyond time allowed.

Goods Traffic—Goods Traffic to be worked by all Trains if found necessary.

Guards must call out the names of Stations on arrival, and see that Passengers change into right Carriages at the Junction.

No official or servant of the Company will be allowed to travel without a ticket or a pass.

No person is to be allowed travel on the Engines without permission to do so.

COLLECTION AND EXAMINATION OF TICKETS.
DOWN TRAINS.

Tralee—Trains to be checked before starting.

At stopping places Guards to collect the fares and issue tickets.

Basin—Guard to issue ticket if necessary.

Blennerville—Tickets to be issued and Blennerville tickets collected.

4

Castlegregory Junction—Tickets to be issued, and Main Line and Branch Trains checked before starting. Castlegregory Junction Tickets to be taken up.

Aunascaul—Tickets to be issued. Passengers to be checked joining Train. Aunascaul tickets taken up.

Lispole—Tickets to be issued and Passengers checked joining Train. Lispole tickets taken up.

Dingle—To collect tickets and have Train examined for lost property, &c , immediately on arrival.

Passengers without tickets will be charged from the Station from which the Train originally started, unless Guard can say where they joined Train

COLLECTION AND EXAMINATION OF TICKETS
UP TRAINS.

Dingle—Tickets to be issued and Trains checked before starting.

Lispole—Tickets to be issued and checked as Passengers join train. Lispole tickets collected.

Aunascaul—Tickets to be issued and checked as Passengers join train. Aunascaul tickets to be taken up.

Castlegregory Junction—Tickets to be issued and Junction tickets taken up. Main Line and Branch Trains to be checked before starting.

Blennerville—Tickets issued and examined as Passengers join Train. Blennerville tickets taken up.

Basin—All tickets taken up. Ticket collector from Tralee to assist in checking.

Tralee—Trains to be searched for Lost Property, &c.

BRANCH.

Castlegregory—Tickets to be issued for Up Trains, and Trains checked before starting. Tickets to be collected on arrival of Down Trains.

Trains examined on arrival for Lost Property, &c.

At Terminal Stations—Stationmasters and Guards must see that brake tubes are properly connected and tested before Train starts, and that all couplings are properly secured; also the van doors are locked. Passengers must not be permitted to open the door whilst Train is in motion.

All Tickets, when collected, to be punched and sent to Tralee. Special care must be taken in punching Return Tickets at Stations not to punch the Return half of tickets unless otherwise directed.

The Engine Bells to be used on county roads, before passing houses, passengers, &c.; using the whistle as little as possible.

The bell to be rung at Terminal Stations five minutes before starting time.

Booking Offices to be opened for the issue of tickets fifteen minutes before time Train is due to start, and closed punctually when time is up.

Dublin time to be observed at all Stations

In starting Train Guard will signal to Driver by green flag and whistle.

To stop, if necessary, for any cause, Guard must use his whistle and brake.

INSTRUCTIONS TO ENGINE DRIVERS AND GUARDS.

Before starting at the beginning of each journey the Train must be examined to see that the brake fittings are in good working order and tested, also that the engine and all vehicles are properly coupled and in working order, and that the tender handbrake is in proper working condition, and carriage and waggon axles oiled and trimmed.

Ordinary stoppages must not be made too quickly, and to avoid this the brake must be applied slightly some distance from where the Train is to be stopped, and the application of it gradually and uniformly increased until the Train comes to a stand. It must at all times be released very cautiousiy to prevent the jerk consequent on the rebound of the carriage buffers and the engine shooting ahead, and to avoid subjecting the couplings to undue strain and the Passengers to discomfort

The Up Trains on approaching the Junction will give one whistle; the Down Trains two, and the Branch Trains three whistles.

Three short sharp whistles will signify to the Guard to put on his hand-brake tightly, and release it on one sharp whistle being given.

Before starting the Guard must see that the proper vacuum is registered by the indicator in his van for the effectual use of the brake.

All Trains must come to a dead stop at the bridge at the top of Glounagalt incline, and, if more than three vehicles are on, to pin down the waggon brakes, and the speed to Scrallaghbeg cottage not to exceed 6 miles an hour. The engine hand-brake must also be used on this incline.

If necessary Driver must stop when passing restive horses, cattle, &c., if he sees any indication of danger.

Guards and all concerned must be particular to see that the carriage doors are not opened when Train is in motion, owing to the close running of train to gate posts, buildings, trees, &c.

Before starting the register of vacuum shown on Engine and Guard's Van must at least be 18 inches, and same *maintained when running*, and on no account is a Train to be made up unless the breaks on all vehicles are in good working order and properly connected. The Driver and Guard must at all times keep the *whole Train* under control with the vacuum brake, and see that same works on each vehicle, and for no cause whatever must a Driver cut off the vacuum between his Engine and the Train.

Before descending the steep incline at Glounagalt (either way) the Engine driver must have a full working pressure of steam (viz., at blowing off point 130lbs to the square inch), and that his guage glass shows sufficient water in the boiler to ensure same against burning (viz., at least 4 inches). All Trains must come to a dead stop at this point, and the wagon hand brakes pinned down *in addition to the vacuum brake*, using the Engine and van hand brake also, and the speed *on no account* to exceed *six miles an hour*, slowing off to five miles an hour when passing Scrallabeg gate crossing, and five miles an hour on approach and crossing Curraduff bridge.

The Guard will also be held responsible to see that those duties are properly performed.

On Glounagalt incline and other steep inclines the Guard must not interfere with the vacuum handle in his van *but leave its application altogether under the control of the driver.*

At Glenmore Bridge the speed must be reduced to five miles an hour, also the approach to Lispole Bridge (either way) to be five miles per hour.

At Tounavane curve the speed to be five miles an hour, and at the approach to Ballydunlea Bridge, on the curve between Blennerville and Tralee, the speed must not exceed five miles an hour.

The speed down Kelly's Height into Castlegregory *must never exceed six miles an hour.*

On main line (between Castlegregory Junction and Dingle) the loads of Trains will be as follows :—One carriage, one

van, and five loaded wagons (or five empty . If ~~four~~ 6 carriages are on Train no waggons must be attached.

Between Tralee and Castlegregory a Train may consist of eight vehicles, but if over this number, a second van and Guard must be provided.

At night time Guards on getting the word to start from Stations must show the Driver a Green Light.

Drivers must use great care when passing Station Platforms, and not proceed faster than *Four Miles an Hour.*

SPEED OF TRAINS, &c.

The speed of Trains on approaching the Junction should not exceed five miles an hour, and should be reduced to two miles an hour when passing over the facing points. Drivers must be prepared to pull up at once if at any station or gate the signals are against them.

The speed between Tralee Terminus and Great Southern and Western Railway Company's Terminus not to exceed two miles an hour. The speed over the crossings on the line to be reduced to ten miles an hour, and over the crossings near Tralee to five miles an hour. The speed on the country roads where the line is Tramway not to exceed twelve miles an hour, and where the line is fenced off not to exceed twenty-five miles per hour, slowing off to ten miles an hour for the sharp curves or down the steep gradients of 1 in 30.

In crossing the road at Blennerville from the curve to the Station the speed must on no account exceed two miles an hour.

In crossing the road at 17¾ miles not to exceed two miles an hour.

At all the oblique crossings of all roads the speed must not exceed five miles an hour. On the sharp curves on each side of the viaduct at 10 miles 58 chains not to exceed five miles an hour.

In crossing Lispole bridge five miles an hour.

A Tablet or Train Staff must be carried with each train or engine, and without this no train or engine must be allowed to travel on the line.

Three Tablets are used, one between Tralee and Castlegregory Junction, one between Junction and Aunascaul, and one between Aunascual and Dingle.

Train Staff between Castlegregory Junction and Castlegregory.

At the Junctions and at Stations where Trains have to cross each other, all signals must be kept at "danger," except when required to be lowered to admit a Train, and when Trains having to pass each other are approaching the Station in opposite directions, and the signals have been lowered for one Train, they must not be lowered for the other Train until both Trains have come to a dead stop, and

the Signalman has seen that the line on which the other Train will arrive has been left quite clear.

The person in charge of the station for the time being is the sole person authorized to receive and deliver the staff through the Guard. The Guard will also be held accountable for this duty being properly performed.

INSTRUCTIONS TO GATEMEN, PLATELAYERS, &c.

On the approach of a Train the Gateman at crossings supplied with signals must first see that the gates are properly closed across the road, and then lower the arm of signal to "all right," and raise them to "danger" when train passes.

The Gatemen, on seeing the gates closed across the road for the approach of a Train where there is no signal, must show a white flag when all is right and a red flag after Train passes. (Lamps to be used instead of flags at night time). At the gates at the Basin a green flag must be shown when the gates are open for a Train and a red flag when Train has passed.

The speed around the curves between Tralee and Basin not to exceed 10 miles an hour, and reduced on approaching crossing gates to five miles an hour.

Milesmen must be particular to see that ballasting and stone do not get into the flange space at the crossings; they must make it their special duty to examine the crossings repeatedly.

R. A. PARKES,

General Manager.

Appendix Three
TIMETABLES

Early handbills with elaborate timetables, which were available from the "visitor" hotels in the 1890s give the impression – at a quick glance – of an intensive service of trains. Close inspection however shows that as with French light railways, most of the trains listed were for special occasions (the most regular being livestock specials for the fairs; excursions on Saints' days etc.). Columns alongside those giving the train times also gave fares in similar-looking units! What the intending traveller made of all this information – given the common inability to understand even the simplest timetable – we cannot imagine! There were normally only two trains in each direction per day, with connections for the Castlegregory Branch.

Basin was dropped as a stopping place or flag stop in the 1920s and not reinstated. Early timetables mention Tonevane as a flag stop, though not an "Official" station and no platform ever existed. The same was true of Puckisland (or Puc Island) between Lispole and Garrynadur. A halt at Ballinasare did not feature until the '20s.

Through trains from Tralee-Castlegregory and Castlegregory-Tralee did not appear until the 1930s but continued up to the end of passenger services in 1939.

On Sundays there were no regular trains, except for many years a monthly working out of Tralee at 3pm of empty stock (and dealers) for Dingle Pig Fair, held on the Monday. Many excursions were run on Sundays to coastal stations en route to Camp Junction and Castlegregory; particularly in the time of Tom O'Donnell MP when great attempts were made to provide extra excursion traffic to improve receipts. There were also a number of Sunday excursions to All-Ireland football matches and other sporting events, especially if Kerry were "at home". On occasion early morning Mass was said in the station yard at Dingle prior to the excursion leaving.

First class was offered from the start, and with only one composite coach available in 1891, a couple of the full-3rds had to be converted until composite stock could be afforded/built in 1898 and 1904/7.

There were no siding/loading facilities at Ballinclare, and special trains for the seasonal Autumn-Spring Fairs were loaded at Annascaul.

1931 Public Timetable

GREAT SOUTHERN RAILWAYS.

TRALEE AND DINGLE.

Single 1 Cl. s. d.	Single 3 Cl. s. d.	Return 1 Cl. s. d.	Return 3 Cl. s. d.	DOWN TRAINS		Week Days am	noon	am	pm	pm	..	Sundays am	pm	pm
				TRALEE	dep.	7 30	12 0	..	5 15	...	..	...	..	...
0 3	0 2	0 6	0 4	Basin	..	...	..	..	...	—	..	...	..	...
0 7	0 5	1 0	0 9	Blennerville	..	flag	flag	..	flag	...	—	...	.	..
1 6	1 0	2 8	1 9	Derrymore	..	flag	flag	...	flag	...	—	...	..	...
1 11	1 3	3 5	2 3	Castlegregory Junc.	arr.	8 10	1240	...	5 55	...		...	..	.
..		..	..	Castlegregory Junc.	dep.	..	1250	..	6 5	...	..	...	..	...
2 6	1 8	4 5	2 11	Deelis	..	..	flag	...	flag	...	..	...	..	...
2 10	1 11	5 0	3 5	Aughacasla	..	..	flag	..	flag	...	..	...	..	...
3 0	2 0	5 8	3 6	Castlegregory	arr.	.	1 20	...	6 35	...	..	...	..	..
..		..	..	Castlegregory Junc.	dep.	9 15		..	6 0	...	..	...	..	...
2 8	1 9	4 8	3 1	Glounagalt	..	flag	—	..	flag	...	..	...	..	...
3 0	2 0	5 8	3 6	Glenmore	..	flag	—	..	flag	...	..	...	..	...
3 5	2 3	6 0	4 0	Emalough	..	flag	—	..	flag	...	..	...	..	...
4 0	2 8	7 0	4 8	Annascaul	arr.	9 18	—	..	6 55	...	..	...	..	...
..	..	..	..	Do.	dep.	9 20	—	..	7 5	...	..	...	..	...
4 9	3 2	8 4	5 7	Garrynadur	..	flag	—	...	flag	...	..	...	..	...
5 1	3 5	8 11	6 0	Lispole	..	9 45	—	...	7 30	...	..	...	..	..
6 0	4 0	10 6	7 0	DINGLE	arr.	10 5	—	...	7 50	...	..	...	..	...

Single 1 Cl. s. d.	Single 3 Cl. s. d.	Return 1 Cl. s. d.	Return 3 Cl. s. d.	UP TRAINS		Week Days am	am	am	pm	pm	pm	Sundays am	pm	.
				DINGLE	dep.		11 0	...	2 30	..	...	..	...	.
1 2	0 9	2 1	1 4	Lispole	..	...	1118	...	2 45	—	...	—	...	.
1 4	0 11	2 4	1 8	Garrynadur	..	..	flag	...	flag	..	...	—	...	.
2 1	1 5	3 8	2 6	Annascaul	arr.	..	1140	...	3 15	..	...	—	...	.
..	..	..	..	Do.	dep.	..	1145	...	3 20	..	...	..	...	.
2 8	1 9	4 8	3 1	Emalough	..	...	flag	...	flag	..	...	—	...	.
3 0	2 0	5 3	3 6	Glenmore	..	...	flag	...	flag	..	...	—	...	—
3 [illegible]	2 6	6 4	4 0	Glounagalt	..	..	flag	...	flag	..	...	—	...	—
4 2	2 9	7 4	4 10	Castlegregory Junc.	arr.	...	1245	...	4 15	..	...	—	...	—
5 1	3 6	9 3	6 2	Castlegregory	dep.	7 40	..	...	3 40	..	...	..	...	—
4 11	3 3	8 8	5 9	Aughacasla	..	flag	..	...	flag	..	...	..	...	—
4 6	3 0	7 11	5 8	Deelis	..	flag	...	...	flag	..	...	..	...	—
..	..	..	..	C'gregory Junc.	arr.	8 10	...	..	4 10	..	...	..	...	—
..	..	..	..	Castlegregory Junc.	dep.	8 20	1249	...	4 20	..	...	—	...	—
4 6	3 0	7 11	5 8	Derrymore	..	flag	flag	...	flag	..	...	—	...	—
5 6	3 6	9 8	6 5	Blennerville	..	...	flag	...	flag	..	...	—	...	—
5 10	3 11	10 3	6 11	Basin	..	...	flag	...	flag	..	...	—	...	—
6 0	4 0	10 6	7 0	TRALEE	arr.	9 0	1 30	...	5 0	..	...	..	...	..

Note.—Trains will stop by Signal at Stations marked "Flag," or on notice to Guard at previous stopping station.

Last Passenger Timetable: 1939

Tralee to Dingle and Castlegregory.

Distance from Tralee	DOWN TRAINS.		Week-Days. 1. Mixed.	2. Mixed.	3. Mixed.
			a.m.	a.m.	p.m.
	TRALEE ... •	dep.	7 30	11 55	5 30
2¼	BLENNERVILLE HALT	,,	F	F	F
6	CURRAHEEN ...	,,	F	F	F
7¾	DERRYMORE HALT	,,	F	F	F
10	CASTLEGREGORY JCT. •	arr.	8 10	12 35	6 10
	Branch: CASTLEGREGORY JCT.	dep.	...	12 45	p.m. 6 20
12¼	Branch: DEELIS HALT	,,	...	F	F
14¼	Branch: AUGHACASLA HALT	,,	...	F	F
15¾	Branch: CASTLEGREGORY T.S.&T.	arr.	...	1 21	6 56
			a.m.		p.m.
	CASTLEGREGORY JUNCTION	dep.	8 15	...	6 15
11¾	CAMP HALT ...	,,	F	...	F
14	GLENAGALT HALT	,,	F	...	F
16	GLENMORE HALT ...	,,	F	...	F
17½	EMALOUGH HALT	,,	F	...	F
20¼	ANNASCAUL ... •	,,	9 20	...	7 20
23	BALLINASARE HALT	,,	F	...	F
24¾	GARRYNADUR HALT	,,	F	...	F
26¾	LISPOLE HALT ...	,,	9 45	...	7 45
27¾	BALLINSTEENIG HALT	,,	F	...	F
31¾	DINGLE ... •	arr.	10 5	...	8 5

• E Tablet. F—Stops on signal to Guard and Driver.

Dingle and Castlegregory to Tralee.

UP TRAINS.		Week-Days. 4. Mixed.	5.	6. Mixed.	7. Mixed.
		a.m.		a.m.	p.m.
DINGLE	dep.	...	...	10 50	2 30
BALLINASTEENIG ...	,,	...	...	F	F
LISPOLE HALT	,,	...	...	11 8	2 45
GARRYNADUR	,,	• ...	...	F	F
BALLINASARE	,,	...	...	F	F
ANNASCAUL	,,	...	...	11 35	3 20
EMALOUGH	,,	...	...	F	F
GLENMORE	,,	...	...	F	F
GLENAGALT	,,	...	...	F	F
CAMP	,,	Sats.	Sats.	12 30	4 10
CASTLEGREGORY JUNCTION	arr.	excepted	only	12 35	4 15
			a.m.		p.m.
Branch: CASTLEGREGORY ...	dep.	8 10	9 50	...	3 35
Branch: AUGHACASLA ...	,,	F	...	...	F
Branch: DEELIS	,,	F	...	...	F
Branch: CASTLEGREGORY JCT.	arr.	8 46	10 26	...	4 10
					p.m.
CASTLEGREGORY JUNCTION	dep	8 50	10 30	12 39	4 20
DERRYMORE	,,	...	...	F	F
CURRAHEEN	,,	...	...	F	F
BLENNERVILLE ...	,,	...	...	F	F
TRALEE	arr.	9 30	11 10	1 20	5 0

F—Stops on Signal to Guard and Driver

Daily Goods Working: 1939-46

(taken from CIE Working Timetables)

Tralee to Dingle.

Distance from Tralee.	Down Trains.			Week Days.	1. Goods.	
					a.m.	
—	TRALEE ...	●W *	dep.	...	7 30	...
2¼	BLENNERVILLE HALT	N	,,	...	...	...
6	CURRAHEEN ...	N	,,	...	...	...
7¾	DERRYMORE HALT ...	N	,,	...	...	...
10	CASTLEGREGORY JCT.	*	arr.	...	8 15	...
	CASTLEGREGORY JCT.	W	dep.	...	8 45	...
11¾	CAMP HALT ...	N	,,	...	...	...
14	GLENAGALT HALT ...	N	,,	...	...	...
16	GLENMORE HALT ...	N	,,	...	...	...
17½	EMALOUGH HALT ...	N	,,	...	...	...
	ANNASCAUL ...	W*	arr.	...	10 4	...
20¼			dep.	...	10 24	...
23	BALLINASARE HALT ...	N	,,	...	...	...
24¾	GARRYNADUR HALT ...	N	,,	...	...	...
	LISPOLE HALT ...	N	arr.	...	10 57	...
26¾			dep.	...	11 7	...
27¾	BALLINSTEENIG HALT	N	,,	...	...	...
31¾	DINGLE ...	● *	arr.	...	11 32	...

Dingle to Tralee.

Up Trains.			Week Days.		2. Goods.	
					noon	p.m.
DINGLE	W●	dep.	...	...	12 0	...
BALLINASTEENIG ...		,,	...	...	...	...
LISPOLE HALT ...		arr.	...	...	12 26	...
		dep.	...	...	12 36	...
GARRYNADUR ...		,,	...	...	...	...
BALLINASARE		,,	...	...	...	...
ANNASCAUL		arr.	...	...	1 9	...
	W	dep.	...	...	1 40	...
EMALOUGH		,,	...	...	...	...
GLENMORE		,,	...	...	...	...
GLENAGALT		,,	...	...	...	...
CAMP		,,	...	...	...	...
CASTLEGREGORY JCT.	W	arr.	...	...	2 58	...
CASTLEGREGORY JCT. ...	W	dep.	...	...	3 18	...
DERRYMORE		,,	...	...	...	...
CURRAHEEN		,,	...	...	...	...
BLENNERVILLE ...		,,	...	...	...	...
TRALEE	●	arr.	...	...	4 0	...

N—No Telephone Communication. *—E Tablet. ●—Engine Turntable. W—Water Column.

Appendix Four
A SELECTION OF TICKETS

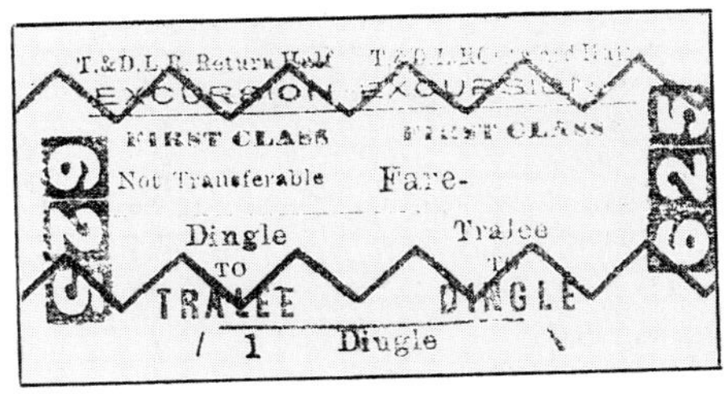

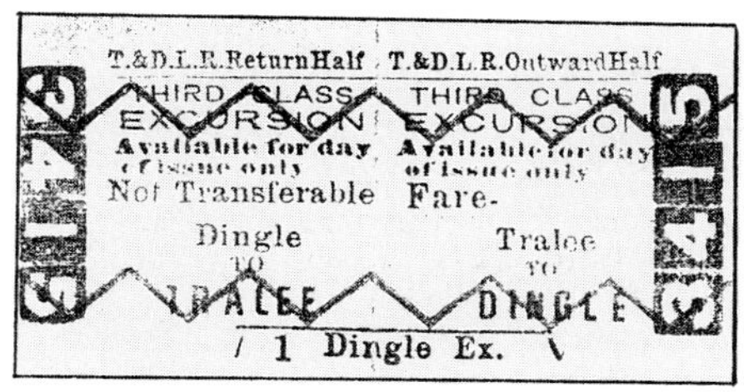

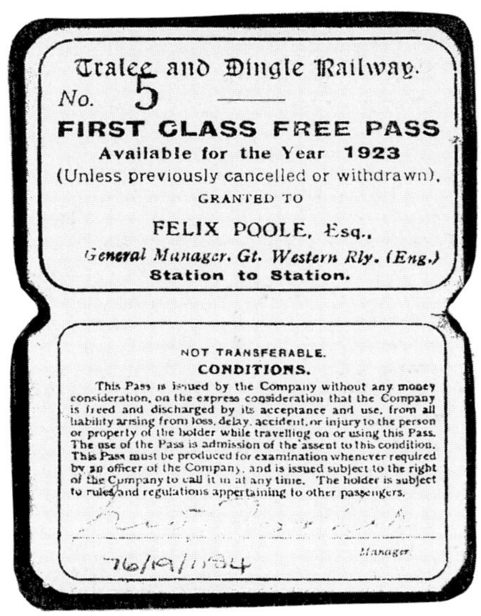

TAILPIECE . . . .

188. A wartime cattle special returning from Dingle Fair, moving away towards Emalough in 1943. *(Fr. F. Browne SJ)*